Using
RTI for
School
Improvement

To my boys, Scott and Wesley: Once again, you have supported me through the long hours and chaos that go with this work. Thank you so very much for your love and encouragement. I am so amazed that God chooses to bless me through you.

To my parents, Mom, Dad, Mimi, and Papa: Your love and support mean more than I can ever express. Thank you for all that you are and all that you do for us.

—Cara Shores

I dedicate this work to my family, Chris, Payton, and Haley. Your unselfish support and encouragement mean so much to me. Payton, your many hours of occupying your sister did not go unnoticed. Haley, the times we worked side by side on our computers were memorable. Chris, your determination to stay awake while I worked through the night was cherished. You each inspire me to do more than I could ever dream. You truly are special blessings straight from heaven above. I love you more than words can say.

—Kim Chester

Cara Shores — Kim Chester

Using RTI for School Improvement

Raising Every Student's Achievement Scores

A Joint Publication

For information:

Corwin Press
A SAGE Company
2455 Teller Road
Thousand Oaks, California 91320
www.corwinpress.com

SAGE India Pvt. Ltd.
B 1/I 1 Mohan Cooperative
 Industrial Area
Mathura Road, New Delhi 110 044
India

SAGE Ltd.
1 Oliver's Yard
55 City Road
London, EC1Y 1SP
United Kingdom

SAGE Asia-Pacific Pte. Ltd.
33 Pekin Street #02–01
Far East Square
Singapore 048763

Printed in the United States of America.

Library of Congress Cataloging-in-Publication Data

A catalog record of this book is available from the Library of Congress.

ISBN: 978-1-4129-6641-2
ISBN: 978-1-4129-6640-5

08 09 10 11 12 10 9 8 7 6 5 4 3 2 1

Acquisitions Editor: David Chao
Editorial Assistant: Mary Dang
Production Editor: Appingo Publishing Services
Cover Designer: Monique Hahn
Graphic Designer: Lisa Riley

Contents

Acknowledgments

Corwin Press would like to acknowledge the following reviewers for their contributions:

Michelle Barnea
Early Childhood Consultant
Independent Consultant
Millburn, New Jersey

Laurie Emery
Principal
Old Vail Middle School
Vail, Arizona

Debi Gartland, PhD
Professor of Special Education
Towson University
Towson, Maryland

Susan N. Imamura
Principal (Retired)
Hawaii State Department of Education
Honolulu, Hawaii

About the Authors

Cara Shores, EdS, began her career as a special education teacher and taught children in both pull-out and inclusive classrooms. She received her master's degree and educational specialist's degree from the University of West Georgia and has since served as Student Support Services Coordinator and District Director of Special Education. Mrs. Shores has trained thousands of teachers and administrators across the United States on practical strategies for inclusion, co-teaching, and increasing achievement for all students through differentiated instruction and RTI. She provides regional and national training for the Council for Exceptional Children. She is co-author of *Response to Intervention: A Practical Guide for Every Teacher.* Mrs. Shores now serves as the President of Wesley Educational Services.

Kim Chester began her career as a general education teacher in an inclusive classroom, where for many years she implemented effective principles of co-teaching and differentiating instruction to meet the diverse needs of her students. After her youngest child was born with cerebral palsy, she went back to school to receive her MEd in special education from Kennesaw State University. Currently, she works as a parent mentor in her local school system, as a region AYP consultant, and as an educational consultant for Wesley Educational Services. In addition, Mrs. Chester serves on various committees, including the Governor's Council on Developmental Disabilities in Georgia. She offers her range of perspectives to educators, parents, and administrators. Mrs. Chester enjoys working with students and teachers in classroom settings, providing practical strategies for raising student achievement through inclusion, co-teaching, differentiated instruction, behavior management, and RTI.

Creating a Vision and Framework

1

Over the past several decades, how best to improve America's public education system has been heavily debated by educators, researchers, politicians, and the general public. It seems that everyone involved in the debate has their own opinion of what would fix the problems—as a result, the staffs of our nation's schools have been subjected to what seems like a constant stream of new programs to be implemented, none of which has apparently had the desired effect.

Yet there is little debate over the fact that changes are needed. The accountability built into the No Child Left Behind (NCLB) legislation has revealed significant gaps in academic performance between the general school population and subgroups of children such as those with disabilities, members of minority groups, and children living in poverty. It is generally agreed by school practitioners that the goal of having every child read on grade level by 2014, as required in NCLB, is not attainable if schools continue on their current track.

This book is about legitimate, effective school improvement through Response to Intervention (RTI). It is not about another new program like those that educators have seen come and go. Taken seriously and implemented effectively, it has the potential to transform classrooms into highly effective, highly motivating arenas of learning. However, it is important to understand that the process will only be effective if implemented in its entirety. We (the authors) do not recommend using only parts of the RTI process or simplifying them to achieve minimum standards.

Our vehicle for change involves a process of identifying students at risk, pinpointing highly effective strategies specifically designed to address the students' areas of need, implementing the strategies with fidelity, and utilizing assessment to determine progress and adjust instruction. It is not a difficult process in and of itself. However, it can only be effective in an atmosphere that is characterized by a commitment to see *all* children succeed.

The process presented in this book is based on levels or tiers of increasingly intensive interventions. As students are identified as exhibiting risk for school failure, they are instructed using interventions designed to eliminate or correct the cause of failure. Their progress is monitored using simple assessment tools. Again, it is not a difficult process, but it does involve a change of mind-set from that found in most public and private schools. There must be a firm commitment at both the district and the school level to provide whatever is necessary to enable all students to be successful academically and behaviorally. Implementation involves rethinking job descriptions and reallocating resources. It involves extensive training for teachers and administrators. It involves changing the way America's schools are run and the way its students are taught. Without this change of mind-set, the process can only have minimal success.

We present this process to you with the combined insights of having served as general education teacher, special education teacher, building administrator, system administrator, consultant, and parent. We fully understand what is involved in running a classroom, a school, and a school system. As consultants, we travel throughout the country, observing in classrooms and talking with teachers. We understand the tendency to stay with what is familiar—to teach the way you were taught. And yet, we believe that full implementation of the process outlined on the following pages will transform classrooms, schools, and districts into highly effective learning environments.

Our school improvement process involves implementation of pyramids of intervention. Pyramids of intervention, as stated above, involve layers of increasingly intensive interventions or strategies designed to address learning or behavioral problems exhibited by students who are at risk for school failure. These pyramids have taken several forms, including tiered reading models and RTI models. In this book, we focus on RTI and its role in the overall school improvement process.

RESPONSE TO INTERVENTION AND TIERED READING MODELS

A review of research literature written since 2000 reveals a huge volume of information regarding Response to Intervention. RTI was first implemented in the 1970s and has since become an accepted means of addressing academic and behavioral problems, especially in young children. After it was included in the 2004 Reauthorization of the Individuals with Disabilities Education Improvement Act (IDEA 2004), RTI has gained momentum as a viable method for identifying students with learning disabilities while ruling out poor instruction as the cause of learning problems.

Much of the research on RTI has involved a three-tiered reading model that incorporates the work of the National Reading Panel (NRP). The NRP was a federally appointed group of reading experts who met for over two years, reviewing research on reading instruction. In April 2000, the panel submitted to Congress its report, which outlined five components essential to reading instruction. The components were identified as phonemic awareness, phonics, fluency, vocabulary, and comprehension, applied as appropriate to the particular grade level's educational standards (National Institute of Child Health and Human Development, 2000). This landmark report was a comprehensive outline of effective reading instruction and was unlike any document previously developed. It clearly specified the elements involved in learning to read and made the information easily accessible to teachers and researchers alike.

In 2001, President Bush included the NRP findings in the No Child Left Behind Act (NCLB). NCLB created an initiative called Reading First, which provided funding and resources to states and districts to establish programs for reading instruction. It also initiated a requirement that all school-wide programs operate according to a plan that contains proven strategies designed to facilitate school-wide reform and improvement. Further, NCLB requires that any strategy considered for this purpose be research-based and likely to produce the desired results (U.S. Department of Education, 2001). This requirement for scientific, research-based strategies would become central to future development of pyramids of intervention.

Acting on the recommendations of the NRP report and NCLB requirements, researchers began intensive studies of the most effective ways to teach reading, assess reading progress, and remediate reading difficulties. Sharon Vaughn and her colleagues at the Vaughn Gross Center for Reading and Language Arts initiated numerous studies, including a four-year project entitled Preventing Reading Difficulties: A Three-Tiered Intervention Model. The project was designed to address reading problems with at-risk students by providing intensive early intervention. The model used in the project involved three tiers, designated as primary, secondary, and tertiary intervention (Vaughn Gross Center for Reading and Language Arts, 2006). At Tier 1, all students received core reading instruction during the reading block. Through varied formal and informal assessments, the teacher determined students' responses to core instruction and identified which students were at risk for reading failure. For students who were not adequately progressing when provided core instruction, Tier 2 provided additional exposure to the core curriculum or to an alternative program or strategy with more intensive instruction. Intensity was increased in that the teacher–student ratio was typically decreased to four to five students per teacher and the student received additional instruction time (usually 30 minutes per day). Using various forms of assessment, teachers determined students' response to Tier 2 instruction. Students who were not adequately responding to Tier 2 instruction began a more intensive program of intervention in Tier 3. The manner of instruction and intensity was further adjusted based on students' responses. At this level, instruction was more intense, group size was smaller, and supplemental instruction lasted longer.

Similar studies have been implemented frequently over the past several years (D. Fuchs, Fuchs, & Compton, 2004; Speece & Case, 2001; Vaughn, Linan-Thompson, & Hickman, 2003; Vellutino, Scanlon, Small, & Fanuele, 2006). Each of the studies cited here involved young children (most often kindergarteners or first-graders) who were identified through curriculum-based measurement as being at risk for reading failure. The students were provided intensive interventions using a highly effective research-based reading intervention for a specific time period. Students' progress was continually evaluated, and instructional adjustment was made based on student response.

As the three-tiered reading model evolved, it was adopted as the basic framework for implementation of RTI (Bender & Shores, 2007; D. Fuchs & Fuchs, 2006; L. S. Fuchs & Fuchs, 2007; Mastropieri & Scruggs, 2005). Just like the previously described reading model, RTI involves tiers (usually three or four) of increasingly intensive instruction provided to students identified as non-responders at the previous tier. The instruction uses high-quality, research-based strategies coupled with ongoing progress monitoring using curriculum-based measurement tools or other brief assessments. After progressing through the tiers as a non-responder, a student may ultimately be determined to have a specific learning disability (Bender & Shores, 2007).

As stated earlier, RTI has a long history but has gained significant attention since its inclusion in IDEA 2004 as a means of determining learning disability eligibility. In order for you to understand the full impact and implications of RTI for school improvement, we feel it is necessary to paint the "big picture" by reviewing the history of the RTI process.

HISTORY OF RESPONSE TO INTERVENTION

The first studies utilizing a Response to Intervention model were conducted by Deno & Mirkin (1977) and Bergan (1977). The Deno & Mirkin study, perhaps the first three-tiered reading study, utilized curriculum-based measurement to assess students' reading skills. Goals based on benchmark assessments were developed for students identified as at risk for reading problems. Students were taught in small groups and assessed through continued use of the benchmark assessments (Batsche et al., 2006).

Bergan's (1977) study involved a behavioral problem-solving process in which the behavior issues were observed and measured in the classroom setting. A behavioral goal was established based on expectations for all students. Interventions specific to the identified problem were implemented, and improved changes in performance were assessed by comparing current behavior to the established goal (Batsche et al., 2006).

These studies served as the foundation for future research and development of two distinct models of what we currently know as Response to Intervention. These models, the Standard Protocol Model (based on Deno & Mirkin, 1977) and the Problem-Solving Model (based on Bergan, 1977), continued to be implemented and evaluated sporadically over the next two decades. Discussions about RTI as a means of identifying specific learning disability (SLD) became more frequent among researchers and policymakers. In 2001, President Bush established the Commission on Excellence in Special Education to study and make recommendations for improvements to the provision of services for students with disabilities (2002). The commission recommended early intervention and curriculum-based assessment practices and suggested changing SLD eligibility determination to a response model. Also in 2001, the National Summit on Learning Disabilities recommended RTI as the most promising method for learning disability eligibility determination (Bender & Shores, 2007). In 2002, similar recommendations were issued by the National Research Council Panel on Minority Overrepresentation and the National Research Center on Learning Disabilities (NRCLD, 2002). Benefits of RTI outlined in these reports included the efficacy of early intervention to prevent or reduce academic difficulties, the ability to rule out poor instruction as a cause of low achievement, more objective means of evaluation to reduce overrepresentation of minority students in special education, and the assurance of quality instruction resulting from the use of scientifically research-based strategies. As Congress began the process of reauthorizing the Individuals with Disabilities Education Act 1997 (IDEA 1997), members took notice of the recommendations and included RTI in the new Individuals with Disabilities Education Improvement Act of 2004. IDEA 2004 does not mandate the use of RTI for SLD eligibility. It does, however, permit its use and prohibits states from requiring the use of the significant discrepancy model (U.S. Department of Education, 2006).

The inclusion of Response to Intervention in IDEA 2004 has resulted in an enormous increase in discussion, debate, and research on the topic. School personnel have found themselves caught up in a widespread debate over how to implement the procedure quickly but effectively. The RTI process seems destined to become labeled a "special education initiative." And yet, the success of RTI relies heavily on the requirement that it be perceived and developed as a function of general education (L. S. Fuchs & Fuchs, 2007; Hilton, 2007). Indeed, it is our opinion that RTI can be successful as a tool for school improvement if, and only if, it is embraced by general education leadership at the state, local, and school levels. It must be developed into a vision for overall school improvement and integrated into every aspect of the school, including curriculum, assessment, scheduling, staff development, and allocation of resources. With that in mind, we will focus the remainder of this chapter and the next four chapters on RTI as a general education practice. This chapter will provide an in-depth discussion of the Standard Protocol and Problem-Solving Models. Chapters 2 through 5 will go into greater detail about specific components of RTI, such as assessment and research-based strategies. In Chapter 6, we will revisit the idea of utilizing RTI as a means of determining eligibility for and providing special education services. Chapter 7 will bring all components of the process together and provide guidance for developing a school or district implementation plan.

TWO MODELS FOR RTI IMPLEMENTATION

The Standard Protocol Model

As discussed in the previous section, the 1977 study by Deno and Mirkin evolved into what is commonly known as the Standard Protocol Model of RTI. The Standard Protocol Model, also referred to as Standard Treatment Protocol, is very similar to the three-tiered reading model described previously. In a Standard Protocol RTI, Tier 1 instruction involves effective implementation of the core curriculum for all students in the general education classroom. The classroom teacher utilizes benchmark assessment or other forms of curriculum-based measurement to assess his or her entire class for mastery of the core curriculum, usually in the area of reading or math. Students performing below a certain level are identified as being at risk for failure in the assessed area. Students are then placed into Tier 2, encompassing small group instruction that is in addition to the core instruction. The small group instruction is readily available to students and has been pre-established based on the most common needs of students in the school. The additional instruction involves a scientific, research-based strategy or curriculum specifically designed to address the students' deficit areas. A goal is established that targets expected improvement. Curriculum-based measurement is administered

Errata

Figure 1.1   Standard Protocol Model

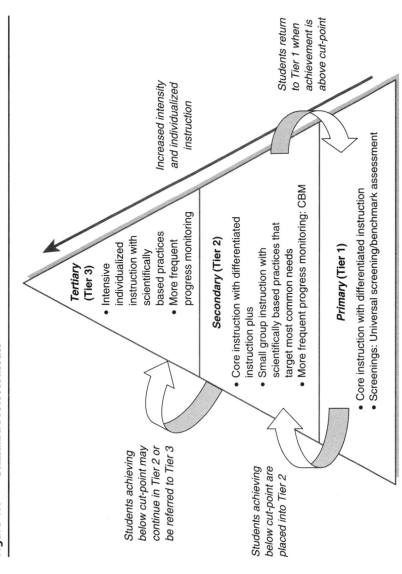

Increased intensity and individualized instruction

Tertiary (Tier 3)

- Intensive individualized instruction with scientifically based practices
- More frequent progress monitoring

Secondary (Tier 2)

- Core instruction with differentiated instruction plus
- Small group instruction with scientifically based practices that target most common needs
- More frequent progress monitoring: CBM

Primary (Tier 1)

- Core instruction with differentiated instruction
- Screenings: Universal screening/benchmark assessment

Students return to Tier 1 when achievement is above cut-point

Students achieving below cut-point may continue in Tier 2 or be referred to Tier 3

Students achieving below cut-point are placed into Tier 2

at regular intervals to evaluate each student's progress toward the goal. Instruction and assessment may be carried out by general education teachers, special education teachers, paraprofessionals, or others who have been trained in the instructional strategy or curriculum. In many Standard Protocol Models, instruction is delivered and evaluated for ten weeks, with the possibility of students participating in three or more of these ten-week sessions. Response to the intervention is operationalized with additional cut-points, which vary widely between studies. Students whose achievement is above the cut-point return to Tier 1, general instruction. Students whose achievement is below the cut-point may continue with the Tier 2 instruction or be referred to Tier 3, which usually involves intensive individualized instruction, often provided through special education (Graner, Fagella-Luby, & Fritschmann, 2005; Speece, Case, & Molloy, 2003; Vaughn et al., 2003). Movement up the pyramid involves more intensive instruction and progress monitoring with each additional level. The intent of the intervention is to remediate problems as soon as they are identified and to move students back down to a lower tier when they have exhibited positive response to the more intensive instruction. Figure 1.1 illustrates a Standard Protocol Model of intervention. Figure 1.2 goes into further detail, outlining the flow of activities in the model.

There is a wealth of information about and examples of Standard Protocol RTIs in the research literature. This model is preferred by

Figure 1.1   Standard Protocol Model

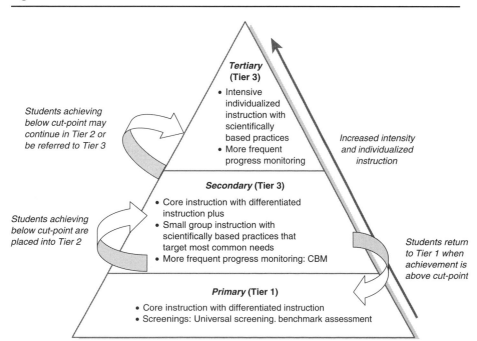

Students achieving below cut-point may continue in Tier 2 or be referred to Tier 3

Tertiary
(Tier 3)
• Intensive individualized instruction with scientifically based practices
• More frequent progress monitoring

Increased intensity and individualized instruction

Students achieving below cut-point are placed into Tier 2

Secondary **(Tier 3)**
• Core instruction with differentiated instruction plus
• Small group instruction with scientifically based practices that target most common needs
• More frequent progress monitoring: CBM

Students return to Tier 1 when achievement is above cut-point

Primary **(Tier 1)**
• Core instruction with differentiated instruction
• Screenings: Universal screening. benchmark assessment

Figure 1.2   Standard Protocol Flowchart

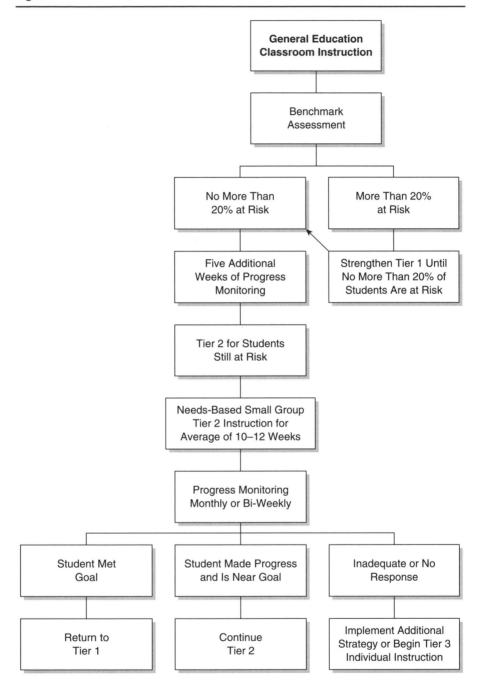

researchers because of (1) the ability to control variables, resulting in high-quality research data; (2) the use of scientific, research-based strategies; and (3) less need for a large variety of strategies to be used in the school, thereby increasing instructional quality or fidelity (Bender & Shores, 2007; D. Fuchs, Mock, Morgan, & Young, 2003). Yet, it is not without weaknesses. With this model, there is less flexibility with interventions. It is designed to provide interventions based on the needs of the majority of students. It does not allow for students who might learn differently and therefore may not respond to the particular intervention chosen. It also calls for considerable restructuring of the school's resources and procedures to allocate time for instruction in the intervention groups. Finally, it has been applied almost exclusively to students in grades K–3, with the majority of studies performed in the area of reading. Although this seems logical, given the Standard Protocol Model's roots in the three-tiered reading model and its goal of early intervention, the model may have significant limitations for application to other content areas or to older students.

In Chapter 4 of this book, we will discuss specific issues associated with school-wide implementation of the Standard Protocol Model. We will provide guidelines and examples in the areas of research-based strategies, fidelity of instruction, scheduling, and staff options. We will also provide an example of full implementation of the model at the school level.

The Problem-Solving Model

The second recognized model of RTI is the Problem-Solving Model, which developed from the Bergan (1977) study discussed previously. It is preferred by practitioners in the school setting in that it allows more flexibility with interventions and focuses more on the individual needs of the student. This model involves a decision-making process employed by a team of professionals who consider the needs of each child and develop strategies based on those specific needs. The team employing the process may be composed of teachers, administrators, school psychologists, or others who have knowledge of the student and/or strategies which might be implemented. This model has been applied to both behavioral and academic problems. When a student in the general education class is identified as at risk for academic or behavioral difficulties, the classroom teacher utilizes the problem-solving team to develop an appropriate RTI plan. Figure 1.3 illustrates the steps in the decision-making process. This figure should help you to see the thought processes involved in implementing this model.

Figure 1.3   Problem-Solving RTI Model

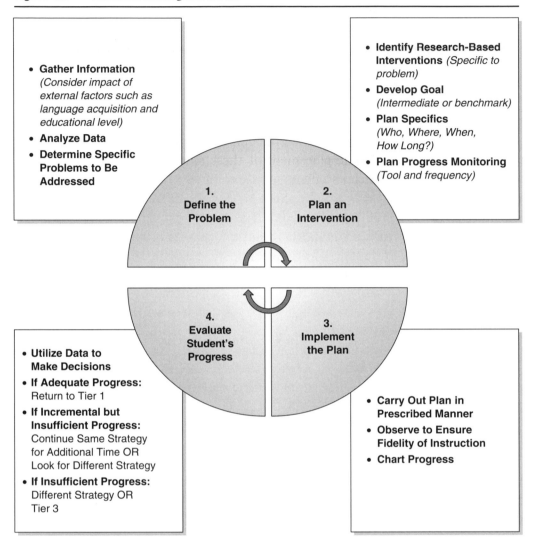

Step 1: Define the problem. Step 1 in this process begins as the team develops a clear definition of the student's presenting problem, whether academic or behavioral in nature. Team members should first gather information related to the student's functioning both within and outside the school setting. We believe this step is critical to the success of the remainder of the cycle. Experiences outside the school often play a definitive role in academic success (Maslow & Lowery, 1998). When students feel unsafe, when they feel hungry, or when they suffer distress due to other external causes, schoolwork falls low on their priority list (Sousa, 2001). In fact, home environment has been shown to be closely correlated

with early reading development (Vellutino et al., 1996). Teachers may not have control over external factors, but understanding their impact will enable the teacher to better communicate with and build a relationship with the student (Payne, 2005). Students who come from deprived, dysfunctional, or violent homes often demonstrate significant benefit from this deeper understanding on the part of the teacher.

If the team is implementing the problem-solving process for students from minority groups, specifically English language learners or African American students, team members should carefully explore factors that often lead to disproportionate placement of these students into special education. African American students are three times more likely to be labeled mentally retarded than Caucasian students (Council for Exceptional Children [CEC], 2002). Cultural norms and societal expectations within the student's culture are sometimes in conflict with the expectations of America's public schools. For example, in some cultures, it is considered disrespectful for children to make direct eye contact with adults. However, in American classrooms, teachers expect their students to make eye contact to show they are paying attention. Although this is a very simplistic example, more significant conflicts between expectations and cultural norms often result in high rates of disproportionality for subgroups of children (CEC, 2002).

When working with English language learners, problem-solving team members must consider the student's level of English proficiency. Cummins' Theory of Language Acquisition (1980) explored the difference between conversational English and academic English. Students who are conversationally proficient are often judged to have the skills necessary to be successful in school. However, many students may be able to participate fully in conversations in English and yet not understand the semantics, structure, and vocabulary of academic content. They are deficient in academic fluency. According to Cummins, academic English proficiency requires much more time for mastery: an average of five to seven years as compared with two years for conversational English. Without taking this into consideration, problem-solving teams may incorrectly determine that a student's learning problems are not associated with language acquisition.

In the case of an English language learner, the team should also consider factors such as the level of proficiency in the native language (Freeman & Freeman, 2004). Studies have shown a direct correlation between proficiency in other languages, especially Spanish, to English acquisition (Klingner & Artiles, 2003; Ordonez, Carlo, Snow, & McLaughlin, 2002; Vaughn, Mathes, Linan-Thompson, & Francis, 2005). Therefore, teams should learn as much as possible about the student's school history prior to education in the United States. If a student never had formal training in the structure of his native language, he has nothing with which to compare the structure of English. Additional factors that may affect student achievement include medical history, psychological stressors such as separation anxiety or post-traumatic stress disorder, and willingness to accept the American culture (Bender & Shores, 2007; Marler & Sanchez-Lopez, 2006). While it is true that the data-based nature of the RTI process often reduces subjectivity in special education referrals, it would be a mistake to ignore the impact of these external factors (Davis, Lindo, & Compton, 2007). A team's lack of understanding of these issues may very well lead to inappropriately determining that the student is non-responsive and thus in need of special education. (See Bender & Shores, 2007, pp. 67–81 for a full discussion of RTI's impact on students from minority groups and children from poverty.)

Another important task to be completed in step 1 is to analyze all relevant data. In Chapter 2, we will discuss in detail the components and uses of formative and summative assessment. It is important to utilize both types of assessment in order to develop an overall picture of student functioning. Summative data allows the members of the team to visualize the overall strengths and weaknesses of the student, while formative data allows them to see how the student functions on a daily or weekly basis and how the student has responded to regular classroom (Tier 1) instruction. This data may be the outcome of benchmark assessments, curriculum-based measurement, standardized criterion-referenced or norm-referenced test results, end-of-chapter tests, end-of-course tests, or a variety of other options. It may be as simple as the results from Exit Cards (also called "tickets out the door"), a brief informal assessment procedure.

The team reviews the available data to develop a picture of the student's functioning, being as specific as possible when determining the cause of the difficulty. For example, the team may determine that the student is functioning in the lowest 20 percent of the class in reading fluency with a score of 15 words per minute on the reading fluency assessment. This provides useful information with which the team can develop a specific goal and strategy. If the team simply said "Johnny can't read" or "Johnny reads below grade level," additional assessment would be needed before a measurable goal could be developed.

Step 2: Plan an intervention. After the student's specific cause of difficulty is identified, the team is ready to plan an intervention designed to address the problem. As we discussed earlier, interventions utilized in the RTI process must have a substantial research base. There are many strategies and curricula available that meet this criterion, and we will go into greater detail about research-based interventions in Chapter 3. There are several issues, however, that we will address now which the problem-solving team must keep in mind.

First, the intervention must specifically address the identified problem. Traditionally, problem-solving RTIs have been found to involve poor-quality interventions (D. Fuchs et al., 2003). Our own experience with the problem-solving process has verified this in that the most common interventions chosen included preferential seating, reduced workload, and increased time to complete assignments. These are not research-based strategies, and they are not specifically geared toward teaching the student a skill. Problem-solving team members must turn to the research literature and independent evaluations of curricular programs to determine which interventions are most appropriate for their students.

Secondly, teachers, paraprofessionals, or other practitioners who are implementing the intervention must be properly trained in its implementation. Whether the intervention is a strategy or a supplemental curriculum, it will have specific guidelines and procedures that must be followed. If these guidelines and procedures are not carefully followed, the research base that substantiated the intervention is no longer valid.

After identifying an appropriate strategy, the team must develop a goal for the student. This goal may be based on expected benchmarks, the functioning level of the remainder of the class, or an incremental step between the student's current functioning and the benchmark. For example, Kade, a first-grade student, reads 20 words per minute according to the reading fluency assessment of the Dynamic Indicators of Basic Early Literacy Skills (DIBELS). The expected benchmark for his class is 40 words per minute. The problem-solving team may decide to implement a specific strategy for ten weeks. The team may set Kade's goal at the benchmark (40 wpm) or may set an intermediate goal, making the required growth rate more manageable. The team decides to set an intermediate goal for Kade at 30 words per minute by the end of the ten-week intervention. If Kade achieves this goal, it would be expected that the strategy would continue for another ten weeks in order to attempt to reach the benchmark of 40 words per minute.

After developing the goal, the team must determine specifics involved in implementing the intervention. Team members must determine the following:

- Who will carry out the intervention (teacher, paraprofessional, or other personnel)
- Where the instruction will occur (general education classroom, separate small group, individual tutoring, etc.)

- When instruction will take place (time of day, number of days per week)
- How long the intervention will be implemented (minutes per day, number of weeks)

Each of these components, once established, will have an impact on the outcome of instruction. For example, if the instruction is supposed to take place for 30 minutes three times per week, but instead is only implemented for 20 minutes two times per week, the outcome could be heavily affected.

Finally, the team must determine how and how often to assess progress. Curriculum-based measurement (CBM) tools are used to assess academic progress in the areas of reading and math particularly (see Chapter 2 for an extensive discussion of curriculum-based measurement and progress monitoring). The team should choose an appropriate CBM tool that will provide valid data of incremental steps of student progress. The team should then decide how often the student will be assessed. An important point to remember is that the more often the CBM assessment tool (also called probe) is administered, the more data will be available to the team. Each score obtained when a CBM assessment tool is given is called a data point. Four data points collected during a ten-week intervention will give only a vague picture of the student's progress. Ten data points during the same time frame will provide a much more detailed picture of incremental and minute positive or negative responses to instruction.

Step 3: Implement the plan. After the team has developed an intervention plan containing all of the elements outlined above, the next logical step is to implement the plan as it was designed. If the RTI plan is well developed, with careful thought given to details, plan implementation is usually quite simple. Instruction should occur in the prescribed manner, with careful attention given to making sure the intervention is implemented just as it was in the research. This component is known as fidelity of instruction. The team should designate one member to monitor the instruction and ensure that it is implemented with fidelity. This most often takes the form of a brief observation conducted by someone who is knowledgeable about the intervention. Some published curricula include a fidelity checklist or listing of required components that can easily be converted into a checklist. Otherwise, the observer can make anecdotal notes verifying appropriate implementation. The notes from this observation become part of the data used to rule out lack of instruction as a reason for poor response to the intervention. It simply documents that the intervention that has been proven effective for students with the specified problem was implemented correctly and found to be ineffective for this particular student.

As the intervention is implemented and progress monitoring takes place, the data generated by the progress monitoring should be charted in order to develop a picture of progress. Charting of data can easily be accomplished with chart paper or computer programs designed for the purpose. This chart will allow the team to quickly determine whether or not the student is exhibiting adequate response to the intervention.

Step 4: Evaluate the student's progress. The final step of the problem-solving process is to utilize the data to make instructional decisions for the student. Team members should consider all aspects of the plan implementation and analyze the CBM data so the team can determine whether or not the student has made adequate progress. Our recommendation for determining progress is to use a method called dual-discrepancy formula, in which the team considers the student's starting and ending performance (slope) as well as the student's end point in comparison to the goal (level; D. Fuchs & Deshler, 2007). Based on the student's progress toward the goal, the team must make a determination of the next step.

As the problem-solving cycle is applied, students progress through a multi-tiered pyramid as they did in the Standard Protocol Model in order to provide more intensive interventions and progress monitoring when needed. The team uses the cycle to develop an intervention plan, and the plan is implemented as designed. If the student showed a positive response to the instruction but did not reach the goal or benchmark, the team may decide to continue the same intervention for an additional time period or may increase the intensity of the intervention by implementing it for a longer session length or more days per week. If the student showed little or no response, the team may try a different intervention or move the student to the next tier of the pyramid. Of course, if the student responded well and reached the goal or benchmark, the team would most likely place the student back in general education in Tier 1. Regardless of the outcome, the team must make its decision based on the data.

The Mixed Model

An option that we often recommend and which some state and local agencies are choosing is one that incorporates both models within a school. With this option, the Standard Protocol Model is chosen and implemented to address the most common academic problems in the school. For example, review of the end-of-year standardized assessment might reveal that most kindergarten students with reading problems are weak in the area of phonemic awareness. The school or district administrators should first examine their core instruction in phonemic awareness to substantiate that students are provided appropriate instruction and given adequate opportunity to learn. They should substantiate that the majority of students are making acceptable progress with this core instruction. Next, they may choose one or more Standard Protocol interventions designed to teach phonemic awareness. They may then schedule for needs-based instruction during the school day, where when a student is identified as deficient in phonemic awareness, he or she can immediately be placed into an intervention group. The Standard Protocol RTI Model would then be followed.

At the same time or following the establishment of these intervention groups, the school or district would train its teachers in the Problem-Solving Model, perhaps developing a core team to assist with implementation. When students are identified as having academic difficulties not related to the deficiencies addressed through Standard Protocol, or when a behavior problem arises, the Problem-Solving Model would be implemented and decisions would be based on students' individual needs. With each model, care should be taken to rely on scientific, research-based interventions, progress monitoring data for decision making, and attention to fidelity of instruction (Hollenbeck, 2007).

This mixed model provides the advantage of having an established intervention available to students as soon as they are identified as having the most common learning problems. Additionally, it may ensure greater fidelity of instruction due to the fact that limited interventions are used. At the same time, students who have different needs can still receive appropriate intervention. Planning for this type of structure will vary by school, depending on available resources and instructional needs.

Cautions Regarding RTI Implementation

We have devoted much more time to discussion of the Problem-Solving Model than to Standard Protocol. Our reasons for this are simple. First, the Problem-Solving process has a history of mediocre or poor implementation. Numerous states have used the process for many years with some success. For example, Minneapolis Public Schools has implemented the model in all of its schools, grades K–12 (Marston, Muyskens, Lau, & Canter, 2003). Heartland Area Educational Agency has implemented the Problem-Solving Model in a majority of its service area schools in Iowa since 1985 (Tilley, 2003). Pennsylvania's Instructional Support Teams, established in 1990, utilize this model as well. Yet there is little empirical data that the Problem-Solving Model has been effective as a tool for early intervention. Specifically, there is little evidence that interventions are implemented with fidelity or that they are effective in remediating or eliminating the presenting problem (D. Fuchs & Deshler, 2007; D. Fuchs et al., 2003). There is also little evidence that student data has been generated and utilized for instructional decision making. In essence, the Problem-Solving Model has a limited research base for treatment of academic problems (D. Fuchs & Deshler, 2007). And yet, as we mentioned earlier, this model is the one that is preferred by practitioners and seems to be the most commonly chosen model for RTI implementation. Therefore, we feel we must place greater emphasis on the components that can make the process successful. Schools and school systems should exercise caution in moving full-force into this model. An enormous amount of planning, staff development, and reallocation of resources is required to put the essential elements in place that will promote effective Problem-Solving RTI implementation (Tilley, 2003). Extreme care must be taken in ensuring fidelity of treatment implementation (D. Fuchs & Deshler, 2007).

RTI IMPLEMENTATION OUTSIDE OF THE ELEMENTARY SETTING

Our discussion thus far has presented models for RTI implementation that have a strong research base for implementation in elementary schools. Research data on RTI in grades 6–12 is extremely limited. This is not surprising, given that RTI is designed as a tool for early intervention. However, most states are requiring implementation in grades K–12. This leaves teachers and administrators in a quandary as to how to apply recommendations for elementary best practices to the secondary school setting. Although there are good examples of implementation at the secondary level (e.g., Minneapolis Public Schools), there are few recommendations in the literature that are specific to this level. Because the overall school structure is so different from the earlier grades, many RTI features do not translate well to the middle and high school settings.

The reality of the situation is that many students at the secondary level will need intensive interventions to address a variety of problems, including poor reading and math skills. In 2004, it was reported that 68 percent of eighth-grade students and 64 percent of high school seniors failed to attain the level of proficient reader (Deshler, 2004). Reasons for this include lack of appropriate instruction in the primary grades, the difficulty of content area work, the cumulative effect of problems that were not as significant in the early grades, excessive absenteeism resulting in acquisition of splinter skills, and the presence of significant behavior problems that impede the student's learning (Hughes & Deshler, 2007). The focus on reading at the secondary level shifts from *learning to read* to *reading to learn*; students who were successful readers in the earlier grades may be deficient in reading *comprehension* (Biancarosa & Snow, 2006). It is improper, then, to assume that all students who are going to have difficulties through their school careers will be identified and remediated in the primary grades.

RTI implementation in middle schools can often be accomplished by adapting many of the practices in place in the elementary grades. Middle schools are usually structured so that students spend most of their day with a team of teachers. The middle school concept was developed in order to provide added support for students in the transitional years from elementary to high school. This team concept allows teachers to get to know their students better and to track their progress on a regular basis. We find that many schools are adjusting their current structure to fit within the RTI framework.

However, the situation is much different at the high school level. Because of the departmental structure of typical high schools in the United States, teachers have limited contact with their students. That contact usually occurs in sixty- to ninety-minute blocks of instructional time. A teacher may see an individual student only once daily or, in some cases, every other day. As a result, there may be no mechanism for identifying and supporting at-risk students. This is clearly illustrated in the statistical phenomenon known as the "ninth-grade bulge." According to a study of high school progress, the promotion rate between ninth and tenth grades is lower than the rate between any other grades. This results in a larger freshman class than any other class in eighth through twelfth grades. Additionally, the study found that a large number of students who failed freshman classes eventually drop out of school (National High School Center, 2007).

In order to address this and other instructional issues, schools must redesign their infrastructure to provide opportunities for supplemental and intensive intervention (Biancarosa & Snow, 2006). They must arrange for support systems, including extended learning time, amid the demands of high school graduation requirements. As a result, the concept of RTI implementation as a school improvement process is perhaps more important at the secondary level than in the earlier grades.

High school faculties must develop a vision of RTI as a school improvement process and realize its application to their students. This begins as the administration seeks to orient the faculty and staff to the concepts of curriculum-based measurement, progress monitoring, and differentiation of instruction. High school teachers often express frustration when faced with the concept of differentiating instruction while maintaining high standards.

Most secondary teachers are unaware of the concepts of progress monitoring. The logical reason for this is the absence of curriculum-based measurement tools applicable to older students. There are very few standardized curriculum-based assessment tools designed specifically for use with adolescents.

With these issues in mind, we now look at the unique challenges involved in RTI implementation at the secondary level. We will offer options for structuring the process at both the middle and high school levels. Throughout the remainder of the book, we will provide examples of strategies and assessment tools appropriate for adolescents.

Middle School and Junior High School Implementation

The Standard Protocol Model is being utilized successfully in middle and junior high schools in the same way as in our earlier description. School-wide assessment data is analyzed and the most significant areas of need are identified. Reading skills, reading comprehension, and math computation and problem solving are the most common areas for intervention. Standard Protocol intervention groups are then formed based on these areas of need. Schools often incorporate needs-based instruction or extended learning time into their vocational or special area segments (also called connections or exploratory). Students receiving Tier 2 interventions are placed into targeted assistance groups during these segments. Progress monitoring is implemented using tools appropriate for the grade level.

The Problem-Solving Model is also widely used at these grade levels. Teams are formed to address students' needs and develop intervention plans. Interventions may be carried out in small groups within the content area classroom or in small group settings.

As we stated earlier, implementation at the middle school level often involves adapting procedures from elementary models. Benchmark assessments may be administered three times per year or every six to nine weeks. The problem-solving process is applied through team meetings involving all teachers who teach the student. Schools with the junior high structure (similar to traditional high school structure) face more of the challenges experienced by high schools and may need to look to secondary models for process development. Without the team concept in place, scheduling becomes a bigger issue. However, as already mentioned, progress-monitoring tools are available for students in these grades.

High School Implementation

As more secondary schools begin developing the RTI process, we see two distinct structures emerging. Both structures contain the foundational characteristics of the RTI models already presented: research-based interventions, progress monitoring, and attention to fidelity of instruction. Students may move between tiers in the same manner as in previously discussed models. What differs between the structures is the direction they take in identifying and remediating student weaknesses. One structure addresses student deficits in basic skill areas, specifically reading comprehension. The other structure addresses weaknesses in actual content knowledge: literature/language arts, mathematics, science, and social studies. We will explore both of these options and present recommendations for implementation.

Basic Skills Structure

Let us begin by examining the first structure, built around student achievement in basic skill areas. In this model, students' performance on general outcome measures, including criterion-referenced tests, high school entrance/placement tests, and/or basic skills tests, is examined. These assessment tools are used as benchmark assessments and identify students who are considered in the deficient range in reading skills and comprehension. The cut-point for deficiency or at risk may be established by the state or district, or it may be standard for the assessment tool. The reason for the focus on reading, specifically comprehension, is that this skill is critical to success in secondary content classes. Students must possess very complex reading skills in order to learn information from content text. These skills include the ability to read with purpose, the ability to glean information and learn from text, the ability to discern meaning of words in context, the ability to discern fact from opinion, and the ability to integrate new information with background knowledge (Biancarosa & Snow, 2006). Students must use these abilities in narrative, expository, technical, and persuasive writings. Students who are deficient in these basic comprehension skills are likely to struggle in content classes.

Tier 1 in this model involves instruction to all students in the general education classroom. Students who are identified as having deficient skills are provided intensive Tier 2 interventions. Tier 2 interventions are carried out in extended learning time provided during and/or outside the school day. These interventions focus on improving broad skills, such as reading comprehension, needed to succeed in content area classes. They often focus on teaching students specific learning strategies that can be used in most or all classes. These strategies are then embedded in the teaching processes used in the content classes. As content teachers overtly demonstrate and utilize the strategies, students are able to generalize them to applicable uses. Frequent progress monitoring is utilized to track student progress. Students are then moved through the pyramid based on their responsiveness to the interventions.

Hughes and Deshler (2007) proposed a model of RTI of this type based on the Content Literacy Continuum (CLC) developed at the University of Kansas Center for Research on Learning. The CLC looks at the skills necessary to learn in each of the content areas. It seeks to answer the following questions about literacy supports available to struggling students:

1. What happens for those students who are reading below the fourth-grade level?
2. What is in place across a school staff to ensure that students will get the "critical" content in spite of their literacy skills?
3. What happens for students who know how to decode but cannot comprehend well?
4. What steps have been taken to ensure that powerful learning strategies are embedded across the curriculum?
5. What happens for students who have language problems? (Hughes & Deshler, 2007)

The continuum answers these questions through five levels of support, beginning with enhanced content instruction and embedded strategy instruction in the general education classroom. For students who are still unsuccessful, the school then provides intensive strategy instruction through strategy classes and/or strategic tutoring. Students may also receive intensive basic skill instruction as needed. Finally, students who prove unresponsive to previous interventions are provided with therapeutic intervention, perhaps by a speech/language pathologist. The continuum is illustrated in Figure 1.4. (For a full description of the process, visit www.kucrl.org or www.smarttogether.org/clc.)

In the RTI model based on the CLC, schools preface RTI implementation with extensive staff development for all content teachers on effective practices in reading and comprehension of academic texts and vocabulary/concept development. It is very important to develop a framework in which all teachers understand that they each play a vital role in literacy. Additionally, teachers are trained in curriculum-based measurement processes, such as maze assessments, and research-based strategies proven effective with older students (Hughes & Deshler, 2007).

Figure 1.4 The Content Literacy Continuum

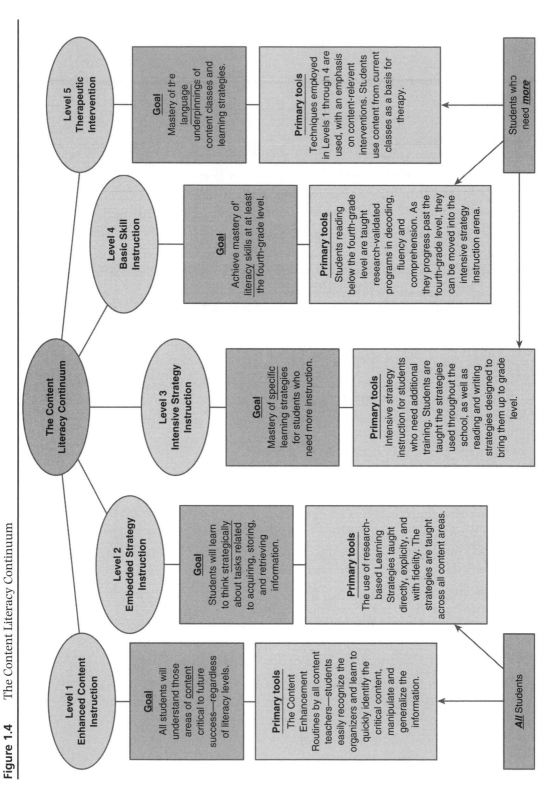

The Content Literacy Continuum

Level 1 Enhanced Content Instruction

Goal
All students will understand those areas of content critical to future success—regardless of literacy levels.

Primary tools
The Content Enhancement Routines by all content teachers—students easily recognize the organizers and learn to quickly identify the critical content, manipulate and generalize the information.

Level 2 Embedded Strategy Instruction

Goal
Students will learn to think strategically about tasks related to acquiring, storing, and retrieving information.

Primary tools
The use of research-based Learning Strategies taught directly, explicitly, and with fidelity. The strategies are taught across all content areas.

Level 3 Intensive Strategy Instruction

Goal
Mastery of specific learning strategies for students who need more instruction.

Primary tools
Intensive strategy instruction for students who need additional training. Students are taught the strategies used throughout the school, as well as reading and writing strategies designed to bring them up to grade level.

Level 4 Basic Skill Instruction

Goal
Achieve mastery of literacy skills at at least the fourth-grade level.

Primary tools
Students reading below the fourth-grade level are taught research-validated programs in decoding, fluency and comprehension. As they progress past the fourth-grade level, they can be moved into the intensive strategy instruction arena.

Level 5 Therapeutic Intervention

Goal
Mastery of the language underpinnings of content classes and learning strategies.

Primary tools
Techniques employed in Levels 1 through 4 are used, with an emphasis on content-relevant interventions. Students use content from current classes as a basis for therapy.

All Students

Students who need *more*

SOURCE: © The Strategic Learning Center.

Tier 1 involves implementation of the effective reading practices in content classes. All students are screened for deficiencies in word analysis skills, fluency, and comprehension. If that information is available through state assessments, those results are used. If not, students are screened through some form of general outcome or curriculum-based measurement. Levels 1 and 2 of the CLC are implemented within the content area classes.

Students identified as at risk move to Tier 2 of the RTI pyramid. They receive intensive supplemental instruction in comprehension, vocabulary, and word-level skills, and teachers facilitate strategy use in the content area classes. Research-based interventions such as learning strategy instruction, study guides, graphic organizers, and class-wide peer tutoring are implemented in the content classes. These interventions are based in Levels 3 and 4 of the Content Literacy Continuum. Support to the general education teacher is provided by a support teacher, but again, the interventions are "embedded" in instruction in the general education classroom. Finally, in Tier 3, students who prove unresponsive are given intensive strategy and/or skill instruction in small group settings in subsequent tiers (Hughes & Deshler, 2007; University of Kansas Center for Research on Learning, 2007).

It is evident that this model requires a focus on climate change within the school. Roles and responsibilities must be redefined, and faculty members must think "outside the box" to develop a structure that will fit within federal and state course and graduation requirements. It requires changes in scheduling, as well. However, it holds great promise in providing intensive skills instruction designed to address significant reading comprehension issues. Because the model is based on literacy instruction, it does not address deficiencies in math abilities. Our next model may prove more applicable in that area.

Content-Specific Structure

The second structure that we see emerging across the country is one based on content-specific skills. All students are assessed using benchmark assessment tools (usually developed at the state or district level) that measure progress in all content classes. The benchmarks are administered at the beginning of the semester, at the midpoint, and at the end. Students who fall significantly below the benchmark are provided with Tier 2 interventions designed to teach learning strategies and address content skill deficits. The interventions may be carried out in extended learning time through computer-assisted instruction, direct instruction in elective classes, or afterschool learning programs. Curriculum-based measurement is used for progress monitoring on a biweekly or weekly basis. Students move up and down the RTI pyramid based on their responsiveness to the interventions.

A key component of this structure, which may also be incorporated into the Basic Skills Structure, is the provision of extended learning time. This concept is being applied in numerous high schools across the country through credit recovery programs, virtual (online) classrooms, and extended day/year programs. In a report prepared for the Center for American Progress, Pennington (2006) identified several principles key to using extended learning time in high schools. These include providing a variety of support services for students who struggle. She stressed that providing additional time cannot, in and of itself, raise achievement. The instruction provided during that time must be different from previous instruction, provide extra support while maintaining high expectations, and engage students in the learning process. As school personnel develop extended learning time options within their schools, they should avoid the creation of traditional remedial-type classes. Groupings should be based on specific student needs. Group size should be kept small. Specific research-based interventions should be implemented with fidelity. Progress monitoring should be used to effectively drive instruction.

Figure 1.5 gives several resources for RTI implementation in the secondary levels. As more schools implement the process, we will undoubtedly see many variations on the structures listed above, and other structures will develop based on the needs and resources of individual schools and districts. We encourage secondary school staff to apply the concepts of an effective RTI process and current research on effective secondary practices to their overall vision of school improvement in order to create a uniquely successful plan.

Figure 1.5   Resources for Secondary RTI Implementation

- University of Kansas Center for Research on Learning
  www.kucrl.org
- National High School Center
  www.betterhighschools.org
- Center for American Progress
  www.americanprogress.org/issues/2006/10/pdf/extended_
  learning_report.pdf
- Research Institute on Progress Monitoring
  www.progressmonitoring.net/CBM_Sec_Res.doc

RTI MODEL FOR BEHAVIORAL INTERVENTIONS

As has been discussed, the Problem-Solving Model originated from a behavioral research study and has been recommended as the model to use to address behavioral problems (D. Fuchs & Deshler, 2007). Because implementation for academics involves so many specific factors, we have until this point presented the model with academic examples of interventions and progress monitoring. The model is easily applied to behavioral interventions. In doing so, the basic structure is the same as one for academic deficits. It still includes research-based interventions, progress monitoring, and observations for fidelity of instruction. As we examine the model more closely, we will highlight similarities to and differences from the previously presented academic models.

Tier 1—School-Wide and Class-Wide Interventions

In a Problem-Solving Model for behavioral issues, Tier 1 involves use of a social skills curriculum focused on the behaviors necessary for success in the general education environment. This may be implemented through the use of class-wide or school-wide behavioral plans, such as Positive Behavioral Interventions and Supports (PBIS; Sandomierski, Kincaid, & Algozzine, 2007; Sugai, Horner, & Gresham, 2002). PBIS has been implemented in schools throughout the United States and has been found to provide effective behavior management in preschool through secondary settings. Its focus is to reduce and prevent inappropriate behavior by teaching and reinforcing appropriate behavior.

The Tier 1 plan should establish and teach expectations, provide reward systems for compliance, and provide consequences for noncompliance. Through its implementation, teachers should be able to manage minor behavior occurrences and implement interventions to increase active engagement (Barnett et al., 2006).

The Tier 1 behavior plan, when implemented with fidelity, should be generally effective for approximately 80 percent of the class. In order to ensure this, leadership teams may review discipline records to identify classes in need of assistance. Classrooms in which large numbers of students receive discipline referrals or engage in off-task or aggressive behaviors should be carefully examined for effective behavior management practices. Just as with academic interventions, it is only after this effective practice has been verified that you should begin looking at nonresponders (Sandomierski, et al., 2007).

Students who experience significant behavioral difficulties despite the PBIS implementation may be identified through universal screening consisting of teacher observation, behavior checklists, and review of discipline referrals. This does not, however, identify students who exhibit withdrawing behaviors. According to Sandomierski and colleagues (2007), there are currently no standardized behavior screening measures that fit this description. Until such tools are developed, schools must continue to use the tools such as those listed above.

Tier 2—Targeted Interventions for Tier 1 Non-Responders

The problem-solving team process is applied in order to clearly define the problem behavior and develop an intervention plan. The team makeup might be identical to that used for academic interventions, but the team could also include behavior specialists, positive behavioral support (PBS) coaches, school counselors, or others with expertise in behavior management. The team should explore whether external factors may be contributing to the behavior problems. This information may be obtained through social histories, parent interviews, parent questionnaires, and physicians' reports (Barnett et al., 2006). The team should also consider whether behaviors might be a response to academic deficiencies—in other words, whether frustration or embarrassment the student experiences over inability to complete assignments is causing outbursts of bad behavior. In one PBIS project school, team members found that over 80 percent of students referred for severe behavioral problems also experienced academic problems (Sandomierski et al., 2007). Students may receive Tier 2 interventions for both academic and behavioral problems simultaneously. In such cases, teams should carefully evaluate and monitor the relationship between behavior and academic functioning.

Behavior observations that document antecedent-behavior-consequence are very helpful in analyzing and monitoring behavior problems and progress (Crimmins, Farrell, Smith, & Bailey, 2007). By carefully documenting and considering the setting, time frame, frequency, duration, antecedents, and consequences of behavior, teams can begin to identify patterns, which leads to effective interventions. Resource D of this book provides an example of a behavior documentation form of this type.

Based on all available data, the team would then design an intervention plan containing proactive, evidence-based behavioral interventions designed to keep the behavior from occurring and break undesirable behavior patterns. Direct instruction of interventions might be carried out one-on-one or in small group settings. Interventions may also be embedded in classroom procedures modified for individuals or groups of children. Group interventions might include social stories (Gray, 2000), social curriculum (Joseph & Strain, 2003), or group counseling (Corey,

1990; Sanders, 2007; Sandomierski et al., 2007; Utay & Lampe, 1995). Additionally, individual interventions such as self-monitoring, daily behavior report cards (Chafouleas, McDougal, Riley-Tillman, Panahon, & Hilt, 2005; Fairbanks, Sugai, Guardino, & Lathrop, 2007), and token economies (Sprick, Garrison, & Howard, 1998) may be implemented within the general education classroom. As stated earlier, the strategies should be proactive and serve the purpose of preventing, eliminating, or replacing undesirable behaviors. Sending students to "time out," the office, or home rarely has a positive impact on behavior change.

Progress monitoring may include careful documentation of the frequency and duration of the targeted behavior in various settings based on the incidence of the original behavior. Behavior checklists, teacher rating scales, and anecdotal records may also be used, along with continued monitoring of discipline referrals. The team must determine a cut-point, or decision rule, that will identify when the student has made sufficient or insufficient progress (Barnett et al., 2006). These decision rules should clearly define what is considered acceptable or unacceptable progress. Short- and long-term goals should be established for the student. After implementation begins, the team will analyze the data to make instructional decisions about responsiveness to the strategy.

Tier 3—Intensive Individualized Interventions for Tier 2 Non-Responders

When students are unresponsive to Tier 2 behavioral interventions, the team must employ more intensive assessment and interventions, in Tier 3. This may be accomplished through closer analysis of previous data and through functional behavioral assessment (FBA; Barnett et al., 2006). FBA seeks to determine why the student is behaving as he or she is. It helps the team to determine how external factors and student characteristics interact to influence the child's behavior (Crimmins et al., 2007). Students at Tier 3 may also be referred for further evaluation to determine the existence of disabling conditions. Just as with academic models, inclusion of special education services at this level will depend on state and local policy. Regardless of whether the child is served within or outside of special education, intensive, individualized research-based interventions should be implemented as part of an overall plan for behavior improvement.

A key component of the behavioral RTI model, as with the academic model, is to have flexible movement up and down tiers. When problem behaviors diminish, students should move back to less intensive interventions whenever possible. Barnett and colleagues (2006) proposed that initial implementation of all tiers simultaneously might be suitable for children with extreme behaviors. In this case, the team should develop a comprehensive plan that includes intensive interventions. As behaviors diminish, interventions are phased out and the student moves to a lower, less intensive tier.

Throughout subsequent chapters, we will present many interventions and examples of RTI implementation for behavioral issues. As with all RTI models, leadership teams should begin with Tier 1: effective instruction and management for all students. When they can verify that this is in place, development of subsequent tiers can proceed.

Partnering With Parents (Chapter 1)

Parents can bring a unique perspective to the RTI team. After all, parents are teachers too—they have been teaching their children since well before they entered school and will continue to teach them until well after they leave school. Combining expertise and varying perspectives increases student achievement as you focus efforts on a common goal. The goal is helping our children to learn.

As you endeavor to implement the RTI process, it is crucial to involve parents at all tiers. Attempts to increase involvement must be more than token gestures. You must make real efforts to inform parents and include them in all aspects of your school program.

Some teachers have the perception that families do not want to be involved, when in fact many simply do not know how to be involved. It is also the case that some parents have the perception that they are not welcome at school—often as a result of their own negative school experiences. Yet, parents and schools both typically want to increase involvement.

Many parents and other concerned adults, such as physicians and mental health professionals, do not truly understand the pyramid of interventions. Often, we see well-meaning but uninformed non-educators fighting the system. The importance of teamwork to a winning game is obvious to everyone in endeavors such as basketball; however, in education, we often forget to work together as a true collaborative team. We believe increasing two-way communication is the best way to create a truly effective team.

There are several ways to communicate the overall RTI process to parents and community members. The student handbook is an obvious method for educating parents. It should provide a clear description of the process. Parent-friendly notices describing the process and how it addresses the needs of all learners is also beneficial. Communication can also be increased through e-mail, interactive phone systems, communication notebooks, newsletters, and meetings. To know the most *effective* method of communication takes knowing your community of parents. It may be necessary to meet at various times of the day and at various locations in the community to truly achieve school and family collaboration.

Throughout this book, we will discuss the importance of partnering with parents as we endeavor to include them as part of the team.

SUMMARY

Response to Intervention is a process that may be used for the identification of learning disabilities in students of all ages. We believe RTI has the potential to have more substantial effect for all students when it is incorporated into a school improvement process. The Standard Protocol Model, the Problem-Solving Model, and the mixed model are all ways to structure the process for school-wide implementation. The process will vary by school structure and grade level. Thus far, we have given you a brief overview of each model. Throughout subsequent chapters, we will go into great detail about the components of effective RTI implementation and will provide recommendations for implementation as a tool for school improvement.

REFERENCES

Barnett, D. W., Elliott, N., Wolsing, L., Bunger, C. E., Haski, H., McKissick, C., et al. (2006). Response to intervention for young children with extremely challenging behaviors: What it might look like. *School Psychology Review, 35*(4), 568–582.

Batsche, G., Elliott, J., Graden, J. L., Grimes, J., Kovaleski, J. F., Prasse, D., et al. (2006). *Response to intervention: Policy considerations and implementation* (4th ed.). Alexandria, VA: National Association of State Directors of Special Education.

Bender, W. N., & Shores, C. F. (2007). *Response to Intervention: A practical guide for every teacher*. Thousand Oaks, CA: Corwin Press.

Bergan, J. R. (1977). *Behavioral consultation*. Columbus, OH: Charles E. Merrill.

Biancarosa, C., & Snow, C. E. (2006). *Reading Next—A vision for action and research in middle and high school literacy: A report to Carnegie Corporation of New York* (2nd ed.). Washington, DC: Alliance for Excellent Education.

Chafouleas, S. M., McDougal, J. L., Riley-Tillman, T. C., Panahon, C. J., & Hilt, A. M. (2005). What do Daily Behavior Report Cards (DBRCs) measure? An initial comparison of DBRCs with direct observation for off-task behavior. *Psychology in the Schools, 42,* 669–676.

Corey, G. (1990). *Theory and practice of group counseling*. Boston: Brooks/Cole Publishing.

Council for Exceptional Children. (2002). *Addressing over-representation of African American students in special education: The prereferral intervention process—An administrator's guide*. Washington, DC: National Alliance of Black School Educators.

Crimmins, D., Farrell, A. F., Smith, P. W., & Bailey, A. (2007). *Positive strategies for students with behavior problems*. Baltimore: Paul H. Brookes Publishing.

Cummins, J. (1980). The entry and exit fallacy in bilingual education. *NABE Journal, 4*(3), 25–29.

Davis, G. N., Lindo, E. J., & Compton, D. L. (2007). Children at risk for reading failure: Constructing an early screening measure. *TEACHING Exceptional Children, 39*(5), 32–37.

Deno, S., & Mirkin, P. (1977). *Data-based program modification*. Minneapolis, MN: Leadership Training Institute for Special Education.

Deshler, D. (2004, January). *We've been waiting for this moment...Are we ready?* Retrieved August 29, 2007, from http://www.kucrl.org

Fairbanks, S., Sugai, G., Guardino, D., & Lathrop, M. (2007). Response to intervention: Examining classroom behavior support in second grade. *Exceptional Children, 73*(3), 288–310.

Freeman, D., & Freeman, Y. (2004). Three types of English language learners. *School Talk: Newsletter of the National Council of Teachers of English, 9*(4), 1–3.

Fuchs, D., & Deshler, D. (2007). What we need to know about responsiveness to intervention (and shouldn't be afraid to ask). *Learning Disabilities Research & Practice, 22*(2), 129–136.

Fuchs, D., & Fuchs, L. S. (2006). Introduction to Response to Intervention: What, why, and how valid is it? *Reading Research Quarterly, 41*(1), 93–98.

Fuchs, D., Fuchs, L. S., & Compton, D. L. (2004). Identifying reading disabilities by responsiveness-to-instruction: Specifying measures and criteria. *Learning Disability Quarterly, 27,* 216–227.

Fuchs, D., Mock, D., Morgan, P. L., & Young, C. L. (2003). Responsiveness-to-intervention: Definitions, evidence, and implications for the learning disabilities construct. *Learning Disabilities Research & Practice, 18*(3), 157–171.

Fuchs, L. S., & Fuchs, D. (2007). A model for implementing responsiveness to intervention. *TEACHING Exceptional Children, 39*(5), 14–20.

Graner, P. S., Fagella-Luby, M. N., & Fritschmann, N. S. (2005). An overview of responsiveness to intervention. *Topics in Language Disorders, 25*(2), 93–105.

Gray, C. (2000). *The new social story book*. Arlington, TX: Future Horizons.

Hilton, A. (2007). Response to intervention: Changing how we do business. *Leadership, 36*(4), 16–19.

Hollenbeck, A. F. (2007). From IDEA to implementation: A discussion of foundational and future responsiveness-to-intervention research. *Learning Disabilities Research & Practice, 22*(2), 137–146.

Hughes, C., & Deshler, D. (2007, April). *RTI in middle and high school: How will the game play out?* Retrieved Presentation at the Council for Exceptional Children's National Conference, Louisville, KY.

Joseph, G. E., & Strain, P. S. (2003). Comprehensive evidence-based social-emotional curricula for young children: An analysis. *Topics in Early Childhood Special Education, 23*, 65–76.

Klingner, J. K., & Artiles, A. J. (2003). When should bilingual students be in special education? *Educational Leadership, 61*(2), 66–71.

Marler, B., & Sanchez-Lopez, C. (2006, April). *Distinguishing learning disabilities from academic difficulties for English language learners.* Retrieved Presentation at the 2006 Council for Exceptional Children's Conference, Salt Lake City, UT.

Marston, D., Muyskens, P., Lau, M., & Canter, A. (2003). Problem-solving model for decision making with high-incidence disabilities: The Minneapolis experience. *Learning Disabilities Research & Practice, 18*(3), 187–200.

Maslow, A., & Lowery, R. (1998). *Toward a psychology of being* (3rd ed.). New York: John Wiley.

Mastropieri, M. A., & Scruggs, T. W. (2005). Feasibility and consequences of Response to Intervention: Examination of the issues and scientific evidence as a model for the identification of individuals with learning disabilities. *Journal of Learning Disabilities, 38*(6), 525–531.

National High School Center. (2007). *Easing the transition to high school: Research and best practices designed to support high school learning.* Retrieved December 12, 2007, from http://www.betterhighschools.org

National Institute of Child Health and Human Development. (2000). *Report of the National Reading Panel. Teaching children to read: An evidence-based assessment of the scientific research literature on reading and its implications for reading instruction.* Retrieved August 21, 2007, from http://www.nichd.nih.gov/publications

National Research Center on Learning Disabilities. (2002). *Common ground report.* Reston, VA: Author.

Ordonez, C. L., Carlo, M. S., Snow, C. E., & McLaughlin, B. (2002). Depth and breadth of vocabulary in two languages: Which vocabulary skills transfer? *Journal of Educational Psychology, 94*(4), 719–728.

Payne, R. K. (2005). *A framework for understanding poverty.* Highlands, TX: aha! Process, Inc.

Pennington, H. (2006, October). *Expanding learning time in high schools.* Retrieved December 10, 2007, from http://www.americanprogress.org/issues/2006/10/pdf/extended_learning_report.pdf

President's Commission on Excellence in Special Education. (2002). *A new era: Revitalizing special education for children and their families.* Retrieved July 26, 2006, from http://www.ed.gov/inits/commissionsboards/whspecialeducation/index.html

Sanders, T. (2007). Helping children thrive at school: The effectiveness of nurture groups. *Educational Psychology and Practice, 23*(1), 45–61.

Sandomierski, T., Kincaid, D., & Algozzine, B. (2007). Response to intervention and positive behavior support: Brothers from different mothers or sisters with different misters? *Positive Behavioral Interventions and Supports Newsletter, 4*(2), 1–5.

Sousa, D. (2001). *How the brain learns* (2nd ed.). Thousand Oaks, CA: Corwin Press.

Speece, D. L., & Case, L. P. (2001). Classification in context: An alternative approach to identifying early reading disability. *Journal of Educational Psychology, 93*(4), 735–749.

Speece, D. L., Case, L. P., & Molloy, D. E. (2003). Responsiveness to general education instruction as the first gate to learning disabilities identification. *Learning Disabilities Research & Practice, 18*(3), 147–156.

Sprick, R., Garrison, M., & Howard, L. M. (1998). *CHAMPs: A proactive and positive approach to classroom management.* Longmont, CO: Sopris West.

Sugai, G., Horner, R. H., & Gresham, F. M. (2002). Behaviorally effective school environments. In M. Shinn, H. Walker, & G. Stone (Eds.), *Interventions for academic and behavior problems II: Preventive and remedial approaches* (pp. 315–350). Bethesda, MD: National Association of School Psychologists.

Tilley, W. D. (2003, December). *How many tiers are needed for successful prevention and early intervention? Heartland Area Education Agency's evolution from four to three tiers.* Paper presented at the National Research Center on Learning Disabilities' Responsiveness-to-Intervention Symposium, Kansas City, MO.

U.S. Department of Education. (2001). *No Child Left Behind Executive Summary.* Retrieved August 21, 2007, from http://www.nationalreadingpanel.org/publications/nochildleftbehind.htm

U.S. Department of Education. (2006, August 14). Assistance to states for the education of children with disabilities and preschool grants for children with disabilities; Final rule. *Federal Register, 71*(156), 46786–46787.

University of Kansas Center for Research on Learning. (2007). *Content Literacy Continuum.* Retrieved December 11, 2007, from http://clc.kucrl.org

Utay, J. M., & Lampe, R. E. (1995). Use of a group counseling game to enhance social skills of children with LD. *Journal for Specialists in Group Work, 20*(2), 114–120.

Vaughn, S., Linan-Thompson, S., & Hickman, P. (2003). Response to instruction as a means of identifying students with reading/learning disabilities. *Exceptional Children, 69*(4), 392–409.

Vaughn, S., Mathes, P. G., Linan-Thompson, S., & Francis, D. (2005). Teaching English language learners at risk for reading disabilities to read: Putting research into practice. *Learning Disabilities Research & Practice, 20*(1), 58–67.

Vaughn Gross Center for Reading and Language Arts. (2006). *Preventing reading difficulties: A three-tiered intervention model.* Retrieved August 21, 2007, from http://www.texasreading.org

Vellutino, F. R., Scanlon, D. M., Sipay, E. R., Small, S. G., Pratt, A., Chen, R., et al. (1996). Cognitive profiles of difficult-to-remediate and readily remediated poor readers: Early intervention as a vehicle for distinguishing between cognitive and experiential deficits as basic causes of specific reading disability. *Journal of Educational Psychology, 88*, 601–638.

Vellutino, F. R., Scanlon, D. M., Small, S., & Fanuele, D. P. (2006). Response to intervention as a vehicle for distinguishing between children with and without reading disabilities: Evidence for the role of kindergarten and first-grade interventions. *Journal of Learning Disabilities, 39*(2), 157–169.

Selecting and Implementing Ongoing Assessment

In this era of standards-based, high-stakes assessments, improving student achievement is central to most school mission statements across the nation. Schmoker (1999) asserts that an emphasis on results is essential for schools to show educational improvement, and when schools improve, students reap lifelong benefits. To truly improve achievement, educators must focus on desired results, set clear and obtainable goals, and discuss progress on these goals throughout the learning process. As educators discuss progress, they must *use* the data to inform, and possibly change, teaching methods. Education for all students will be improved as educators focus on appropriate assessments that yield viable results and strive to obtain the conditions that promote success.

A variety of assessments are given throughout the school year, each serving a different function that provides us with diverse information about student performance. Common functions include assigning student grades and ranking schools and students. These large-scale assessments are limited in their ability to *immediately* increase student learning. Classroom assessments, however, are powerful instructional tools for improving the learning of students. Yet, the very mention of the word "assessment" conjures up negative emotions for some teachers. On numerous occasions, we have asked teachers to describe the feeling they get when asked about assessments and data. The most common response is fear. When asked to elaborate, teachers typically respond that they fear the data from assessments will be used to "catch" them doing something wrong or that the data will not portray their hard work. On the contrary, the data from assessments should be used for more practical purposes, such as increasing student learning through informed instructional decision making. When decisions regarding assessment are made with the students in mind, the outcomes become more relevant to what we are striving to achieve in the classroom.

One of the essential components of Response to Intervention is the reliance on data for instructional decision making. In order to assess whether a student is making progress, you must use valid, reliable data derived from a variety of sources. The data must show small increments of change and reflect student response to increasingly intensive instruction. This is most often achieved through the use of benchmark assessments in Tier 1 and curriculum-based measurement (CBM) in Tier 2 and above. The process of utilizing this data for instructional decision making is called progress monitoring.

As we explore assessment in this chapter, we will begin by looking at some basic ideas regarding the process. We will discuss the difference between formative and summative assessment and give practical methods for using both formal and informal formative assessment for daily instructional decision making. We will develop an overall picture of utilizing data to plan, evaluate, and restructure your instruction.

Additionally, we will discuss the use of curriculum-based measurement, functional behavioral assessment, and progress monitoring inherent in Tier 2 and above. These practices increase student achievement and are essential in understanding students' strengths, weaknesses, and progress toward goals.

DATA UTILIZATION

Data is all around us, but all too often, teachers are not given the training, time, or tools to interpret the data. DuFour (2004) describes this by saying educators suffer from the DRIP syndrome: Data Rich/Information Poor. To illustrate this point, a parent of a second-grader was recently given a DIBELS scoring booklet during a parent–teacher conference. When asked what the scores meant, the teacher said she did not know, because teachers were merely instructed to administer the assessment to all students and send the scores to the central office. The data was intended to give the teacher relevant information for instructional purposes, not to file away at central office or in a parent's keepsakes. Without instructional relevance, those scores were useless and the time used for administering the test was wasted.

Teachers' responsiveness to data is a key factor in determining success. Educators must begin to interpret their student data, as well as the data of their colleagues' students, in order to have a method of comparison. Interpreting requires organizing and displaying the information in a way that clearly presents students' progress. Charts or graphs can be easily developed using tools such as Microsoft Excel or Chart Dog, a free data management tool available at www.interventioncentral.com.

DuFour (2004) describes professional learning communities in which teams have access to and utilize the ideas, materials, strategies, and talents of every member of the team. This type of collaboration is very helpful in utilizing data to raise student achievement. As teachers collaborate, they begin to ask key questions about their students and the progress toward learning goals. The questions that originate from these collaborative teams are ones such as

- Which students are most at risk?
- What diagnostic information do I have about my students to inform instruction?
- What classroom interventions have I tried?
- What interventions do I plan to try next?

To truly benefit all students, the educators must honestly confront the answers to these questions. This means accepting the challenges presented without excuse, looking at individual students' scores rather than just the class average, and asking whether individual students have made progress on specified goals. Educators can then use this evidence to enhance student learning.

Integrating Assessment and Instruction

With this collaborative process in mind, we will now turn our focus to various types of assessment that should be utilized in Tier 1 of the RTI process. It is here, in the general education classroom, that teachers should begin to utilize assessment for the purpose of delivering high-quality instruction to students. When this is accomplished, assessment powerfully influences student learning and the degree of student engagement (Wiggins, 1998).

The degree of student engagement is based on the nature of the assessment. Authentic assessments with feedback and opportunities to revise learning processes can be more engaging than mastery measurement approaches, such as multiple-choice tests. The nature of the feedback also affects engagement. Feedback should be genuine and cannot be merely in the form of praise. It must be specific feedback on how a student performed in relation to the stated goal. One way to provide this feedback is to develop graphs containing student performance data. Graphs clearly illustrate student progress and present precise data to teachers, administrators, students, and parents. Consider the following scenarios.

Scenario 1: A parent of a third-grade student attends a school conference to discuss the child's struggles in reading comprehension. The teacher reports the student's test scores from traditional multiple-choice tests to the parent: 85, 60, 82, 83, 60, 62. Immediately, the parent experiences a sense of despair and has no direction for assisting with improvement. The teacher has recorded and reports the data to the parent but has no specific direction for intervening. The teacher stresses her concern over the grades and how the deficit will negatively affect the transition that occurs in third grade from *learning to read* to *reading to learn*. However, the data is not portrayed or analyzed in a way that informs instruction. Thus, the child receives no change in instruction, leading to no change in performance.

Scenario 2: A parent of a third-grade student attends a school conference to discuss the child's struggles in reading comprehension. The teacher discusses the child's overall performance by displaying a progress-monitoring graph that depicts his reading comprehension before and after intervention (see Figure 2.1). The teacher quickly informs the parent of the pattern of weakness that she was able to distinguish while previously analyzing the data. She explains to the parent that the child's scores of 85, 82, and 83 were from narrative text. Narrative texts are easier for many readers because they draw the reader into the story, they have predictable story lines, and they utilize common vocabulary. She continues by explaining that expository text delivers information that has a variety of text patterns, such as problem–solution, cause and effect, and time-order. Multiple text patterns can even be combined in one expository text; therefore, the student must be skilled at adjusting his or her reading strategy.

The teacher explains that some weeks ago, using this information, she developed a plan of action that included targeted instruction for improving expository reading skills after the first four scores were analyzed. She had implemented the plan by incorporating a two-column question-and-answer graphic organizer.

The teacher continues to explain the plan and her research to the parent. She explains that the National Reading Panel (2000) found that graphic organizers are particularly appropriate for expository texts, enabling readers to utilize illustrations of the concepts and their relationships.

The teacher shows the parent the graph seen in Figure 2.1, which portrays comprehension scores from narrative and expository text after implementing the graphic organizer intervention. She points out that the

Figure 2.1 Third Grade Student's Progress Monitoring for
Comprehension of Narrative and Expository Text

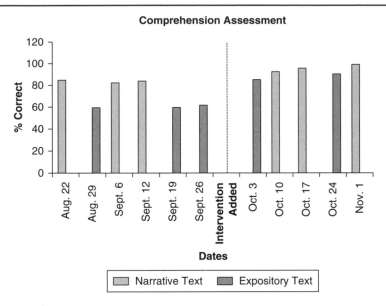

Comprehension Assessment

expository text scores increased to 85 and 90, while the narrative text
scores were 92, 95, and 99. She explains that the explicit use of graphic
organizers improved the student's comprehension scores of not only the
expository text but also the narrative text. The teacher gives the parent
various graphic organizers to use at home that were found to be useful in
the classroom. The parent is willing to try these, because she can visibly see
the improvements made in her child's progress. As a team, the parent and
teacher contributed to increasing the child's ability to comprehend text.

In comparing these two scenarios, note that the people involved and the
initial scores are identical. The outcomes, however, are very different. The
true impact comes from using the data to provide specific feedback to teachers, parents, and students so they can make necessary instructional changes
as a team. Providing feedback does not have to be a time-consuming,
impractical task. At times, feedback is informal. An example of this would
be a teacher who walks around the room during independent work, stop-
ping at a student's desk to specifically comment on how he may improve
fluency and accuracy of long division steps by using the acronym DMSB
(Daddy, Mother, Sister, Brother—for Division, Multiplication, Subtraction,
Bring Down). Another example is to use a checklist or rubric to give feedback to students working in small groups.

As you provide explicit feedback to students, they will begin to self-
assess and regulate their own learning, leading them to become mature

learners. Black and Wiliam (1998) assert that student achievement is increased when student self-assessment is incorporated within formative assessment. Figure 2.2 shows an example of student self-assessment used to promote student engagement as well as an awareness of strengths and needs.

Formative assessments provide the teacher with practical information used to alter instruction for increased student learning. Formative assessments can be both formal and informal. One such informal assessment consists of determining the readability of subject matter material for students (Northey, 2005). Teachers can assess the readability of their textbooks by developing a simple readability tool. To do this, the teacher chooses a page from a student text and reads it aloud at an accomplished reader's speed to determine appropriate rate. The teacher notes five basic comprehension questions that students should be able to answer after reading the passage. She then gives the same reading passage to her students. She tells them to read the passage silently and record their stop time from a digital clock display or a countdown timer. The students should then answer the five comprehension questions, reread the passage, and list unknown words. Students who read significantly slower than the teacher's predetermined rate, make more than two errors on the comprehension questions, and list five or more unknown words do not have access to text information. This data allows teachers to determine which students need varied forms of access to print material (e.g., recorded texts or reading guides).

Assessment and instruction are integral components of an effective lesson. Teachers should incorporate various types of ongoing assessments

Figure 2.2   Self-Assessment Checklist

Mathematics Self-Assessment Checklist: Multiplying Fractions

		Name: _____ Date: _____
Yes	No	I can simplify the fractions if not in lowest terms.
Yes	No	I can multiply the numerators of the fractions to get the new numerator.
Yes	No	I can multiply the denominators of the fractions to get the new denominator.
Yes	No	I can simplify the resulting fraction if possible.

that include access to materials, skill attainment, progress toward goals, and student engagement. Daily informal and formal assessments provide a guide for targeted instruction throughout the week.

ASSESSMENTS COMMONLY USED IN TIER 1

There are a variety of assessment tools available to today's educator. When striving for fair assessment, teachers must incorporate various types of assessments that lead to valid consensus and portray a complete picture of students' current levels of functioning. It is unfair to base important decisions on the outcome of one assessment. Every assessment has limitations. Incorporating various assessments is not always easy, due to limited time and resources. Educators must consider the efficiency and feasibility of the different approaches and then choose and utilize assessments in the most effective way (McMillan, 2000).

In the next section, we will explore several types of assessments that may be used in each tier of the RTI pyramid. We will also discuss how each one may be used for instructional decision making.

Formative and Summative Assessments

Two types of assessments available for use in the classroom are formative and summative assessments. Formative assessments are given frequently throughout the unit and are used to adjust and confirm instruction. Also known as assessment *for* learning, formative assessments give immediate evidence of progress and provide an opportunity to make changes to instruction in order to improve the quality of student learning. Formative assessments inform instruction by telling teachers what was learned and where the gaps are in students' skills and thought processes. They provide teachers with additional information for differentiation, such as how to regroup students for enrichment or re-teaching. It is imperative that the teacher's purpose in using formative assessments is to continually assess the impact of instruction and improve student learning. Formative assessments include, but are not limited to, self-assessments, anecdotal records, quizzes, question-and-answer time within the lesson, homework, observation, projects, checklists, simulations, conferences, and Exit Cards. In order to meet the goal of improving student learning, the information gained from formative assessments must be used to guide the instructional process, not merely recorded in the grade book. Figure 2.3 (teacher checklist) and Figure 2.4 (Exit Card, or "Ticket out the Door") are examples of formative assessment tools used for feedback on student learning.

Figure 2.3   Student Performance Checklist

Objective: Writing a Persuasive Paragraph

Student:	Identifies a position and clearly supports with factual information	Organization is logical and maintained throughout	Effectively addresses needs and characteristics of audience	Language choices enhance the text
James	Y	Y	Y	Y
Sara	N	N	N	N
Payton	Y	Y	Y	Y
Haley	Y-weak	Y-weak	Y	Y
Nathan	Y-weak	Y	N	N

Figure 2.4   Ticket Out the Door for a Bill of Rights Unit

List your basic freedoms as a United States citizen.

Summative assessments are very common in classrooms across the country. These assessments are more comprehensive and are used at the end of a unit or instructional period in order to evaluate the effectiveness of the educational program; thus they are termed assessments *of* learning. Summative assessments do not provide the instantaneous, contextualized response useful for helping teachers and students during the learning progression. They do, however, provide accountability for teachers, schools, and school systems as they judge students' cumulative learning experience. Summative assessments include chapter and unit tests, final exams, final projects, statewide tests, national tests, and entrance tests (e.g., SAT or ACT). Summative assessments determine whether students have mastered explicit educational objectives; therefore, it is too late to use data from summative assessments for immediate instructional change.

To illustrate the importance of formative assessments, let's compare a formative assessment to a physical exam. When a doctor examines her patient, she devotes extensive time to understanding and communicating methods for improving health. For example, after Heather's yearly physical, she is told that she has high cholesterol. Her doctor tells her to get more exercise, change her diet, and take a prescription medication. She is advised that in three months, she should return to have her cholesterol checked again so that her plan can be adjusted.

Likewise, the intent of formative assessments is to diagnose and prescribe the appropriate intervention in order to be educationally healthy (DuFour, DuFour, Eaker, & Karhanek, 2004). In much the same way, formative assessments guide our instruction daily in order to increase the learning outcomes indicated on the final summative assessments. For improving students' learning along the way and comprehensively, both types of assessments must be understood and used effectively.

Benchmark Assessments

Benchmark assessments, sometimes referred to as universal screening tools, are commonly used in classrooms to provide a clear picture of student learning. The term "benchmark" actually means a standard by which others can be measured. Specifically, benchmarks allow us to gauge students' strengths and weaknesses against set criteria or against the performance of other students. In Tier 1, general education instruction, benchmark assessments are used as universal screening tools, administered to all students at regular intervals, typically three to four times or more per year. They may also be given to individual students as screening tools for identifying specific student needs.

The results of benchmark assessments indicate the effectiveness of the educational program. Individual students' performance can be compared with the performance of other students (e.g., lowest 20th percentile) or the benchmark goal (e.g., 40 words per minute). They can be used to determine strengths and weaknesses of the student, the curriculum, and instruction. The results should then be used to guide instruction including the need for intervention or enrichment.

In the RTI process, benchmark assessments are used for screening purposes in order to identify students in Tier 1 instruction who are at risk for not meeting the standard. This allows the teacher to monitor the lowest-achieving students more frequently and provide needed assistance through Tier 2 interventions.

One well-known benchmark assessment tool for reading in kindergarten through sixth grade is Dynamic Indicators of Basic Early Literacy Skills (DIBELS). DIBELS are a set of standardized quick, instructional assessment probes that assess students in the areas of phonemic awareness, phonics, fluency, vocabulary, and comprehension.

In some instances, no standardized benchmark tools are available for the content area or grade level being evaluated. School districts may create their own assessments based on local or state curriculum. Creating benchmark assessments requires thoughtful consideration of critical standards-based components. Once the vital skills have been identified, educators must represent these on the assessment in a manner that produces clear results that can be used to interpret students' weaknesses and plan instructional interventions.

The most common purpose of benchmark assessment is to evaluate how well the students have mastered material to date. Some benchmarks, however, are used to predict how well students will do on future summative assessments. Determining the purpose of your assessment is critical in order to appropriately choose benchmark test items. The most important factor is to develop benchmark assessments in order to adjust instructional strategies to increase student learning. Benchmark assessments must extend beyond simply outlining the data to also providing a means for interpreting the data for instructional changes.

Behavior Data Analysis for Schools and Individuals

Student behaviors and academics are two intertwined factors that must be addressed within the classroom. Behavior must be a primary focus within schools, because academic interventions are unsuccessful in unmanaged environments. Marzano (2003) emphasizes that the teacher's most important role in the school is classroom manager. In order to effectively manage behaviors, teachers must be aware of behavior problems throughout the school as a whole, as well as behavior problems for individual students. Being aware of these behaviors includes systematically collecting and analyzing school-wide and individual student data in order to determine contributing factors to inappropriate behavior, such as time of day, location in the school, or specific teacher or subject matter. This information can be obtained through office discipline referrals, anecdotal records, behavior checklists, bus discipline referrals, suspension records, and parental notices.

Often, collecting and analyzing this type of data across the school reveals school-wide behavior problems. For example, we have worked in many schools where, after collecting and analyzing the data, we became aware of instances in which a certain hallway in the school was unsupervised or that a specific teacher needed professional development in behavior management. In addition, we have been able to pinpoint specific periods of the day in which individual students displayed inappropriate behavior. One such example was of a student who always displayed inappropriate behavior during the ten o'clock hour. With this information, the teachers investigated further and determined the child was continually hungry at this time but was unable to express his need to eat; in fact, he did not even realize his hunger. Before moving on to Tier 2 strategies, we must first systematically review and analyze both behavior and academic data.

TIER 2 AND ABOVE: ASSESSMENT OF INDIVIDUAL STUDENTS' PROGRESS

Progress Monitoring

As students move from Tier 1 to Tier 2, assessments provide more focus on individual student progress. Teachers must utilize data to closely observe the student's response to research-based interventions and adjust instruction accordingly.

Progress monitoring is a key component of effective Tier 2 instruction. It has been used since the early 1970s. Simply stated, progress monitoring is assessing students to monitor their academic progress in core educational skill areas. For example, in reading, educators measure students' fluency and accuracy in reading text. Educators monitor progress and use the results to set appropriate individual goals and adjust instruction as needed. Implementing progress monitoring requires determining students' current levels of performance, as well as identifying learning objectives. Students' academic functioning is evaluated on a regular basis—weekly, biweekly, or monthly, based on individual students' needs. Actual and expected rates of learning are compared. This informs the teacher of students' progress, which allows him or her to make appropriate instructional decisions. The National Association of State Directors of Special Education (2005) has identified nine essential characteristics for progress monitoring to be useful in an RTI context.

Progress monitoring should:

1. Assess the specific skills embodied in state and local academic standards.
2. Assess marker variables that have been demonstrated to lead to the ultimate instructional target.
3. Be sensitive to small increments of growth over time.
4. Be administered efficiently over short periods.
5. Be administered repeatedly (using multiple forms).
6. Result in data that can be summarized in teacher-friendly data displays.
7. Be comparable across students.
8. Be applicable for monitoring an individual student's progress over time.
9. Be relevant to development of instructional strategies and use of appropriate curriculum that addresses the area of need.

In summary, the student's progress is documented and instructional strategies are adapted to meet the student's learning needs. Benchmark assessments and curriculum-based measurements are a part of progress monitoring.

The Office of Special Education Programs (OSEP) has funded the National Center on Student Progress Monitoring (www.studentprogress .org) in order to assist educators in implementing effective progress monitoring. Under the "Tools" navigation tab on this Web site there is a Review of Progress Monitoring Tools, such as DIBELS, AIMSweb, and EdCheckup. This Tools Chart may be helpful as educators compare tools in order to choose the one most appropriate for their district or school. Figure 2.5 provides information on some of the most frequently used progress-monitoring tools available.

Figure 2.5   Progress-Monitoring Resources

Web Site	What It Offers
National Center on Student Progress Monitoring www.studentprogress.org	National technical assistance and dissemination center to assist states and districts as they implement progress monitoring in grades K–5. It is funded by the Office of Special Education Programs.
DIBELS—Dynamic Indicators of Basic Early Literacy Skills http://dibels.uoregon.edu/	Data system that allows teachers to generate automated reports.
Intervention Central www.interventioncentral.org	Numerous free downloads to assist with administering probes and graphing student data.
STEEP—System to Enhance Educational Performance www.isteep.com	Program that matches interventions to student needs.
AIMSweb www.edformation.com	Computer software that graphs and analyzes student scores.
Classworks www.classworks.com	Program that specializes in localized data-driven curriculum solutions.
Thinkgate/Testgate www.thinkgate.net	Program that provides individual student response analysis.
EdCheckup www.edcheckup.com	Online assessment system that administers and scores tests. Class and student reports are generated. Provides guidelines for setting goals and evaluating progress.
Review of Progress Monitoring Tools www.studentprogress.org/chart/chart.asp	Evaluation process regarding the scientific rigor of commercially available tools that monitor students' progress.
McGraw-Hill www.ctb.com/mktg/ypp/ypp_index.jsp	Program that assesses students weekly and graphs scores with instructional recommendations (Yearly ProgressPro).

Curriculum-Based Measurements (CBM)

Curriculum-based measurements (CBM) are research-based methods of monitoring student progress. Educators use curriculum-based measurements as indicators of academic competence in fundamental content areas (math, reading, writing, and spelling). Research shows that curriculum-based measurements increase student achievement (Fuchs, Deno, & Mirkin, 1984) and help teachers identify when instructional changes are needed

(Fuchs, Fuchs, Hamlett, Walz, & Germann, 1993). Administration of curriculum-based measurements typically takes one to five minutes and can be given to a whole class or an individual student, depending on what is being measured. Frequency of administration is determined by how often educators need information for decision making. We recommend that CBM be administered monthly to biweekly in Tier 2 and biweekly to daily in Tier 3. Obviously, the more data points obtained, the more accurate the analysis.

Curriculum-based measurements are standardized in that they are given and scored in the same manner each time. CBM differs from traditional assessment in that most scores are obtained by counting the number of correct responses, causing the measurement to be extremely sensitive to the slightest skill improvement. Figures 2.6, 2.7, and 2.8 provide examples of scoring procedures for common CBM assessments.

Figure 2.6   Curriculum-Based Measurements

There are many curriculum-based measurements that can be purchased online or accessed for free through www.interventioncentral.org.

Reading Fluency

- Given to an individual
- Scored: Number of words correctly read in the passage—middle score recorded

Mathematics

- Can be given to an individual or group
- Scored: Number of correct digits
- Single skill probes (same type problems)
- Multiple skill probes (mix of problems with different math operations)

    Example:

$$\begin{array}{r} 67 \\ \times\ 12 \\ \hline 134 \\ 670 \\ \hline 804 \end{array}$$ Traditional score of 1; CBM score of 9

Spelling

- Can be given to an individual or group
- Scored: Pairs of letters in a word that are placed in the proper sequence

    Example:

    Spelling Word: Dictionary   Traditional score of 1; CBM score of 9

Writing

- Can be given to an individual or group
- 1 minute think time and 3 minute write from a story starter
- Scored: (1) number of words written, (2) number of letters written, (3) number of words correctly spelled, or (4) number of writing units placed in correct sequence

Students' scores are compared to their own prior performance, rather than peers', which increases motivation. Specifically, the data from curriculum-based measurements can be used to identify individual student levels, students at risk of failing, effectiveness of instruction or intervention, and progress monitoring.

The majority of standardized CBM tools available are designed for use in elementary grades. The most common elementary CBM measures assess basic skills in the areas of math computation, reading fluency, spelling, and writing. It should be noted that DIBELS, which we discussed in the earlier section on Benchmark Assessments, can also serve as a CBM tool for progress monitoring. It is appropriate for both because it identifies student progress toward the benchmark and measures small increments of progress when administered on a frequent basis.

There are currently few standardized and readily available curriculum-based measurement tools for secondary schools. However, much research is being done in this area. The Research Institute on Progress Monitoring (RIPM; www.progressmonitoring.net) gives some secondary resources for creating content-related curriculum-based measurements in the areas of reading, content area learning, and writing.

Students who are fluent readers in early grades may begin to experience reading difficulties when the focus shifts to comprehension. This shift usually occurs at third or fourth grade. As these students become involved in content area classes that require reading information from different types of text, they may experience multiple learning problems. Because most middle and high schools do not teach specific reading classes, teaching students to comprehend content-related material becomes the responsibility of content area teachers. However, most content teachers focus on the content instruction itself rather than reading comprehension. As a result, students may fail to learn content due to their deficit in reading comprehension. Therefore, assessing students' ability to read and comprehend content-specific knowledge is critical. Students who struggle to read and comprehend have little hope of retaining vital concepts.

The most commonly recommended method for assessing older students in the area of reading involves the use of three-minute maze passages (Espin & Foegen, 1996). Maze passages can be created from human-interest newspaper articles or basal readers. A maze passage consists of a passage of about 400 words at an appropriate readability level in which every seventh word is replaced with a set of three choices (Stecker, Fuchs, & Fuchs, 1999): one correct (the original word from the text) and two incorrect, all with a similar number of letters. If the seventh word is a name, go on to the next word. Students must choose the correct word for the context. In assessing a student's performance on a maze passage, the following items should be counted as incorrect: skipped items, two circled items, choice cannot be distinguished. Mark a line through incorrect choices and count correct choices to obtain a score. After three consecutive errors, stop scoring and count correct choices to that point. An example of a maze passage assessment is included in Figure 2.7.

In the area of written expression, students' general writing performance can be analyzed by having students respond in writing to a narrative prompt for seven minutes. The score is computed by adding the number of correct word sequences and subtracting the number of incorrect word sequences (Espin et al., 2000). This same measure can be used for progress monitoring using a five-minute sample. Possible writing prompts include:

- One day my friend and I went to the aquarium.
- It was the last day of summer vacation.
- I was the first to see the flames.

The passage is scored by counting the correct word sequences, which is any two adjacent, correctly spelled words that are syntactically and semantically correct (Videen, Deno, & Marston, 1982).

Finally, curriculum-based measurements for content area learning consist of using a vocabulary-matching technique. Students match terms with definitions in a five-minute period. This measure assesses performance and monitors students' progress in content area learning. Teachers consider their particular curriculum and develop appropriate measures (Espin, Busch, Shin, & Kruschwitz, 2001). The first step consists of creating a list of potential vocabulary terms. These terms must represent the curriculum for the entire year or semester. The textbook glossaries, past lectures, and resource materials are all good sources to use. The next step

Figure 2.7   Sample Maze Passage

A Tea Party of Sorts

The Tea Act resulted in a drop/shop/make in the cost of tea. British declare/leaders/hurried thought Americans would be overjoyed to save/clip/give money and thus forget about their battle/yelled/sunset against unjust taxation. The Americans responded hours/quite/knows the opposite though. After three weeks of/it/so deliberating the fate of three ships full/came/hall of tea, the Americans took action. With/Which/Whom many dressed as Mohawk Indians, a procession/immediately/accomplished moved from the Old South Meeting House of/to/in the harbor. They accomplished their mission of/us/so ridding the boats of 90,000 pounds in/up/of tea into the water. It was an/in/he unusual tea party for sure.

consists of developing definitions for each term. Again, the glossary is a good resource for this step. The definitions should be clear, explicit, and approximately 15 words in length. Each week, the educator chooses 20 terms and their matching definitions plus two additional definitions that do not match a term. Each probe will have 20 terms and 22 definitions. Typically, the probe will have terms on the left side with a blank for an answer space and the definitions with letters on the right side of the page. Students then choose the correct definition for each term.

Figure 2.8   Vocabulary Matching (Geometry)

1. Acute Angle	a. A positive angle that measures less than 90 degrees
2. Skew Lines	b. Two angles that share both a side and a vertex
3. Solid	c. A statement that is assumed to be true without proof
4. Great Circle	d. A line segment, line, or plane that divides a geometric figure into two congruent halves
5. Bisector	
6. Radius	e. A statement that can be easily proven once a theorem is proved
7. Scalene Triangle	f. The statement made by interchanging the hypothesis and the conclusion of a statement
8. Locus	
9. Diameter	g. A line segment that connects two points on a curve
10. Isometry	h. The line segment joining two points on a circle and passing through the center
11. Corollary	
12. Converse	i. The line segment connecting two nonadjacent vertices in a polygon
13. Adjacent Angles	j. A line that intersects two other lines
14. Vertex	k. The circle formed by the intersection of a plane passing through the center of a sphere
15. Pyramid	
16. Chord	l. The longest side of a right triangle that is opposite the right angle
17. Diagonal	m. A transformation of a figure that does not change the distances of any two points in the figure
18. Kite	
19. Axiom	n. A quadrilateral with two disjoint pairs of congruent adjacent sides
20. Hypotenuse	o. The set of all points (usually forming a curve or surface) satisfying some condition
	p. The union of all line segments that connect a given point
	q. The distance from the center to a point on a circle
	r. Two lines that are not in the same plane
	s. A three dimensional object that completely encloses a volume of space
	t. A triangle with three unequal sides
	u. A polyhedron with four faces

Assessing Progress Using CBM Benchmarks

In order to analyze progress, teachers must have clear benchmarks indicating adequate response in terms of performance. These benchmarks may be obtained from the assessment tool being utilized, the curriculum being implemented, or perhaps state or local department of education guidelines. For instance, the DIBELS reading fluency benchmark for the beginning of second grade is 45 words per minute. A student who is reading less than 45 words per minute is considered at risk for failure.

Over time, curriculum-based management data can be used to graphically illustrate a child's relative rate of progress. Data points obtained from CBM assessment tools can easily be charted. A progress-monitoring graph should include a vertical axis labeled with the academic skill being measured and a horizontal axis labeled with the number of instructional weeks the intervention will be in place.

Before instructional intervention occurs, a student's baseline data is determined by taking the median score from three initial curriculum-based measurement probes. The teacher or team must then set a performance goal based on the baseline, the number of weeks planned for intervention, and the expected rate of progress. After the performance goal is calculated, it is plotted on the graph with a line connecting the student's initial performance and anticipated performance goal. This line is referred to as the goal line or aimline.

In Figure 2.9, the second-grader read 22 words per minute on his first fluency probe. His initial fluency score was recorded for August and the DIBELS benchmark goal of 90 was indicated for June. A line was then drawn to connect the two data points to visually determine throughout the year whether the student was on track to obtain the end-of-year benchmark of 90 words per minute. Each week, multiple forms of fluency data were obtained and plotted on the graph. As you can see, this student made adequate progress and achieved the benchmark set for the class.

In the RTI process, most Standard Protocol interventions are set up for a specified number of weeks. In contrast to the example above, the teacher and/or interventionist will determine the goal based on the number of weeks of intervention. The goal may be incremental—a first step to reach the benchmark. For example, Juan, a second grader, has an oral reading fluency (ORF) baseline of 25 words per minute, based on the median score of three administrations of the benchmark assessment. In his school, the expected oral reading fluency benchmark for the end of second grade is 90 words per minute. Juan's teacher arranges for him to receive Tier 2 interventions through her school's Standard Protocol small group instruction.

The time frame for this intervention is fifteen weeks. Juan's teacher knows that most students in her class increase their reading fluency by 1.5 to 2.0 words per week. By multiplying these numbers times fifteen weeks, she estimates that Juan could increase his ORF by 22 to 30 words per week. Adding these numbers to his baseline score of 25 words gives an estimated ORF score of 47 to 55 words per minute. She decides to set his goal at 50 words per minute. This is an incremental goal, designed to eventually get Juan to the benchmark of 90 words. She then determines that, in order to achieve this benchmark, Juan may need an additional twenty weeks of instruction (40 words divided by 2 words per week). She and the intervention specialist will closely monitor his progress. At the end of the initial fifteen weeks, they will determine whether he is responding sufficiently to the intervention. They will then determine the next instructional step, based on his response during the initial standard protocol intervention period. In

Figure 2.9 Reading Fluency Progress Monitoring Graph

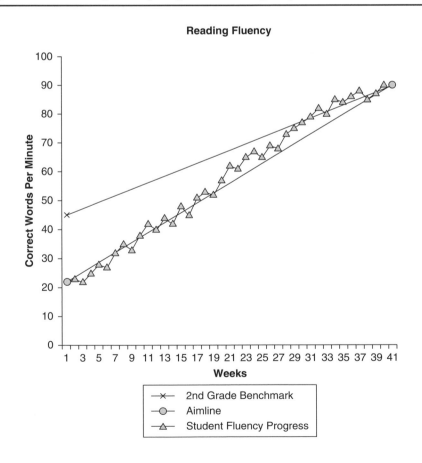

this case, it would be inappropriate to set the benchmark of 90 wpm as the goal with only fifteen weeks of planned instruction.

Educators analyze the data points to look for progress made during the intervention phase. Certainly, the goal is for students to be on or above the aimline. Students who achieve this on a consistent basis are expected to make their final benchmark goal. For students who are significantly below the aimline, educators must use professional judgment to determine effectiveness of instruction by considering a variety of factors. We will explore many of these factors in Chapter 5.

Functional Behavior Assessments

Another important type of classroom assessment is functional behavior assessment. A functional behavioral assessment is designed to determine the cause or function of a behavior prior to developing an intervention. Interventions that are implemented before investigating a behavior's cause (function) are typically ineffective and often cause additional behavior problems. The very nature of functional behavior assessment is to solve problems in a systematic manner. Perspective is broadened as educators look beyond the behavior to find the causes and appropriate interventions. In general, educators use observations, interviews, rating scales, and manipulation of events to explore behavior. The most effective of these methods is observation and documentation of the ABCs of behavior: antecedents (conditions or stimulus preceding behavior), behavior (response to the stimulus), and the consequence (result of the behavior). After establishing these points, the educator must then hypothesize the function of the behavior—for example, whether the behavior functions to garner attention, to avoid interactions, or to fulfill sensory needs. With the function of the behavior identified, specific interventions can be implemented. It is imperative to monitor progress with the new intervention to determine effectiveness and adjust as needed. This information should be displayed visually, in a graph. Functional behavior assessment allows you to make decisions based on clear evidence and continually review and assess progress.

Resource D of this book contains a brief tool to conduct a simple ABC behavioral assessment. It is designed to help teachers begin to see patterns of behavior linked to factors such as times of day, peer group, and physical location. It may be used to begin development of a Tier 2 plan. Some children will require a much more extensive tool. Special education teachers often have the expertise to complete more thorough assessments for children in the RTI pyramid. They can provide invaluable guidance and assistance in this process.

Partnering With Parents (Chapter 2)

Parents should be aware of assessments used at all tiers of the pyramid. Notice we did not say they must give permission. The benchmark assessments and curriculum-based measurements given do not typically require permission, but parents should be aware of administration and purpose. Again, this can be communicated easily through newsletters, parent–teacher conferences, phone calls, or other established methods. It is important to remember that parent permission is required for students being individually evaluated for special education services. Lastly, parents should know the expected length of progress monitoring. The length of progress monitoring is based on the type of intervention, school system procedures, and intensity of support.

Parent–teacher conferences are ideal settings for discussing *results* of assessments. If schools have communicated types of assessments and their purpose, parents will have an understanding of the assessment and increased ability to comprehend the results given to them. The data should be given in a graphic representation for parents to visualize their child's progress. This step also helps the teachers to analyze the data. It is not necessary to always schedule a parent–teacher conference to relay information about a particular assessment. We understand that time constraints make this impossible at times. Once parents are well informed and have a base of information regarding their child's assessments, teachers can deliver well-defined data to the parents by phone or by a note home. Remember, as decisions are being made, parents should be involved. Their input and support is critical to the child's success.

SUMMARY

Multiple forms of assessment are necessary at all tiers of the pyramid. Whether they use formative, summative, benchmark, or curriculum-based measurements, teachers must align curriculum goals to suitable assessments that reveal relevant information. Teachers must use assessment results to guide instruction while they work to meet the varied needs of their students. As teachers analyze the data individually and as a team, they begin to see the complete picture and make student-specific decisions that lead to increased student achievement.

Imagine an archer who spends most of his time preparing arrows to shoot toward his target every day. It would seem ridiculous for that archer to not see how close he came to the bull's-eye when he shot. Many teachers spend much of their day crafting and shooting instructional arrows with student achievement as their bull's-eye; yet, they often leave out the important last step of the cycle by not verifying how close they are to the mark. Administering assessments is only the beginning. Using the data for instructional decision making completes the process and gets each instructional arrow closer to the coveted bull's-eye.

REFERENCES

Black, P., & Wiliam, D. (1998). Inside the black box: Raising standards through classroom assessment. *Phi Delta Kappan, 80*(2), 139–148.

DuFour, R. (2004, May). What is a "professional learning community"? *Educational Leadership, 61* (8), 6–11.

DuFour, R., DuFour, R., Eaker, R., & Karhanek, G. (2004). *Whatever it takes: How professional learning communities respond when kids don't learn.* Bloomington: Solution Tree.

Espin, C. A., Busch, T., Shin, J., & Kruschwitz, R. (2001). Curriculum-based measures in the content areas: Validity of vocabulary-matching measures as indicators of performance in social studies. *Learning Disabilities Research and Practice, 16,* 142–151.

Espin, C. A., & Foegen, A. (1996). Validity of three general outcome measures for predicting secondary students' performance on content-area tasks. *Exceptional Children, 62,* 497–514.

Espin, C. A., Skare, S., Shin, J., Deno, S. L., Robinson, S., & Brenner, B. (2000). Identifying indicators of growth in written expression for middle-school students. *Journal of Special Education, 34,* 140–153.

Fuchs, L. S., Deno, S. L., & Mirkin, P. K. (1984). The effects of frequent curriculum-based measurement and evaluation on pedagogy, student achievement, and student awareness of learning. *American Educational Research Journal, 21,* 449–460.

Fuchs, L. S., Fuchs, D., Hamlett, C. L., Walz, L., & Germann, G. (1993). Formative evaluation of academic progress: How much growth can we expect? *School Psychology Review, 22,* 27–48.

Marzano, R. J. (2003). *What works in schools: Translating research into action.* Alexandria, VA: Association for Supervision and Curriculum Development.

McMillan, J. H. (2000). Fundamental assessment principles for teachers and school administrators. *Practical Assessment, Research & Evaluation, 7(8).* Retrieved August 2007, from http://PAREonline.net/getvn.asp?v=7&n=8

National Association of State Directors of Special Education, Inc. (2005). *Response to intervention: Policy considerations and implementation.* Alexandria, VA: NASDSE.

National Center on Student Progress Monitoring. (2006). Retrieved March 9, 2006, from http://www.studentprogress.org

National Institute of Child Health and Human Development. (2000). *Report of the National Reading Panel. Teaching children to read: An evidence-based assessment of the scientific research literature on reading and its implications for reading instruction: Reports of the subgroups* (NIH Publication No. 00-4754). Washington, DC: U.S. Government Printing Office.

Northey, S. S. (2005). *Handbook on Differentiated Instruction for Middle and High Schools.* Larchmont, NY: Eye on Education, Inc.

Schmoker, M. (1999). *Results: The key to continuous school improvement.* Alexandria, VA: Association for Supervision and Curriculum Development.

Stecker, P. M., Fuchs, L. S., & Fuchs, D. (1999). Using curriculum-based measurement for assessing reading progress and for making instruction decisions. *Effective Reading Instruction for Individuals with Learning Disabilities Online Academy: Teaching Reading to Individuals with Learning Disabilities.* Downloaded May 15, 2007, from http://www.onlineacademy.org/modules

Videen, J., Deno, S. L., & Marston, D. (1982). Correct word sequences: A valid indicator of writing proficiency in written expression (Research Report No. 84). Minneapolis: University of Minnesota, Institute of Research on Learning Disabilities.

Wiggins, G. (1998). *Educative assessment: Designing assessments to inform and improve student performance.* San Francisco: Jossey-Bass.

Determining Appropriate Research-Based Interventions

A new phenomenon is occurring in education in which the "art" of teaching is becoming the "science" of teaching (Marzano, Pickering, & Pollock, 2001). Teaching should not just be about the fun and creative activities—it should also be about the planned systematic research approach that increases learning. We believe that school improvement efforts should be based not solely on intuition, but rather on experience *and* research-based practices. At the core of effective teaching is the classroom teacher. In fact, recent research on teaching shows that the most important factor affecting student achievement is the classroom teacher (Wright, Horn, & Sanders, 1997). For this reason, in this chapter we will focus on specific research-based strategies that teachers can implement in their classrooms throughout all tiers of instruction in order to maximize their impact on achievement.

As discussed in Chapter 1, research-based strategies are required by our nation's federal education laws: the Individuals with Disabilities Education Improvement Act of 2004 (IDEA 2004) and the No Child Left Behind Act of 2001 (NCLB). In particular, NCLB states that only strategies and methods proven effective by scientifically based research should be included in school reform programs (Comprehensive School Reform Program Office, 2002). IDEA 2004 also references the use of research-based strategies, specifically as it relates to the identification of students who are learning disabled and as it relates to providing Early Intervening Services to students at risk for failure (U.S. Department of Education, 2006).

There is an ongoing debate among researchers and practitioners concerning an appropriate definition for research-based strategy. NCLB uses the term "scientifically based instructional strategies" in its requirements for their use in targeted assistance schools. The act defines "scientifically based research" to mean research that involves the application of rigorous, systematic, and objective procedures to obtain reliable and valid knowledge relevant to education activities and programs and includes research that

- employs systematic, empirical methods that draw on observation or experiment;
- involves rigorous data analyses that are adequate to test the stated hypotheses and justify the general conclusions drawn;
- relies on measurements or observational methods that provide reliable and valid data across evaluators and observers, across multiple measurements and observations, and across studies by the same or different investigators;
- is evaluated using experimental or quasi-experimental designs in which individuals, entities, programs, or activities are assigned to different conditions and with appropriate controls to evaluate the effects of the condition of interest, with a preference for random-assignment experiments, or other designs to the extent that those designs contain within-condition or across-condition controls;
- ensures that experimental studies are presented in sufficient detail and clarity to allow for replication or, at a minimum, offer the opportunity to build systematically on their findings; and
- has been accepted by a peer-reviewed journal or approved by a panel of independent experts through a comparably rigorous, objective, and scientific review (NCLB, sec. 9101).

In essence, the law requires that programs and interventions implemented in schools meet this high standard through quality of evidence, quantity of evidence, reliability, validity, and ease of replication. In 2004, Congress adopted this same definition for scientifically based research in IDEA (U.S. Department of Education, 2006; sec. 300.35). Therefore, RTI involves determining a student's response to scientific, research-based interventions that meet this standard.

As schools seek to implement the RTI process, we see interventions of varying types in use. For our purpose, we have divided these interventions into four distinct categories: research-validated curriculum, research-based supplemental materials, research-based practices, and research-based learning strategies.

In most research literature, research-validated curriculum refers to the state and/or local curriculum, including textbooks and structured programs that are in place to teach the curriculum. Most states have moved to curricula based on national standards. They provide state-approved textbook lists from which local districts may choose. These materials become the core curriculum and are used to teach students in general education classrooms.

Supplemental materials are often used for Tier 2 or Tier 3 interventions. They should align with the core curriculum (Vaughn & Roberts, 2007) and provide more intensive instruction in one or more skills. These materials must also meet the scientifically based research (SBR) requirements. They may be in a printed format, a computer software format, a combination of print/software, or kits.

We find that many schools are seeking out this type of intervention. There are some distinct advantages to using a published program. For example, products can be chosen for their ability to target specific skills, such as alphabetics or reading comprehension. They usually provide sequential lessons with specific guidance for the teacher, sometimes even going to the point of being scripted. When this guidance is followed carefully, fidelity of instruction improves significantly over less structured interventions. With proper training, paraprofessionals and other non-certified persons such as tutors may provide the instruction (L. S. Fuchs & Fuchs, 2007; Vaughn & Roberts, 2007).

Computer-assisted instruction (CAI) is being implemented more frequently to address individual student needs. In order to become successful adult learners, students must learn to work independently. One effective method of promoting independent learning is with the computer. Computers are typically engaging for students and can free the teacher to provide intensive instruction to other students in small group settings. It is very important, however, to use quality computer programs to meet individualized student needs; the computer is not intended to be merely a babysitter.

Computer-assisted instruction is used for drill and practice, tutorials, and simulations (Cotton, 1991). Educators are using CAI as stand-alone computer learning or as a supplement to teacher-directed instruction. Stennett (1985) found that well-designed and well-implemented CAI produced significant improvements in achievement when used *as a supplement* to traditional instruction rather than independently of teacher-directed instruction. Multiple research studies show that students who use CAI have a faster rate of learning and longer retention of information than with conventional instruction alone (Cotton, 1991). CAI offers more objectivity, appropriate pacing, opportunities for feedback, individualized learning, and engagement. It is important to match students' needs to appropriate CAI by utilizing classroom data from assessments.

Using purchased materials for interventions, despite its advantages, has some disadvantages. Firstly, using purchased materials is cost-prohibitive for some schools and districts. Because students exhibit a wide variety of skill deficits, it is difficult to provide one or more programs to address all needs.

Additionally, it cannot be assumed that all products on the market meet NCLB/IDEA requirements for scientifically based research. In reality, the extent to which these products meet this standard varies widely. For example, some publishers have valid and reliable internal research but have no independent review of their products. Others have research that is poorly designed, which essentially limits reliability and validity. There are some that have a strong research base, often with development through a research university and replication in large school systems. The dilemma for educators is trying to determine which products meet the standards and which do not. They cannot take for granted that the products they are considering for purchase meet the requirements.

Since 2004, publishers have begun making considerable efforts to establish this research base for their products or to make known the research that they have. In an effort to make their products marketable, some companies compare their materials to National Standards or the recommendations of the National Reading Panel. Others may provide student achievement data from districts that have used their program for some time. Still, most publishers do not have research results that meet the NCLB/IDEA standards.

In an effort to assist schools in finding research-based strategies, the U.S. Department of Education established the What Works Clearinghouse (WWC) through the Institute for Education Sciences. The What Works Clearinghouse provides reviews of research on a variety of scientific research–based interventions, including published materials. The reviews include a rating system, which delineates, on a scale of positive to negative, the amount of effect on student achievement that was documented in the research studies. The information is presented in easily interpreted charts and additional narrative information. It is important to note that the WWC considers evidence only from studies that meet the NCLB/IDEA requirements. Research studies of less rigor and individual system data outside of a research study are not considered in the ratings. (The WWC can be accessed at http://ies.ed.gov/ncee/wwc.)

In addition, the Florida Center for Reading Research has evaluated many reading programs currently on the market at the request of schools in their state. (The results of their evaluations are available at www.fcrr .org/FCRRReports/.) There are other organizations that make similar recommendations concerning research-based strategies and interventions—

several of them are listed in Resource A of this book. When looking at various evaluation sites, we consider only ratings done by U.S., regional, or state departments of education or leading research universities. The information should always include the standard of research considered and the basis on which recommendations are made.

We also recommend that educators wishing to purchase materials contact the publisher and ask for their research base. As we mentioned earlier, most publishers are working very hard to provide this information. Many times, the information is available on the company's Web site. If not, you may call the publisher and ask that they provide you with the information.

Our third type of intervention involves research-based practices. These are overarching concepts that are considered best practice for Tier 1 classroom instruction. They are broad concepts, not specific enough to pinpoint and address targeted deficits. The Access Center, developed by the U.S. Office of Special Education Programs, provides valuable information and teaching modules on many of these practices. The Center was part of a grant whose funding ended in 2007; however, the Web site is still maintained, at www.k8accesscenter.org.

Our last type of intervention involves research-based learning strategies, appropriate across grade levels and content areas for addressing specific skill deficits often found in students with poor achievement. In implementing the RTI process, many schools are choosing to focus on the use of these instructional strategies to provide Tier 2 and Tier 3 interventions. These types of strategies often have a strong research base that meets the NCLB/IDEA standards (L. S. Fuchs et al., 2003; L. S. Fuchs et al., 2004; Saenz, Fuchs, & Fuchs, 2005).

These types of interventions have some advantages over purchased programs, beginning with their cost-effectiveness. Most involve minimal investment and are taught through materials already available in the school, such as the basal textbook. They may be very beneficial in addressing specific skill deficits, such as inability to glean information from text. They are often most effective when taught systematically to students in intervention tiers, then embedded into the general education instruction. This provides generalization of the skill to multiple content areas.

However, just as with published materials, there are disadvantages to their use. The person who is teaching the intervention must do so in a systematic way through modeling, coaching, guided practice, independent practice, and application to the curriculum. This requires a deep understanding of the strategy itself and how it is best used in content instruction. These strategies, although they have a definite structure, often do not have guidance materials such as teacher guides or scripts.

Therefore, fidelity of instruction may not be as strong as with supplemental materials or scripted programs. When these learning strategies are being used, extra steps must be taken to ensure fidelity. We recommend that, prior to using this type of instructional strategy, teachers receive explicit instruction in its effective use. They may need ongoing guidance from instructional coaches or persons who are considered experts in the strategy.

We believe there is benefit to incorporating both programs and learning strategies in RTI intervention options. Some students will benefit most from a program specifically designed to teach their deficit skills, as in the areas of alphabetics or phonics. Other students need to be taught metacognitive strategies that will increase their learning in the general curriculum. The decision for the type of intervention to be used should be based on the needs of the student.

Most educators agree that research-based practices are more valid methods of instruction than general teaching practices. However, identifying multiple strategies, implementing the strategies with instructional fidelity, and training staff members to use them is often a challenge for schools. For this reason, we believe targeted professional development is critical for successful school improvement. In an effort to accomplish this for a variety of interventions, it is helpful to incorporate a systematic staff development plan that provides for training in small increments into the overall school improvement plan (Eaker, DuFour, & DuFour, 2002).

Best practices should be employed for all instruction, including individualized strategies. Once strategies have been selected, they must be employed with the same intensity and structure as recommended in the research. It is important to remember that modeling and demonstration of key concepts are critical for students to obtain the explicit instruction that they need in order to learn. Students also need opportunities to practice, apply, and receive descriptive feedback. Flexible grouping may be needed for various interventions.

Effective approaches to instruction require a commitment from administrators and use of all resources, including parents. The system of supports that is required includes utilizing every person in the building and establishing a flexible schedule for meeting students' needs. Once this system is established, schools may develop a vast bank of interventions available to address a wide variety of students' needs.

In this chapter, we will not discuss published textbooks or supplemental materials, due to the large number available and the complexity of each program. Instead, our focus will be to provide you with information on a variety of research-based practices and learning strategies, the last two categories that we outlined above. We have chosen to highlight strategies that are applicable across grade levels and content areas. As we discuss interventions throughout this chapter, keep in mind that this is just a sampling of many possible strategies and that these are good practices for all students. The determination of a particular strategy and location for delivery of services will depend on the student's needs both behaviorally and academically, as well as the structure of your school's Response to Intervention model.

TIER 1: BEST PRACTICES IN TEACHING

We begin by examining practices that may be incorporated into Tier 1 instruction. These practices are not considered instructional strategies; instead, they are ways to structure the general education classroom to promote learning for all. These factors must be in place in order to create a solid foundation for effective teaching and learning.

School-Wide Behavior Management

In the 2000 *Executive Summary on Youth Violence*, the U.S. Surgeon General reported an escalating rate of disruptive behavior. As we visit schools on a regular basis, it is clear that the unruly behaviors are impeding student learning. For this reason, teachers frequently request assistance with behavior management. To address these concerns, we will present practical fundamental approaches that should be evident in all settings within the school.

Educators are in need of preventive and positive, rather than reactive and aversive, approaches to behavior. School-wide behavior management provides the support and foundation for promoting appropriate behaviors of all students throughout the building (OSEP Technical Assistance Center on Positive Behavioral Interventions, 2007). School-wide positive behavior supports focus on three levels of strategies to improve learning for all: primary or Tier 1 (school-wide procedures), secondary or Tier 2 (classroom procedures), and tertiary or Tier 3 (individual procedures).

The foundation of effective behavior management can be found at the primary level of supports, which is intended for all students and staff and is in effect in all settings of the school. These strategies should be effective for at least 80 percent of the school population. If more than 20 percent of the school population is requiring secondary supports, the school-wide behavior plan should be strengthened. The National Technical Assistance Center

on Positive Behavioral Interventions and Supports outlines seven components that should be evident and effective for a comprehensive school-wide
system of discipline:

1. An agreed-upon and common approach to discipline,
2. a positive statement of purpose,
3. a small number of positively stated expectations for all students
   and staff,
4. procedures for teaching these expectations to students,
5. a continuum of procedures for encouraging displays and mainte-
   nance of these expectations,
6. a continuum of procedures for discouraging displays of rule-
   violating behavior, and
7. procedures for monitoring and evaluating the effectiveness of the
   discipline system on a regular and frequent basis (OSEP, 2007).

In order to increase support and longevity, every adult in the school
should have input as the foundational plan is being created and implemented. The final product should be executed with sincerity by all members of the school, including all staff, students, and parents.

Classroom Behavior Management

Having an effective school-wide behavior plan is an advantage to
classroom teachers, because consistency and support are created when
they mirror each other. However, some schools are not implementing
comprehensive procedures, leaving teachers to independently create their
own classroom behavior plan in a well-structured, proactive, and supportive manner.

In many of our workshops, classroom management has been a topic of
discussion and concern based on its impact on student learning. In poorly
managed classrooms, teachers cannot teach and students cannot learn
(Marzano, 2003). One of the first large-scale systematic studies of classroom
management was completed in 1970 by Jacob Kounin (Marzano, 2003). He
found that effective classroom management had four critical components:
"withitness," smoothness and momentum during presentations, clear
expectations, and variety and challenge during seatwork (Kounin, 1970;
Marzano, 2003). Let us examine each of these more closely.

Withitness

"Withitness" is being aware perceptually and cognitively of what is taking place in the classroom. To accomplish this, teachers must have full view

of every child in the classroom and be able to attend to multiple tasks at once. Along those same lines, Wolfgang (2004) found that teachers who expressed their awareness to the class benefited from increased engagement and decreased misconduct from their students. Teachers must make their students feel they have "eyes in the back of their head" by being aware of behaviors and handling them proactively, appropriately, and immediately.

Smoothness and Momentum

Smoothness and momentum in the classroom requires specific planning and practice. Much time is wasted when transitions are not smooth. Expectations and procedures for minimizing transition time must be explicitly stated and practiced. *CHAMPs: A Proactive and Positive Approach to Classroom Management* by Randy Sprick (Sprick, Garrison, & Howard, 1998) is a practical tool for specifically stating expectations and minimizing transition time. CHAMPs is an acronym for "conversation, help, activity, movement, and participation," which clarifies expectations for students at all times of the day. During seatwork, the teacher displays pictures for each of the areas listed above which might include students working quietly (conversation), raising their hand for assistance (help), completing work at their desk (activity), no movement in the classroom (movement), and students actively engaged (participation). Equally important to smooth transitions is keeping the momentum with appropriate pacing. Downtime should be kept to a minimum. Teachers should keep progressing through the lesson at a steady pace to promote student engagement.

Clear Expectations

Clear expectations begin on the first day of school, with specific rules and procedures. These must be visibly posted, actively discussed, and often revisited. "Rules" and "procedures" differ in purpose: Rules are general expectations, while procedures are specific expectations for particular behaviors (Marzano, 2003). For instance, a general rule would be to respect others, while a procedure would define expectations for obtaining assistance in class. Both rules and procedures are significant components of an effectively managed classroom.

Variety and Challenge

Variety and challenge are important to keep students focused and engaged. When students become bored or are not challenged, inappropriate behaviors often emerge. Students may create their own variations to a task, work with very little thought, or create their own excitement in the form of misbehavior (Kounin, 1970). To minimize inappropriate behaviors, teachers should provide activity and instruction that challenge students at their level of learning. In addition, teachers can provide variety through flexible grouping and varied styles of teaching and learning. Since the early 1970s, many resources have been developed to improve classroom management. Resource A provides a list of resources for proactive discipline and positive behavior supports.

Often, teachers say they cannot differentiate their lessons because their students cannot transition well and have difficulty with the variances differentiation brings. We urge teachers to address the root of the problem: The real issue is not differentiation but rather behavior. Therefore, teachers should address the problem behaviorally in order to incorporate necessary teaching strategies. Teachers must directly teach expectations for transition times as well as instructional times. Once behavior management is addressed, teachers can effectively begin to implement strategies of differentiation to meet students' needs.

Differentiated Instruction

"Differentiated instruction" is a teaching theory based on the belief that instruction should vary and be adapted to meet the individual needs of students. Specifically, this means providing many avenues in which students of varying abilities, interests, or learning styles can learn the content. In addition, differentiation provides greater student responsibility and ownership for learning, as well as opportunity to work collaboratively with peers.

Initially, differentiated instruction was designed and implemented in the general education classroom for gifted students. It was developed to address concerns that these children were not being appropriately challenged. As classrooms became increasingly diverse, differentiated instruction was seen as an effective method for meeting all students' needs by adapting the content, process, product, and learning environment for students based on individual readiness, interest, and learning profile.

For a classroom to truly be considered a differentiated classroom, it must include several key characteristics (Tomlinson, 1999). Teachers must have a clear understanding of essential concepts in the curriculum as well as their students' unique differences. Teachers use their understanding of students' differences to determine effective methods for delivering content. In order to do this, the teacher must integrate assessment and instruction. The results from assessment will guide decision making and allow the teacher to adjust content, process, product, or learning environment to support students in their readiness level, interest, or learning profile. As the teacher makes adjustments, the students participate in respectful work that is of interest and is appropriately supported through teacher and peer collaboration. The purpose in this is to encourage maximum growth and individual student success. To have a truly differentiated class, teachers must be flexible and willing to make necessary instructional decisions.

Differentiation is not one instructional strategy. It is composed of many research-based theories and practices. A key element of differentiation requires teachers to look at students' readiness levels to instruct and support students slightly above their functioning level in order to appropriately challenge and advance learning. Vygotsky (1978) researched this process and termed it the Zone of Proximal Development. More recent research supports this process as well (Fleer, 1992; Jacobs, 2001).

As a teacher begins to differentiate, he or she cannot implement every aspect at once. It is most effective to systematically differentiate in a manner that is beneficial to the students and manageable to the teacher. We recommend that teachers begin with one area (content, process, or product) or by differentiating one unit and then building the process in future units. In our discussion of differentiated instruction, we will discuss pre-instruction assessment, flexible grouping, active practice and feedback, tiered lessons, anchor activities, and "think-alouds."

Pre-Instruction Assessment

Pre-assessments are used to determine what students know about a topic before it is taught. As teachers begin the process of differentiation, we encourage them to incorporate pre-assessments from the beginning. Specifically, teachers should evaluate pre-assessment data regularly to determine flexible group memberships and to verify student strengths and needs. By utilizing pre-assessments, teachers have a means of showing student progress throughout instruction. Methods commonly used for pre-assessments include teacher-prepared pre-tests, KWL charts, demonstration, discussion, show of hands, observations, and checklists.

Flexible Grouping

Flexible grouping occurs when an assessment or instruction reveals the need for review, re-teaching, practice, or enrichment. These groups must be temporary and allow students to receive appropriate instruction at all levels. Groupings can be heterogeneous or homogenous. These are specifically based on readiness, interest, reading level, skill level, background knowledge, or social skills. Heterogeneous groups are suitable for critical thinking activities, open-ended discussions, and hands-on experiments. Homogenous groupings are appropriate for drill and practice, math computation, studying for tests, and answering recall questions (Jones, Pierce, & Hunter, 1989).

Practice and Feedback

Practice and feedback are effective outcomes of flexible grouping and are found to be highly effective. The Center for the Improvement of Early Reading Achievement (2001) states that the effectiveness of small group instruction may exceed individual or whole group instruction because children often benefit from listening to their peers respond and receiving feedback from the teacher. Students are more likely to participate in small groups, leading to more interaction and engagement. As students work together, higher-order cognitive processes are practiced, leading to more advanced outcomes. In summary, combining forces can produce a better product. For small group instruction to be effective, the educator must provide organization and clarity of activity through explicit directions.

Tiered Instruction

"Tiered instruction" is a specific differentiated instruction strategy used to teach one concept while meeting the different learning needs in a group (Tomlinson, 2001). It is an instructional framework that we find easy to implement with some planning and one that allows all students to be taught at their zone of proximal development. Tiered instruction is best implemented when pre-assessment reveals multiple learning levels within the class. In tiered instruction, assignments, lessons, and strategies can be tiered based on students' learning profiles, readiness levels, and interests. Tiering can be applied with varied adjustments to the challenge level, complexity, resources, outcomes, processes, or products (Heacox, 2002). All children benefit from tiered instruction, as each student is appropriately challenged and focused on essential learning concepts.

The first step in planning for tiered instruction is to examine the concepts or standards and assess students' learning profiles, readiness levels, and interests in that area. From the assessment information, teachers should choose an activity or project that is focused on the key concepts in the standard and create different instructional groups with appropriate scaffolding (supports). Tiered instruction will take place as the teacher adjusts the activity to provide for different levels of difficulty or complexity of thought.

Planning for tiered instruction begins as the teacher reviews the standard and determines what *all* students should know at the end of the lesson or unit. This ensures that instruction is focused on essential concepts that are critical for every child to understand. Next, the teacher determines what additional information or what higher level of thought processes will be used to instruct the next higher group. This may be thought of as "What do I want *most* of my students to know?" Finally, the teacher looks at the *few* students in the class who have already mastered or perhaps exceeded the standard. She then develops an activity for this group, again relying on complexity of thought or extension of knowledge. To effectively differentiate, the teacher must plan instruction that exceeds the bare minimum and reaches students in the "most" and "few" categories of learning. Within these levels, students are appropriately challenged. Figure 3.1 provides an example of a planning rubric that may be used for planning a tiered lesson. Again, this offers structure for differentiating instruction in the general education classroom.

Figure 3.1   Tiered Instruction Planning Guide

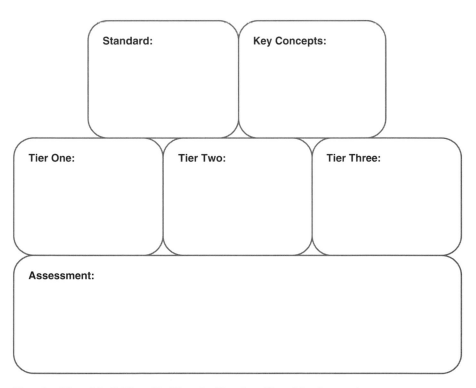

Planning Tiered Activities: Six Ways to Structure Tiered Assignments

- Challenge (Bloom's Taxonomy)
- Complexity (Introductory to Abstract)
- Resources (Reading Levels, Types of Terminology)
- Outcomes (Various Outcomes With Same Resources)
- Process (Various Ways of Learning With the Same Outcome)
- Product (Multiple Intelligences)

Anchor Activities

"Anchor activities" (Tomlinson, 1999) are essential in a differentiated classroom because students will most certainly complete assignments at different times. Anchor activities guide students from one activity to another without wasted time. This allows teachers to work with individuals or small groups of students who need more explicit teacher-directed instruction. Anchor activities are effective methods for keeping students engaged in content-related material. Silent reading, journals, vocabulary practice, math problem of the day, learning centers, spelling practice, science trivia, and Web site of the week are all examples of anchor activities. In order to make the most effective use of anchor activities, teachers must establish clear expectations for student behavior and performance. Checklists, anecdotal records, student conferences, learning journals, rubrics, and peer review are all methods of assessing progress within anchor activities (Tomlinson, 1999).

Think-Alouds

A "think-aloud" is a differentiated strategy for students who struggle with processing information. Thinking aloud has been found to make students' silent knowledge more explicit (Smith & Wedman, 1988). This process involves describing thought processes aloud as a problem is solved or a concept learned. Think-alouds are a form of explicit instruction as the educator models cognitive and meta-cognitive processes that good readers use to construct meaning and monitor comprehension. Students should practice think-aloud procedures as a class, in partners, and then independently. Throughout this process, students should begin to monitor their own comprehension and self-correct errors (Davey, 1983).

In order to utilize think-alouds, teachers must select a passage and preview the material with a student perspective. Educators should take note of any difficult concepts or unknown words in order to model appropriate thought processes. As the educator reads the passage aloud, the students follow along silently and listen for how meaning is constructed. Teachers should make predictions, explain mental pictures, share analogies that link prior knowledge with new information, express confusing points (monitoring comprehension), and demonstrate fix-up strategies to address areas of difficulty. It is important to provide practice opportunities for students to apply what they have observed.

Consider this example of a think-aloud, in which the teacher reads the following short passage:

> The children were filled with excitement as they opened the gate and entered Sarah's birthday party. They couldn't believe their

eyes! Balloons, streamers, confetti, presents, and sweet treats completely transformed the backyard to a party wonderland. It seemed the birds and crickets were even singing "Happy Birthday." Before long, the children realized that this was no ordinary party. Every child had a present! They had come to celebrate a friend's birthday, but Sarah had a surprise for them.

Teacher think-aloud:

- I predict the friends will have their own personal birthday cakes and more presents than Christmas morning.
- I can see the balloons, streamers, confetti, presents, and sweet treats.
- I imagine hearing the birds and crickets singing "Happy Birthday."
- I have had many birthday parties, so I can relate to the excitement of having a birthday.
- I don't really understand why Sarah wanted to surprise her friends. I am going to keep reading to see what she has in store.

Graphic Organizers

Graphic organizers are effective differentiation strategies that affect student achievement in the classroom by providing a "big picture" view of concepts and by helping to organize the relationships between concepts. Organizers are especially helpful in representing abstract information in concrete forms. Commonly used graphic organizers include webs or concept maps, sequence chains, flowcharts, and Venn diagrams. *Before instruction*, organizers can be used to activate prior knowledge and provide a conceptual framework for new information. *During instruction*, students use graphic organizers to process the information. *After instruction*, organizers are used for summarizing, elaborating, organizing, structuring, and assessing learning. It is important to model new graphic organizers and provide guided practice before expecting students to complete them independently (Jones et al., 1989).

Let us now look at a classroom example in which the teacher incorporates various differentiated instruction strategies into her classroom practices.

Ms. Chapman begins a unit on citizenship by giving a brief pre-assessment. This pre-assessment is in the form of a ticket out the door, a single piece of paper with student's name and answers to the following prompts: What is a citizen? What is an immigrant? How is your family heritage related to these terms? Based on the student responses, Ms. Chapman divides the class into ability groups to address these fundamental concepts. The activities are tiered for three ability groups based on students' levels of understanding and need for direct instruction. Group number 1 needs the most support; therefore, the teacher provides direct explicit instruction for learning the differences between immigrants and citizens. They use graphic organizers to illustrate reasons a person would come to our country as an immigrant and the benefits of being a citizen. Group 2 researches and presents the life of famous citizens and immigrants. Group 2 has moderate teacher assistance in the form of daily discussions and structure through rubrics and checklists. Group 3 has a student-directed activity as they trace family heritage and create an exhibit to display how their heritage relates to citizens and immigrants. Group 3 receives a rubric and mini-check in stages to be sure they are progressing properly. As all students work on their projects, anchor activities are used to keep them engaged when they complete assignments or need assistance. Ms. Chapman establishes various anchor activities for this unit of study. They include daily learning journals in which students summarize the most important concepts learned that day. These journals also contain peer reviews of the effectiveness of their group. Books at various reading levels pertaining to citizenship and immigration are provided in the room. For students who cannot read these texts independently, Ms. Chapman has recorded not only the text but also a think-aloud to guide students through small sections of the text. While reading the books, students record their progress in a reading log, along with any questions or comments the students have as they read the books. Throughout this unit, each child is participating in effective differentiated instruction.

Differentiated instruction is critical at all levels of instruction, elementary through high school. In order to meet the needs of a diverse group of students, educators must continually assess students' progress toward learning goals. These assessments will guide the teacher in making instructional decisions for increasing student achievement. Deliberately using students' background knowledge, interests, and learning profiles to differentiate content, process, product, and learning environment within the classroom will enable the teacher to meet individual needs.

TIERS 2 AND ABOVE: INTERVENTIONS TO MEET SMALL GROUP OR INDIVIDUAL LEARNING NEEDS

Interventions used in Tiers 2 and 3 are designed for students who have not shown progress with strategies in Tier 1. These interventions are targeted to meet specific student needs and should be implemented in combination with Tier 1 strategies in order to enhance and supplement the comprehensive curriculum. Interventions should be taught through a systematic, structured plan and monitored to document progress in order to make instructional decisions that increase learning.

Research-based interventions have a high probability of increasing performance (D. Fuchs & Fuchs, 2005). As stated earlier, in an effort to directly affect student achievement in the classroom and provide immediate support to teachers, we have narrowed our discussion to research-based *instructional strategies*, rather than research-based *curricular programs*. These instructional strategies should be used in conjunction with a research-validated curriculum, whether core or supplemental. The following summary of strategies is not by any means an exhaustive list. This is merely a sampling of strategies and resources that are available to educators as they search for interventions to meet individual student needs.

Behavior Management

As discussed previously in this chapter, it is beneficial to have a sound, proactive, positive, and consistent disciplinary system at all levels of the school. Once this is in place, we begin looking for more intense strategies for students who do not respond adequately. We have found that the individualized supports are more effective when coupled with a strong behavioral management foundation. Certainly, teachers should still implement positive, proactive, and consistent procedures as seen in Tier 1, but with added intensity based on individual student needs. Behavior Monitoring Charts, positive behavior support plans with reinforcement, verbal/visual cuing, social skills training, visualizations, and mentoring are a few of the general strategies designed to meet individual or small group behavior needs. It is critical to match each student's behavior to a strategy based on specific behavior assessments. Research-based behavior interventions generally fall under the broad theoretical categories of Applied Behavior Analysis and Social Learning Theory.

Applied Behavior Analysis (ABA) is commonly implemented in schools. In ABA, the functional relationships between antecedents, behaviors, and consequences are examined to determine the function of the problem behavior (Alberto & Troutman, 2006). When the function is identified, replacement behaviors can be made to the inappropriate behavior to serve the same function.

Consider the analogy depicted in Figure 3.2. Payton is continually oversleeping and being late to school. The problem or behavior (B) is not being tardy but rather not getting up when the alarm clock sounds. Being tardy is the consequence (C). The antecedent (A) that occurs just before Payton falls back to sleep is that he hits the "snooze" button, resulting in waking up late and ultimately being tardy. An appropriate plan of action would be to directly affect the behavior by adjusting the antecedent (what occurs just before the behavior). In order to do this, Payton decides to move the alarm clock across the room so that he must get up to turn off the alarm clock. By doing this, he wakes up enough to make a conscious decision to stay awake, get ready, and be on time to school.

Within ABA, educators consider how the consequence rewards the behavior in question. We know behaviors will continue to occur as long as they are being reinforced. Often, it is difficult to see how the consequence is rewarding the child, as illustrated in the following example: A child yells out in class, the other children laugh, and the teacher removes the child to In-School Suspension (ISS). The child's behavior is actually reinforced in two ways in this scenario. First, the child receives attention from peers, and second, the child is allowed to avoid the task at hand. In order to break this cycle, the child's need for attention and avoidance of task should be examined by the teacher. It could be that the child truly needs attention but does not know how to obtain it in an appropriate manner. This may require the teacher to "catch" the child behaving appropriately, so she can provide the needed attention. The child may require more intense social skills training. As for the behavior of task avoidance, the educator must analyze whether the child *can* in fact complete the task but refuses to or whether the child cannot complete the task. The interventions will differ based on the reason the child wants to evade the assignment. If the child cannot perform the task, the teacher will address the behavior academically. If the child has the ability to but will not perform the task, the

Figure 3.2   ABC Scenario

A ntecedent	B ehavior	C onsequence
⟶	⟶	
Hits snooze on alarm clock located by the bed	*Falls back to sleep*	*Late for school*
Action Plan: Change location of clock away from bed		
Gets out of bed to turn off alarm clock	*Awake enough to stay up*	*On time for school*

teacher will need to address it behaviorally, through the established behavior management system for that child. This will more than likely include reinforcement for appropriate behavior. It is this type of systematic evaluation and manipulation of antecedent, consequence, and behavior that research has proven effective in behavior change.

In contrast to Applied Behavior Analysis, Social Learning Theory emphasizes the importance of learning from others by modeling, imitating, and observing (Bandura, 1977). Within this theory, it is believed that not all types of learning are affected by direct reinforcement. Rather, people learn from observing others and then modeling expected behaviors through role-play. Many children know intellectually what to do, but they are unable or have never been asked to physically do it.

To teach appropriate behaviors, modeling and role-play have been highly effective in schools. Consider the following scenario. Mr. Lee has reviewed classroom rules and procedures regularly. He noticed that a few students were not following his most valued rule: Respect others and yourself. He spent much time discussing the disrespectful behaviors and had the students repeat the rule back to him. It appeared they understood the meaning of the rule. Mr. Lee even employed a T chart in which the class discussed what respect looks like on the left-hand side and what it sounds like on the right-hand side. This seemed to help a few of the students, but Mr. Lee noticed the behaviors were still evident at times. He took this small group of students and began to role-play, allowing each child to explicitly model specific behaviors found on the T chart. Each child was able to change roles and experience what true respect looks like, sounds like, and even feels like.

From these overriding theories, numerous strategies have evolved. Marzano (2003) has done extensive analysis of research-based strategies in the classroom. We will highlight two specific strategies that have been found to be highly effective in the classroom. These are self-monitoring and cognitive-based strategies. The self-monitoring strategies require students to be aware of their own behavior, record targeted behaviors, and compare their behavior with goals predetermined by the teacher and student. If the goals are reached, the student is rewarded. When using this process, it is important to meet with both the child and his or her parents to clearly define expectations and procedures for the strategy. Various forms and checklists can be used for recording purposes. Marking cards and charts or moving counters are simple ways of recording behaviors as well. Gradually, the record-keeping and rewards are diminished as appropriate until the student can perform the behavior without keeping a record and meeting with the teacher.

Cognitive-based strategies fall under the categories of social skills training and problem solving (Marzano, 2003). These strategies equip students with a means for dealing with social situations. The following four steps are explicit and systematic steps for assisting students who need to increase self-control (Marzano, 2003, pp. 88–89):

1. Notice when you are becoming angry, annoyed, frustrated, or overwhelmed, and stop whatever you are doing.
2. Ask yourself, "What are the different ways I can respond to this situation?"
3. Think about the consequences for each of your options.
4. Select the action that has the potential for the most positive consequences for you and others.

It is important to explicitly discuss the purpose and details of the strategy with the student and his or her parent. After the teacher has modeled the strategy steps, the child should have ample opportunity to practice the agreed-upon protocol before trying it in the classroom. Lastly, a cue to remind the student to use the steps may be necessary initially.

The behavioral strategies presented here are all considered cognitive strategies in that they cause students to actively think about and problem solve about their behavior. Cognitive strategies, however, are not solely for behavior management. Many are used for academic purposes, as you will see in the next section.

Cognitive Strategy Instruction (CSI)

Many struggling students have difficulty regulating their own learning. Cognitive strategy instruction (CSI) provides support for learners as they discover individual strategies allowing them to access knowledge and extend to higher-level understanding. Visualization, verbalization, making associations, chunking, questioning, scanning, underlining, accessing cues, and mnemonics are examples of specific cognitive strategies for learning and remembering. The focus in CSI should be on not only the specific strategies but also the implementation process. The implementation process is systematic and explicit. It involves teaching prerequisite skills that must be used within the strategy, describing with cues, teaching incremental steps, modeling, verbally rehearsing, practicing with assistance, practicing independently, and then generalizing to other settings. The University of Nebraska at Lincoln has compiled various cognitive strategies that can be accessed at www.unl.edu/csi.

Consider the following example of a child, Haley, who requires cognitive strategy instruction to understand and retain information. Visualization was used to assist Haley with spelling irregular words (words that did not follow general spelling rules). After several weeks of modeling and guided practice, the teacher began to provide more independent practice and asked Haley how she could remember the *ow* in *crown*. The teacher knew this could be difficult because the class had just been studying words that had the same *ow* sound but were spelled differently, such as b*ou*nd. Haley thought for a moment and said, "It's easy. I can see a crown on top of a queen's head in the shape of a *w*." Haley visualized the *w* shape to cue herself that the *ow* sound was made with a *w* and not a *u*. On her spelling test that week, Haley paused when the word *crown* was called out, made a gesture toward her head as a cue to herself, then wrote the word correctly. Later, with no teacher prompt, Haley expressed that she remembered the *oo* in *door* by visualizing two knobs on a single door. The teacher could see that Haley had effectively made it through the implementation process for visualizing and was now generalizing the steps to new situations on her own. The progress was documented and shared with Haley's parents, who began using similar strategies with her as they worked on homework.

Strategic Instruction Model

For more than thirty years, the University of Kansas Center for Research on Learning (2008) has conducted research on strategies designed to address the varied needs of diverse learners. The majority of the research was conducted in middle and high school settings. The Strategic Instruction Model (SIM) is a model that incorporates a variety of research-based strategies to be used with content area subject matter. The purpose of SIM is to promote effective teaching and learning within the classroom by focusing on what is important, what can be taught to help students learn, and how to effectively teach students (University of Kansas Center for Research on Learning, 2008).

Strategic Instruction Model strategies are typically taught to small groups of students that range from six to twelve children. A strategy can often be taught and mastered within three to four weeks, with one hour of instruction per day. Within each strategy, there is an eight-stage instructional methodology that must be carefully followed to ensure that students master and generalize the strategy. Two types of interventions are addressed within this model: teacher-focused interventions and student-focused interventions.

The teacher-focused interventions address how teachers present the content. Specifically, Content Enhancement Routines are explicit teaching procedures that assist the teacher in organizing and presenting the information. This systematic and graphic process aids the learner in comprehension and retention of critical content objectives. The routines include instructional procedures for *Planning and Leading Learning, Exploring Text, Topics & Details, Teaching Concepts,* and *Increasing Performance.*

The student-focused interventions provide specific skills and approaches needed for learning. These models were developed and researched across various settings and with general and special education teachers. Specifically, the Learning Strategies Curriculum addresses students' needs in the areas of *Reading, Storing & Remembering Information, Expressing Information, Demonstrating Competence, Social Interaction, Motivations,* and *Math.*

The Strategic Instruction Model is certainly systematic and explicit as it addresses the many varied needs of learners across all settings. Each strategy has impressive data to show the increase in student achievement. The benefit lies within the structure and support each research-based intervention holds. The limitation is in the accessibility of the model. In order to utilize the Strategic Instruction Model, teachers must receive intensive training from certified members of the International Training Network. The training typically occurs throughout the year and gives teachers the opportunity to master individual strategies through implementation and problem solving. While this model requires a commitment of time and professional development resources, we feel the proven gain in terms of amount, rate, and retention of learning is well worth it.

Math

Concrete, Representational, Abstract (CRA)

Many students struggle in the area of math. This is often because students are asked to learn math concepts in abstract form. It is important to begin math instruction with the appropriate base of understanding, which often requires a concrete approach to learning. Concrete, Representational, Abstract (CRA), a three-part instructional strategy used in mathematics to promote student learning and retention, specifically defines the steps to teaching in this manner.

CRA's three phases build upon each other and are implemented to provide a conceptual structure for meaningful connections to be made. The concrete stage, or Stage 1, is the "doing" stage, in which educators model with manipulatives (The Access Center, 2004). These materials can include colored chips, cubes, base 10 blocks, pattern blocks, and fraction blocks. Visual, tactile, and kinesthetic experiences should be considered. Stage 2, also known as the representational stage, is the "seeing" stage, in which the concrete models are transformed into pictorial representations (The Access Center, 2004). This includes drawing pictures or using stamps to illustrate the concepts. The last and final phase, Stage 3, is the abstract "symbolic" stage, in which abstract symbols are utilized (The Access Center, 2004). These mathematical symbols include numbers, letters, and signs (e.g., 2, 6, $3x$, +, −). The premise for CRA is that students should learn the concepts before learning "rules." Students who use concrete manipulatives develop more precise and comprehensive mental representation that leads to increased motivation and on-task behavior, understanding, and application of these concepts (Harrison & Harrison, 1986). CRA is most effective when used for understanding concepts in early number relations, place value, computation, fraction, decimals, measurement, geometry, money, percentage, number bases, word problems, probability, and statistics (The Access Center, 2004). Figure 3.3 depicts a progression from concrete (with chips) to representational (with the number line) and then finally to abstract (with numbers).

Figure 3.3   Concrete, Representational, Abstract (CRA)

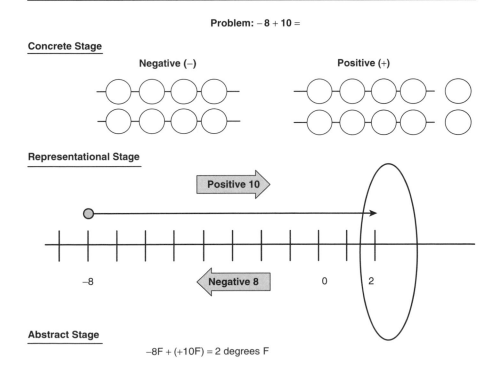

Problem: −8 + 10 =

Concrete Stage

Negative (−)   Positive (+)

Representational Stage

Positive 10

−8   Negative 8   0   2

Abstract Stage

−8F + (+10F) = 2 degrees F

Schema-Based Instruction

Problem solving is a critical skill that often confounds struggling learners. It involves combining knowledge, skills, and strategies in application to new problems. The National Council of Teachers of Mathematics places problem solving as a central theme in the *Principles and Standards for School Mathematics* (2000).

Schema-based instruction has been found to improve math word problem skills for elementary and middle school students (Jitendra, 2002; Miller, 1998). Placing word problems into categories before choosing a method to solve them is especially helpful for low-achieving students (Jitendra et al., 2007). According to the concept of schema-based instruction, most addition and subtraction problems fall into three major categories or types. These problems involve a change, a grouping, or a comparison. The first step in schema-based instruction is to identify the problem type and then translate the problem from words into a meaningful graphic representation (Jitendra, 2002).

Explicit modeling, guided practice, and feedback are essential during the stages of implementation. Furthermore, teachers should scaffold instruction by providing written rules as students are learning the procedures. Students should not be asked to use schema-based instruction independently until they have received direct instruction, scaffolding, and practice in first identifying the sets and then solving the problems through explicit guidance (Jitendra, 2002). Figures 3.4 through 3.6 illustrate addition and subtraction schema-based problem types with a graphic representation. Examples in these figures are for basic computation skills

Figure 3.4   The Change Set

The first problem type is the "change" set, which involves a change from the beginning set that results in the ending set. Consider the following example of a change set.

Haley had 12 ladybugs (beginning). Then, 3 ladybugs (change set) flew away. How many ladybugs does Haley have now (ending)?

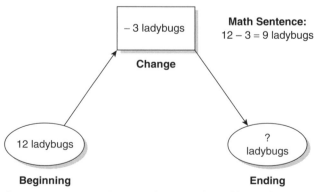

SOURCE: Jitendra, A. (2002). Teaching students math problem-solving through graphic representation. *TEACHING Exceptional Children, 34*(4), 34–38.

Figure 3.5 The Group Set

The second problem type is the group set. It does not involve a change of object amounts. Rather, it involves understanding part-whole relationships and knowing that the sum of the parts equals the whole (Jitendra, 2002). To illustrate this type of word problem, consider the following.

Wesley received 6 gift cards for his birthday. He used 2 from his favorite game store. How many gift cards were left?

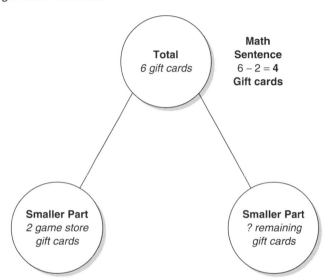

SOURCE: Jitendra, A. (2002). Teaching students math problem-solving through graphic representation. *TEACHING Exceptional Children, 34*(4), 34–38.

Figure 3.6 The Compare Set

The third problem type is the "compare" set, in which two sets have the same unit of measurement. Students focus on the phrase more than or less than to compare these sets (Jitendra, 2002). Consider the following example.

Payton kicked 16 goals (referent set) during the soccer season. Anna kicked 8 fewer (difference set) goals than Payton. How many goals did Anna kick (compare set) during the soccer season?

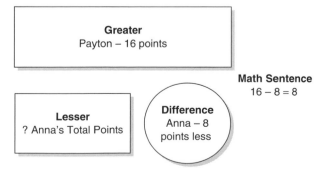

SOURCE: Jitendra, A. (2002). Teaching students math problem-solving through graphic representation. *TEACHING Exceptional Children, 34*(4), 34–38.

typically seen at the elementary level. Additional problem types for multiplication and division can be found in *Teaching Mathematics to Middle School Students with Learning Difficulties*, edited by M. Montague and A. K. Jitendra (2006).

General Content Strategies for Analyzing Information

In their book *Classroom Instruction that Works*, Robert Marzano and colleagues (Marzano, Marzano, & Pickering, 2001) summarized extensive research to present concise information about research-based interventions. They highlighted nine strategies that have high probability of enhancing student achievement for all students in all subject areas at all grade levels. Of these nine, we have chosen to highlight the top two instructional strategies that showed the largest effect size. These are *Identifying similarities and differences* and *Summarizing and note taking*. Specifically, we include these strategies for middle and high school students who struggle with comprehension and gleaning information from text. Either the teacher or the student, depending on the level of support needed, can lead either strategy. When students require explicit teacher support and focus, teachers lead the strategy. As students become proficient at using teacher-directed strategies, students can begin to lead these strategies themselves, which allows for more creativity to work and think. Teachers, however, should continue to guide and monitor students. Graphic organizers are also useful in each of these strategies, to aid students in understanding and visualizing. For specific instructions on implementing each of these strategies, see Marzano et al., 2001.

Identifying Similarities and Differences

Marzano et al. (2001, pp. 13–28) emphasize that identifying similarities and differences might be the "core" of all learning, because it enhances students' understanding of and ability to use knowledge. Identifying similarities and differences is appropriate for any content area in which students are asked to analyze concepts. Seeing similarities and differences is a fundamental cognitive process (Gentner & Markman, 1994). Breaking concepts into similar and dissimilar characteristics increases understanding and ability to solve complex problems by exploring the concepts in a simplified manner. Teachers should explicitly teach similarities and differences through discussion and inquiry. Students' understanding and ability to use knowledge is enhanced when they are guided through the process of identifying similarities and differences and then are provided the opportunity to identify these independently. Identifying similarities and differences involves comparing, classifying, creating metaphors, and

Figure 3.7   Comparison Graphic Organizer (Alternate Form of Venn Diagram)

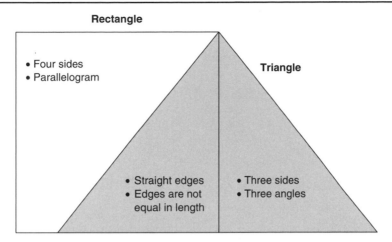

creating analogies. In these methods, students must analyze similarities and differences between concepts.

Comparing. Effective comparison requires recognition of significant characteristics that will improve students' understanding of similarities and differences between the compared items. Consider the following scenario. Students are asked to compare the West and Northeast regions of the United States. It would be insignificant to focus on family members who live in each region as a defining characteristic. More significant characteristics would include a comparison of climate or topography within these regions. When using the strategy of comparing, teachers should provide a comparison task that includes elements being compared, as well as characteristics to compare. Teachers assess students' descriptions of how items are similar or different in relation to the given characteristics. Two graphic organizers are typically used for comparison: the Venn diagram and the comparison matrix. Figure 3.7 provides an example of a comparison graphic organizer.

Figure 3.8   Example of Classification Chart

Herbivores	Omnivores	Carnivores
Eat plant material	Eat plants and meat	Eat meat
Sheep	Chickens	Wolves
Horses	Humans	Cheetahs
Rabbits	Chimpanzees	Dragonflies
Snails		Eagles

Classifying. Classifying requires organizing elements into groups based on their similarities. Classifying is shown in many real-world settings, such as grocery stores. Some students may need more structured tasks, in which teachers define the elements and the classifications for the elements. Figure 3.8 provides an example of a classification chart.

Creating Metaphors. Metaphors are used to experience and understand one thing in terms of another (Lakoff & Johnson, 1980). Socrates used the following metaphor: "Education is the kindling of a flame, not the filling of a vessel." In his metaphor, he depicts the similarity of education to lighting a flame as opposed to just filling a vessel. Teachers often use metaphors in casual conversation, such as "My class is a zoo!" Creating metaphors involves an implied comparison between two essentially unlike things: a classroom and a zoo. These are used to provide strong images and connect to background knowledge. Metaphors are used to give concreteness, clarify the unknown, express the subjective, and assist thought (Weaver, 1967). When using metaphors, teachers should go from the known to the unknown and from the concrete to the abstract. Teachers construct images and models of teaching based upon their prior knowledge and experiences (Johnson, 1987). The level of support provided by the teacher will depend on the student's level of understanding. The teacher may explicitly guide students in how the items are alike at the abstract level. Once students understand the process, the teacher may provide the first element and necessary background knowledge to complete the second element of the metaphor. Graphic organizers assist students in visualizing the abstract pattern between the two elements. Figure 3.9 provides an illustration of metaphors.

Creating Analogies. Creating analogies involves identifying relationships between concepts (Marzano et al., 2001). This involves making associations and discovering similarities between two unrelated elements. Specifically, students relate their background knowledge to unknown concepts.

Figure 3.9   Metaphors

Life Element 1	*Is a*	*Teacher* Element 2
Literal Pattern: Physical, mental, and spiritual experiences that represent existence	Abstract Relationship: *Life experiences are lessons that teach us along the way.*	Literal Pattern: Educates students

A teacher-directed analogy may be a complete analogy, such as *plane* is to *air* as *boat* is to *water* (plane:air::boat:water), where the teacher ascribes a known relationship to newly introduced elements. The teacher could also leave the very last element out of the analogy, such as *mason* is to *stone* as *carpenter* is to _____ (mason:stone::carpenter:_____). In a student-directed analogy, the teacher supplies the initial elements and the student invents the last two elements of the analogy, demonstrating understanding of how the teacher-supplied elements are related. To illustrate this strategy, consider *water* is to *liquid* as _____ is to _____ (water:liquid::_____:_____). Teachers can assess students' understanding of a concept through their analogies.

Summarizing Strategies

Summarizing and note taking are two of the most useful academic skills students can have (Marzano et al., 2001, pp. 29–48). Note taking is important for middle and high school students across all content areas. Students' comprehension is improved as they analyze content to find the most essential information and rephrase it in a way that makes sense to them. Synthesizing, a higher-order thinking skill, is closely related to summarizing because students must learn to analyze information, identify key concepts, and define extraneous information (Hidi & Anderson, 1987). Students must have skills in analyzing the information at a deep level in order to substitute, delete, and keep information as well as have an awareness of the basic structure of the presented information.

Teaching students to recognize various text structures is essential to summarizing and comprehending what is read or heard (Armbruster & Anderson, 1987). Six different text structure summary frames direct student attention to specific content by using a series of questions. Students should be asked to question what is unclear, clarify those questions, and predict what will happen next in the text. We will briefly discuss specific strategies for summarization: reciprocal teaching, rule-based strategy, summary frames, and note taking. Again, for a full explanation of these strategies, see Marzano et al. (2001).

Reciprocal Teaching. Reciprocal teaching (Marzano et al., 2001; Oczkus, 2005; Palincsar & Brown, 1984; Promising Practices Network, 2005) is a dialogue between teachers and students in regard to content reading in all subject areas. The specific purpose of reciprocal teaching is to bring meaning to small portions of text. Reciprocal teaching is one of the most effective summarizing strategies available to teachers to analyze information at a deep level (Rosenshine & Meister, 1994). It was initially intended to coach poor readers to use reading strategies employed by good readers to improve reading comprehension. Small groups of three to four students are effective for providing practice and receiving feedback. During this strategy, students interact with the text to construct meaning by using prior knowledge, experiences, and text information to predict, clarify, question, and summarize.

- *Predicting* consists of an educated guess. Guessing what may happen next gives a purpose for continuing to read and obtain information. Students should use the information they already have, as well as information obtained from headings, subheadings, and questions to effectively predict.

- *Clarifying* consists of explaining concepts and defining words, which allows students to focus attention on the text. This step often leads to re-reading the material, reading ahead, or asking questions; therefore, it should be incorporated during reading.

- *Questioning* leads to asking questions that can be answered by the text. Students must first identify what is important enough to question, then test their understanding with those questions.

- *Summarizing* is merely having the students put the information in their own words. Students must identify, paraphrase, and incorporate the important information from the text in their own words. This is typically done after predicting, clarifying, and questioning. In addition, text can be summarized in a group or individually.

As with most strategies, the teacher must provide modeling and support to students as they learn how to implement the reciprocal teaching strategy. Eventually, the students become proficient in this strategy and require minimal teacher support. Figure 3.10 provides an example of teaching practices for reciprocal teaching.

The "Rule-Based" Strategy (Marzano et al., 2001). The rule-based summary strategy has a set of rules or steps that a student must take to generate a summary (Brown, Campione, & Day, 1981). Merely having these rules posted will not teach the students how to summarize. It is essential that teachers explicitly present these rules through strategies such as modeling and think-alouds. The rules include (Marzano et al., 2001, p. 32):

- Delete trivial material that is unnecessary to understanding.
- Delete redundant material.
- Substitute superordinate terms for lists (flowers for daisies, tulips, and roses).
- Select a topic sentence, or invent one if it is missing.

Figure 3.10 Teaching Practices for Reciprocal Teaching

- Use any combination of the four strategies: predicting, questioning, clarifying, summarizing
- Incorporate best practices with reciprocal teaching:
  - Think-alouds
  - Cooperative learning
  - Scaffolding (modeling, guided practice, feedack)
  - Metacognition
- Before reading
  - Activate prior knowledge
  - Review strategies: predicting, questioning, clarifying, summarizing
  - Predict based on clues from text
  - Set a purpose for reading (clarify unknown words or possible questions)
- During reading
  - Teacher coaches students in predicting, questioning, clarifying, summarizing
  - Clarify words or ideas
  - Ask question about portions of text
  - Predict what is about to happen
  - Summarize text
- After reading
  - Discuss previously made prediction
  - Review strategies used
  - Clarify words or ideas
  - Ask questions to each other (higher-level questions)
- Summarize what was read

SOURCE: Oczkus, L. D. (2005). *Reciprocal teaching strategies at work: Improving reading comprehension, grades 2–6.*

Summary Frames (Marzano et al., 2001). Summary Frames consist of a series of questions provided by the teacher to students. The questions are based on the type of passage being studied. Summary Frames assist students in recognizing text structure. As students complete the Summary Frames individually, as a group, or in pairs, they begin to truly implement effective summarization skills that are essential for learning. After the questions in each Summary Frame have been answered, students use the information to write a summary. Marzano et al. (2001) highlight six types of frames, which include:

- The Narrative Frame
- The Topic-Restriction Illustration Frame
- The Definition Frame

- The Argumentation Frame
- The Problem/Solution Frame
- The Conversation Frame

Figure 3.11 provides an example of a narrative Summary Frame.

Note-Taking Strategies

Note-taking skills correlate with summarizing skills in that they both require students to determine what is most important. Marzano et al., (2001) describe four generalizations from Beecher's research (1988). The first generalization is that verbatim note taking is the least effective way to take notes (Bretzing & Kulhary, 1979). In verbatim note taking, efforts center on writing every word, not synthesizing or analyzing the information. The second generalization states that notes should be a work in progress. Scheduled time and teacher support should be a part of the routine for students to revisit, revise, and update notes. The third generalization is that notes should be used as study guides for tests. Marzano et al., (2001) continue by saying the utilization of well-designed notes to prepare for exams or other summative assessments can be highly effective. Lastly, less is not more when it comes to note taking. Research shows that there is a significant connection between the amount of notes taken and student achievement (Marzano et al., 2001; Nye, Crooks, Powlie, & Tripp, 1984).

We will conclude by discussing classroom practice in note taking. Teacher-prepared notes are explicit models of what the teacher finds important and precise models of how to structure notes (Marzano et al., 2001). Teachers should prepare notes in both linguistic and nonlinguistic formats, which include idea webs, sketches, and outlines (Nye et al.,

Figure 3.11   Narrative Frame Summary Questions

Who are the main characters and what distinguished them from others?

When and where did the story take place? What were the circumstances?

What prompted the action in the story?

How did the characters express their feelings?

What did the main characters decide to do? Did they set a goal, and if so, what was it?

How did the main characters try to accomplish their goal(s)?

What were the consequences?

SOURCE: Marzano et al., 2001, p. 35

1984). Each of these has distinct advantages for different learning styles. Informal outlines use indentations to indicate importance, and webbing uses a larger circle to depict importance with a line connecting circles to show relationships. Webbing limits the amount of information that can be recorded. To receive the benefit of both, a combination of both note-taking formats can be used. In the combination technique, the left column is reserved for informal outlines, the right is for webbing, and the bottom portion is for summarizing (Marzano et al., 2001). This method incorporates key attributes of effective note taking.

Summarizing and note taking are critical to student understanding. Explicit teacher guidance is essential as students learn to effectively summarize and record critical information. Teachers should continue to support and encourage consistent implementation while students become more independent and effective with this strategy. Figure 3.12 is an example of a note-taking guide.

Figure 3.12   Combination Note-Taking Guide

Outline Notes:	Webbing:
Summarization:	

SOURCE: Marzano, R., Pickering, D., & Pollock, J. (2001). *Classroom instruction that works: Research-based strategies for increasing student achievement.* Alexandria, VA: McREL.

Partnering With Parents (Chapter 3)

Parents should know specific strategies being implemented with their child across all tiers. Parents can be active team participants as strategies are being discussed, and they at least need to be notified of chosen strategies. Not only should parents know the strategies, they should also know the timeline of implementation. Strategies and materials for use at home should be considered during school intervention meetings. Be sure to consider parent expertise and ability to perform specific strategies. If parents are unable to aid students with particular approaches, consider computer-based programs or checklists to assist the parent. Many research-based strategies, such as those found in Marzano et al. (2001) can be implemented at home with a little teacher guidance.

SUMMARY

Educators are required to implement research-based strategies more than ever before, to guarantee quality instruction. Response to Intervention is designed to increase effectiveness of these strategies by requiring the research base for Tier 2 and above. The strategies described in this chapter have been found to be effective for students across many grade levels and content areas. We feel that these strategies are best implemented with a team approach; no longer can one person meet the varied needs of students. It truly does take the team to research, implement, and evaluate the effectiveness of these strategies. Lastly, these strategies are most effective when they are implemented in positive, supportive environments in which all of the child's strengths and needs are acknowledged and systematically addressed. It is important to remember that the interventions presented here for Tiers 2 and 3 must be implemented within a well-designed RTI plan.

We realize many educators and administrators are immersed in the day-to-day challenges of education, which leaves little time to sort through the research. Fortunately, there are many resources available to guide schools in the process of identifying research-based strategies. Resource A of this book is provided to guide educators, schools, and systems as they begin to meet students' needs with research-based practices.

REFERENCES

The Access Center (2004, October). *Concrete-representational-abstract instructional approach.* Retrieved August 2007 from http://www.k8accesscenter.org/training_resources/CRA_instructional_approach.asp

Alberto, P. A., & Troutman, A. C. (2006). *Applied behavior analysis for teachers* (7th ed.). Upper Saddle River, NJ: Prentice Hall.

Armbruster, B. B., & Anderson, T. H. (1987). Improving content-area reading using instructional graphics. *Reading Research Quarterly, 26*(4), 393–416.

Bandura, A. (1977). *Social learning theory.* New York: General Learning Press.

Beecher, J. (1988). *Note-taking: What do we know about the benefits: ERIC DIGEST #37.* Bloomington, IN: ERIC Clearinghouse on Reading, English, and Communications. (ERIC Document Reproduction Service No. EDO CS 88 12).

Bretzing, B. H., & Kulhary, R. W. (1979, April). Notetaking and depth of processing. *Contemporary Educational Psychology, 4*(2), 145–153.

Brown, A. L., Campione, J. C., & Day, J. (1981). Learning to learn: On training students to learn from texts. *Educational Researcher, 10,* 14–24.

The Center for the Improvement of Early Reading Achievement (2001, September). *Put reading first: The research building blocks for teaching children to read.* Retrieved July 2007 from http://www.nifl.gov/partnershipforreading/publications/reading_first1.html

Comprehensive School Reform Program Office. (2002, August). *Scientifically based research and the comprehensive school reform program.* Retrieved September 2007 from http://www.ed.gov/programs/compreform/guidance/appendc.pdf

Cotton, K. (1991, May). *Computer assisted instruction.* Retrieved September 2007 from http://www.nwrel.org/scpd/sirs/5/cu10.html

Davey, B. (1983). Think alouds: Modeling the cognitive processes of reading comprehension. *Journal of Reading, 27*(1), 44–47.

Eaker, R., DuFour, R., & DuFour, R. (2002). *Getting started: reculturing schools to become professional learning communities.* Bloomington, IN: National Educational Service.

Fleer, M. (1992). Identifying teacher-child interaction which scaffolds scientific thinking in young children. *Science Education, 76,* 373–397.

Fuchs, D., & Fuchs, L. S. (2005). Responsiveness to intervention: A blueprint for practitioners, policymakers, and parents. *Exceptional Children, 38*(1), 57–61.

Fuchs, L. S., & Fuchs, D. (2007). A model for implementing responsiveness to intervention. *TEACHING Exceptional Children, 39*(5), 14–20.

Fuchs, L. S., Fuchs, D., Prentice, K., Burch, M., Hamlett, C. L., Owen, R., et al. (2003). Enhancing third-grade students' mathematical problem solving with self-regulated learning strategies. *Journal of Educational Psychology, 95*(2), 306–315.

Fuchs, L. S., Fuchs, D., Prentice, K., Hamlett, C. L., Finelli, R., & Courey, S. J. (2004). Enhancing mathematical problem solving among third-grade students with schema-based instruction. *Journal of Educational Psychology, 96*(4), 635–647.

Gentner, D., & Markman, A. B. (1994). Structural alignment in comparison: No difference without similarity. *Psychological Science, 5*(3), 152–158.

Harrison, M., & Harrison, B. (1986). Developing numeration concepts and skills. *Arithmetic Teacher, 33*, 1–21.

Heacox, D. (2002). *Differentiating instruction in the regular classroom: How to reach and teach all learners, grades 3–12*. Minneapolis, MN: Free Spirit Publishing.

Hidi, S., & Anderson, V. (1987). Providing written summaries: Task demands, cognitive operations, and implications for instruction. *Reviewing Educational Research, 56*, 473–493.

Jacobs, G. (2001). Providing the scaffold: A model for early childhood/primary teacher preparation. *Early Childhood Education Journal, 29*(2), 125–130.

Jitendra, A. (2002). Teaching students math problem-solving through graphic representation. *Teaching Exceptional Children, 34*(4), 34–38.

Jitendra, A. K., Griffin, C., Haria, P., Leh, J., Adams, A., & Kaduvetoor, A. (2007). A comparison of single and multiple strategy instruction on third grade students' mathematical problem solving. *Journal of Educational Psychology, 99*, 115–127.

Johnson, M. (1987). *The body in the mind: The bodily basis of meaning, imagination, and reason*. Chicago: University of Chicago Press.

Jones, B., Pierce, J., & Hunter, B. (1989). Teaching children to construct graphic representations. *Educational Leadership, 46*, 20–25.

Kounin, J. S. (1970). *Discipline and group management in classrooms*. New York: Holt, Rinehart & Windston.

Lakoff, G., & Johnson, M. (1980). *Metaphors we live by*. Chicago: University of Chicago Press.

Marzano, R., Pickering, D., & Pollock, J. (2001). *Classroom instruction that works: Research-based strategies for increasing student achievement*. Alexandria, VA: McREL.

Marzano, R. J. (2003). *What works in schools: Translating research into action*. Alexandria, VA: Association for Supervision and Curriculum Development.

Marzano, R. J., Marzano, J. S., & Pickering, D. J. (2003). *Classroom management that works: Research based strategies for every teacher*. Alexandria, VA: Association for Supervision and Curriculum Development.

Miller, S. P. (1998, September). Validated practices for teaching mathematics to students with learning disabilities: A review of literature. *Focus on Exceptional Children, 31*(1), 1–24.

Montague, M. & Jitendra, A. K. (2006). *Teaching Mathematics to Middle School Students with Learning Difficulties*. New York, NY: The Guilford Press.

National Council of Teachers of Mathematics. (2000). Principles and standards for school mathematics. Reston, VA: Author.

No Child Left Behind Act. (2001). Section 9101[37]. Retrieved March 12, 2008, from http://www.ed.gov/policy/elsec/leg/esea02/index.html

Nye, P., Crooks, T. J., Powlie, M., & Tripp, G. (1984). Student note-taking related to university examination performances. *Higher Education, 13*(1), 85–97.

Oczkus, L. D. (2005). *Reciprocal teaching strategies at work: Improving reading comprehension, grades 2–6: Videotape viewing guide and lesson materials*. Retrieved September 2007 from http://www.reading.org/publications/bbv/videos/v500/

OSEP Technical Assistance Center on Positive Behavioral Interventions. (2007). *School wide positive behavioral supports*. Retrieved July 2007, from http://www.pbis.org/schoolwide.htm

Palincsar, A. S., & Brown, A. L. (1984). Reciprocal teaching of comprehension fostering and comprehension monitoring activities. *Cognition and Instruction*, *1*(2), 117–175.

Promising Practices Network. (2005). *Programs that work: Reciprocal teaching.* Retrieved September 10, 2007 from http://www.promisingpractices.net/program.asp?programid=144

Rosenshine, B., & Meister, C. (1994). Reciprocal teaching: A review of the research. *Review of Educational Research*, *64*(4), 479–530.

Saenz, L. M., Fuchs, L. S., & Fuchs, D. (2005). Peer-assisted learning strategies for English language learners with learning disabilities. *Exceptional Children*, *71*(3), 231–247.

Smith, P. L., & Wedman, J. F. (1988). Read-think-aloud protocols: A new data source for formative evaluation. *Performance Improvement Quarterly*, *1*(2), 13–22.

Sprick, R. S., Garrison, M., & Howard, L. (1998). *CHAMPs: A proactive and positive approach to classroom management.* Longmont, CO: Sopris West.

Stennett, R. G. (1985). *Computer assisted instruction: A review of the reviews.* London: The Board of Education for the City of London. (ERIC Document Reproduction Service No. ED 260 687.)

Tomlinson, C. A. (1999). *The differentiated classroom: Responding to the needs of all learners.* Alexandria, VA: ASCD.

Tomlinson, C. A. (2001). *How to differentiate instruction in mixed-ability classrooms* (2nd ed.). Alexandria, VA: ASCD.

University of Kansas Center for Research on Learning. (2008). *Strategic Instruction Model.* Retrieved April 7, 2008, from http://www.kucrl.org/sim/index.shtml

U.S. Department of Education. (2006, August 14). Assistance to states for the education of children with disabilities and preschool grants for children with disabilities; Final rule. *Federal Register*, *71*(156), 46786–46787.

U.S. Surgeon General. (2000). *Executive summary youth violence: A report of the surgeon general.* Washington, DC: Public Health Service. Retrieved March 1, 2008 from http://www.surgeongeneral.gov/library/youthviolence/summary.htm

Vaughn, S., & Roberts, G. (2007). Secondary interventions in reading: Providing additional instruction for students at risk. *TEACHING Exceptional Children*, *39*(5), 40–46.

Vygotsky, L. S. (1978). *Mind in society.* Cambridge, MA: Harvard University Press.

Weaver, R. (1967). *A rhetoric and handbook.* New York: Halt, Rinehart, and Winston.

Wolfgang, C. H. (2004). *Solving discipline and classroom management problems: Methods and models for today's teachers* (6th ed.). Hoboken, NJ: John S. Wiley and Sons, Inc.

Wright, S. P., Horn, S. P., & Sanders, W. L. (1997). Teacher & classroom context effects on student achievement: Implications for teacher evaluation. *Journal of Personnel Evaluation in Education*, *11*, 57–67.

Providing Effective Instruction for All

Tier 1

In the previous chapters, we have presented details involving various elements that are essential in implementing an effective pyramid for RTI implementation. We will now combine these elements to discuss the process of establishing this pyramid in the school, basically moving from concepts and recommendations for best practices to the reality of implementation. As we develop our pyramid, we will offer numerous suggestions for each step in the process based on successful practices we have observed in schools.

STEP 1: DEVELOP A VISION THAT PROMOTES RTI

The first step toward development of a successful RTI process should be a concerted effort to develop a culture in which all parties share and are committed to the concept that all students will achieve. Within this culture, there is an understanding among all staff members that student failure is not acceptable. In their work on Professional Learning Communities, DuFour and his colleagues (DuFour, DuFour, Eaker, & Karhanek, 2004) devoted much of their discussion to the process of creating a culture within a school that embraces the vision of change. They stressed that the implementation of a pyramid of interventions in a school involves a structural change that should not be seen as a new program but should instead be incorporated into the larger process of developing a Professional

Learning Community. They asserted that structural changes produce little lasting impact unless they are embedded in the school's culture, which includes the "assumptions, beliefs, expectations, values, and habits that constitute the norm for that school" (DuFour et al., 2004, p. 172).

We have found this to be true of every change initiative with which we have been involved. Despite strong research evidence that school culture plays a significant part in sustainability of reform (Huberman & Miles, 1984; Sindelar, Shearer, Yendol-Hoppey, & Liebert, 2006), educational leaders at the state, district, and building levels often consider this foundational step to be unnecessary or too time-consuming. Instead, in their haste to implement programs, they develop regulations outlining structural requirements of these programs and impose them on schools whose culture is rooted in traditional methods of teaching and learning. Administrators and teachers at the school level see rules and procedures that do not fit with the culture of their school. Often they view the program as a new fad and figure they will "tough it out" until the fad has passed. They implement the new program for a period of time, sometimes giving considerable effort to making the program work. However, they have no understanding of the foundational ideas essential to the program's success. They have no vision or buy-in necessary for problem solving when difficulties arise. Eventually, they become disillusioned. Without a culture change at this level, the new program soon gives way to the traditional methods that were in place prior to the attempted change.

This phenomenon has been clearly illustrated through the implementation of inclusion and co-teaching, a process with which we have extensive experience as teachers, administrators, and consultants/trainers. For the past two decades, schools across the country have worked to include more students with disabilities in general education classrooms. One method of service delivery is co-teaching, in which two teachers are assigned to teach together in the general education classroom. When implemented appropriately, this model can have great success in improving instruction for all students. However, co-teaching rarely works if the foundational groundwork of team building, proper scheduling, personality matching, and training in models of co-teaching do not occur (Friend, 2005). Simply placing two teachers together and telling them to co-teach is rarely successful. In our experience, inclusion most often fails due to problems with the adults rather than problems with the children. These problems, which usually involve lack of communication, could easily be avoided if foundational issues were addressed prior to the first day of co-teaching. When time is set aside to develop a communicative culture in the school and within each team, the odds of success increase considerably. But this involves a culture change, moving from the concept of one teacher being in charge of his or her classroom and students to the notion of collegial decision making and shared responsibility. Without the culture change, the teachers rarely form a true partnership.

The same will be true for RTI. Attention must be given to the development of core beliefs and attitudes (Hollenbeck, 2007; Tilley, 2003). Schools that proceed with implementation without working on the foundational concepts underlying the process will find themselves facing challenges that seem insurmountable. The broad concept of pyramids of interventions belongs to a group of change initiatives that encompass all programs operated within the school. They are most effective when viewed as an integral part of the school improvement plan. Their effectiveness is greatly diminished when they are designated as belonging to special education or another component of the school (Hilton, 2007). Schools with successful implementation integrate the pyramid into every aspect of instruction, discipline, assessment, scheduling, curriculum design, staffing, allocation of resources, and parental involvement. Leaders within these schools begin implementation by developing a vision and climate that promotes the use of research-based strategies and assesses their effectiveness through curriculum-based measurement. Teachers begin to rely heavily on data to prescribe their next steps in teaching students. In this atmosphere, administrators and teachers refuse to place blame for student failure. Instead they constantly search for solutions to eliminate it.

In his discussion of RTI sustainability, Hilton (2007) identified four areas that are essential for school reform at the district and school level. They are (a) district-level practices that encourage reform, (b) strong school leadership, (c) teacher buy-in, and (d) key teacher leadership. We will examine each of these areas briefly in this chapter in order to build the foundation for an effective Tier 1 process. In Chapter 7, we will discuss these issues again, going into much greater detail as we develop a system plan for implementation.

District-Level Practices That Encourage Reform

At the district level, superintendents should have at least a general knowledge of the components of RTI and how they fit into the framework of school improvement (Hilton, 2007). There should be close collaboration between individuals in charge of curriculum, school improvement, special education, English language instruction, staff development, counseling programs, Title I/federal programs, and any other state or federal initiatives that involve student achievement. We recommend that these people work together to develop a thorough action plan for district-wide development. This team should carefully consider the current practices and needs of the district in all aspects of implementation. Adequate resources should be allotted to provide extensive staff development in the RTI process, research-based strategies, progress monitoring, and data utilization for instructional decision making. Resources should also be identified for the purchase of tools and materials. Districts may use funds designated for general education, such as those designated for curriculum and assessment, school improvement, and other areas as governed by state and federal guidelines. Districts may also utilize special education VI-B funds in the form of those designated for Early Intervening Services through IDEA.

It is our recommendation that districts develop a realistic timeline that allows for foundational practices to be developed and strengthened before moving on to the next step. In their review of Problem-Solving Model implementation in the Minneapolis Public Schools, Marston and colleagues cited a requirement for full implementation in a three-year time period as being a significant cause for concern (Marston, Muyskens, Lau, & Canter, 2003). Their recommendation was to implement gradually, carefully choosing schools for initial implementation. We reiterate that recommendation here. Districts may choose to begin with a small number of elementary schools, follow with middle and high schools in a feeder pattern (if state requirements include these levels), and complete by replicating the process in all schools. This gives school system personnel time to carefully and methodically evaluate the effectiveness of the project and address problems before full implementation. Of course, we are aware that there are states that are requiring immediate implementation at all levels. Even for districts that fall under these guidelines, we suggest a methodical and deliberate plan that begins with a vision for school improvement. Administrators should be realistic in their evaluation of and expectations for school change, allowing sufficient time and resources for buy-in and acceptance of the concepts that serve as the building blocks of RTI (Hollenbeck, 2007).

There is one final step in establishing the vision for RTI that must be addressed at the system level if it has not been mandated by state regulations. That is, school systems must choose which model of RTI to implement. Many states have developed guidelines that determine the model to be used for all school systems within the state. In instances where the choice has been left to the district, we recommend that district-level teams choose the RTI model to be used. In Chapter 1, we discussed both the Standard Protocol Model and the Problem-Solving Model in detail. We also briefly discussed using both in a mixed model. All have advantages and disadvantages when used in a non-research setting. Team members should carefully consider all components of each and choose the process that can be implemented with the greatest fidelity and with the allocation of adequate resources. A school system should not attempt to simply copy what another system has done without careful consideration of how it will apply to their own schools. A host of elements such as school-specific resources, teacher training, and staff commitment will affect the RTI process and will vary widely between sites (D. Fuchs & Deshler, 2007). This makes it impossible to duplicate programs from one school to another without some modifications.

After choosing the model or models to be utilized, the system must determine how many tiers to include in the pyramid—again, only if this has not been determined by state regulations. As illustrated in Chapter 1, most pyramids presented in research studies involve three tiers, with Tier 1 encompassing general education, Tier 2 involving research-based interventions as supplemental instruction, and Tier 3 encompassing individual instruction, often delivered through special education services. There are systems, however, that utilize pyramids containing four, five, or six tiers, all involving increasingly intensive levels of intervention.

L. S. Fuchs and Fuchs (2007) recommend utilizing only three tiers. They base this recommendation on the reasoning that multiple tiers of intensive intervention begin to resemble special education services. If schools are utilizing RTI to determine eligibility for special education, these increasingly intensive levels may distort the decision of whether the student is in need of special education services. They argue that the research-based scientific interventions employed outside of special education should represent a format and intensity that can be implemented by general educators, including well-trained and supervised teacher assistants or paraprofessionals.

In contrast, a four-tiered model was developed for statewide implementation by the Georgia Department of Education (Bender & Shores, 2007). In their model, Tier 1 involves all students within the general education classroom, and Tier 2 provides supplemental instruction for at-risk students through a Standard Protocol Model. Tier 3 utilizes the Problem-Solving Model for students who remain unsuccessful or who need strategies not included in readily available standard protocol interventions. Tier 4 encompasses multidisciplinary evaluation and subsequent services through special education if students are found eligible.

A variety of other models are being developed throughout the United States and Canada. School systems that are charged with choosing the number of tiers should carefully examine the needs of their students and the resources available for implementation and should choose the most appropriate model for increased student achievement. For the remainder of our discussion, we will utilize the three-tiered model recommended by L. S. Fuchs and Fuchs (2007).

Strong School Leadership, Teacher Buy-In, and Key Teacher Leadership

The building principal is key to the success or failure of Response to Intervention in the school improvement process. This has been proven time and again in our work with entire school districts. Given equal system-level support and guidance for change, individual schools within the district often exhibit vast differences in program success. Vaughn and Roberts (2007) identified effective leadership as an essential factor in RTI implementation, emphasizing the importance of leaders who are "committed to prevention-oriented practices" and "curriculum leaders who are willing to assure that scientifically based research practices are implemented" (Vaughn & Roberts, 2007, p. 45). Principals should have extensive knowledge about the process and what is required for implementation and sustainability (Hilton, 2007). They must develop their own set of beliefs about how the process can be most effective. When the principal conveys to his or her staff that the process is worthwhile for raising student achievement, teachers are more likely to follow and give considerable effort to embrace the process.

We encourage principals to develop a school-level implementation team. Involving classroom teachers in the decision-making process encourages their ownership of the program. When teachers take on a leadership role in process development, they may act as liaisons between the rest of the faculty and the administration. Those faculty members not on the team are more likely to give input to member-colleagues regarding their concerns and suggestions. Research on successful school reform and its sustainability revealed that teachers were most likely to embrace a reform movement when the process fit within their beliefs, when it helped the hardest-to-teach students, and when they received ongoing support and training (Sindelar et al., 2006). These may all be addressed by and through a leadership team. The principal and leadership team should convey to teachers their commitment to raising student achievement through the pyramid. They should take time to listen to and address teacher concerns and to ensure their support in the change process.

As we stated earlier, these components will be discussed in much more detail in Chapter 7. At that point, we will illustrate how to develop the leadership team at the district and building levels in order to create a multi-year implementation plan.

STEP 2: STRENGTHEN INSTRUCTION FOR ALL STUDENTS

After the system and school have embraced the RTI concept and have developed a foundational plan, they should proceed by examining and strengthening Tier 1, their core instruction for all students. We recommend that schools set a goal of having 80 percent of their students meet or exceed standards with Tier 1 instruction only (Harn, Kame'enui, & Simmons, 2007). Research has revealed that the number of students requiring Tier 2 interventions is directly related to the quality of the core instruction at Tier 1 (Kamps & Greenwood, 2005). A primary component in the development of an effective RTI process is the assurance of quality instruction for all students (Vaughn & Fuchs, 2003). In the absence of this assurance, poor instruction serves as the cause of failure for a large number of students. This inflates the number requiring Tier 2 interventions, which puts undue stress on both the human and financial resources of the system.

Quality Standards-Based Curriculum

Schools must substantiate that students are receiving effective instruction using a strong, research-based, standards-based curriculum. Marzano (2003), in summarizing research on school-level factors for reform, identified the implementation of a guaranteed and viable curriculum as the factor that had the most impact on student success. He went on to analyze the amount of time required to teach the content found in most state and local curricula. He found that without adding instructional time to the school calendar, it was impossible to teach all of the content. His recommendation was simple: Choose the most essential components and teach them to deep levels of understanding. That is the premise of national content standards.

Over the past few years, many states have revised their curricula to reflect national standards. This was most likely initiated in the wake of NCLB's requirement that all programs and curriculum in schools be scientifically research-based (U.S. Department of Education, 2001). Once it has been established that the school's curriculum is research-based and of high quality, then the school's leadership must ensure that it is being implemented effectively.

Schools should analyze their summative and benchmark assessment data to determine strengths and weaknesses in curriculum and instruction. Completion of a needs assessment may be helpful in identifying areas that require further attention. We have included one such tool in Resource E of this book. An action plan should be developed outlining prioritized needs for the school. Deficit areas should be quickly but comprehensively addressed in order to bring instruction to acceptable standards. Some identified needs may call for a change in materials, instructional practices, or schedules. Others may require staff development or personnel adjustments. The school's administration must ensure that instruction is effective through continued data analysis, extended observations, and frequent walk-throughs in classrooms. As the instructional leader, the principal is ultimately responsible for the instruction in each classroom. This is only possible when he or she spends time viewing instruction, holding teachers accountable for effective instruction, and providing resources and support when deficits are discovered.

Classroom Environment

In order to provide high-quality instruction to all students, teachers must establish a classroom environment conducive to learning. In Chapter 1, we discussed the fact that students must have their basic needs met before learning can occur. One of these needs is safety. It is an easy assumption that a student must feel physically safe in the classroom. However, it is also imperative that a student feel emotionally safe. Learning new concepts involves risk-taking—students need to know that if they make a mistake, they will be affirmed and gently redirected, not ridiculed or made to feel outcast. In the absence of this, students become vulnerable and are unwilling to take the risk of learning. In her work on differentiated instruction, Carol Ann Tomlinson calls this the "weather" of the classroom. When a teacher affirms her students and assures them that they are going to be supported and guided through the learning process, they are more likely to take the risk of learning (Tomlinson, 2003). We often ask teachers to give examples of classrooms with good and poor weather. After generating these examples, we then ask them to evaluate the weather in their own classroom and to determine whether they would like to be a student in that classroom. We feel it is a question that every teacher must consider on a frequent basis.

Formative Assessment

Another component of high-quality instruction is the use of formative assessment to guide instruction. In Chapter 2, we discussed formative assessment, including pre-assessment, curriculum-based measurement, and progress monitoring, to assess and guide instructional decisions. First and foremost, this data must be analyzed to determine whether the majority of students in the class are making progress. Benchmark assessments administered to the entire class will quickly make it clear. In the event that most students are not making acceptable progress, the administration should intervene to assist the teacher in improving the quality of instruction.

When evaluating the use of assessment and progress monitoring, care should be taken to ensure that teachers understand not only how to administer the chosen assessment tools but also how to use the information to adjust instruction for students who are at risk and for those who need enrichment. Data should be used to form flexible instructional groups based on readiness and needs. These groups will be further explored in our discussion of differentiated instruction.

Backward Design

A major obstacle to combining assessment and instruction is that many educators see assessment as something done *after* teaching and learning. When you assess *before*, *during*, and *after* instruction, you get a clear picture of the overall learning. If you are to use assessment to drive instruction, you must begin with the end result in mind.

To accomplish this, we recommend that teachers incorporate *backward design* into their daily instructional practices. Backward design is a process of designing final assessment as the first, rather than the last, step in instructional planning. It focuses on desired results first, as the initial step in the planning process. It involves beginning with the end result as the primary focus prior to planning the lesson (Wiggins & McTighe, 2005).

This concept is evident in many real-world settings. For example, a married couple that has decided to have a new home built rather than purchase an existing one typically does not contract with a builder to have just *any* house built—much time is spent looking through house plans. When the desired outcome has been decided upon, the buyers continue to adjust that blueprint to make the home comfortable and accessible for all family members. Every activity in the building project is completed with the final outcome in mind. Backward design incorporates this same thought process. You continually keep the educational goals in mind, making adjustments to your plan as you proceed, while keeping the end product accessible and attainable to the original goals established for learning.

When teachers use backward design, they begin by determining exactly what they want their students to know, understand, and do at the completion of the unit. They must consider state standards, classroom goals, and students' interests. Once desired outcomes are clearly identified, the educator may begin to plan meaningful assessments that show acceptable evidence of learning. In other words, they may decide how they will answer the question "What is acceptable evidence for my students to show me they understand the information I've taught?" This evidence should be the result of multiple assessment instruments, both formal and informal, that not only assess factual knowledge but reveal application and synthesis of the content to deep levels of understanding. This acceptable evidence is divided into categories based on the level of understanding required. Some concepts in the curriculum are sufficiently mastered if the student learns basic factual knowledge (e.g., dates of battles of the Revolutionary War). These concepts are often assessed through quizzes, homework and classwork assignments, completion of graphic organizers, observations, self-assessments, and other simple assessment tools. Other concepts are fundamental, enduring ideas that must be understood at a deeper level and applied to universal themes (e.g., the quest for freedom and liberty). These enduring understandings are most often assessed through the use of performance tasks that require students to process, analyze, and synthesize the information. A performance task based on our example above might be to ask students to imagine they are citizens of the British Colonies in 1775. They are to write a letter to their relatives in Europe explaining why British rule is no longer acceptable. This type of performance task reveals how well students have mastered content that can be built upon throughout the year and often can be applied across disciplines (Wiggins & McTighe, 2005).

Using a combination of assessments should produce multiple types of data that may then be analyzed to determine students' progression of learning in relation to the stated objectives. One assessment is only a snapshot; multiple assessments provide a photo album of assessment evidence so that teachers may truly evaluate student understanding (McTighe & Thomas, 2003). As teachers continually examine the assessment evidence, they can make adjustments and restructure the learning plan as necessary.

Teachers must be very careful in what they choose as their end result. If the focus becomes raising high-stakes test scores, the result is narrowing of the curriculum. If, instead, the focus is on mastery and deep understanding of major concepts, overriding ideas, and real-world questions, students are more likely to engage in meaningful learning and comprehend large amounts of content knowledge.

After developing appropriate assessment tools, educators may begin to develop learning plans geared toward achieving desired results. In planning lessons, teachers should include a variety of activities, materials, and teaching methods appropriate for engaging all learners in complex thought. This may involve the use of independent work, group activities, learning stations, computer-assisted instruction, and a variety of other arrangements and techniques (Wiggins & McTighe, 2005).

Figure 4.1 presents a backward design framework for instructional planning.

Differentiated Instruction

Backward design complements and fits easily within our next component of effective classrooms: differentiated instruction. Differentiated instruction has been widely promoted for the past ten years or so as a highly effective way to address the multiple levels of learning present in today's classrooms (Bender, 2005). Differentiated instruction involves providing a variety of avenues that allow all students to achieve at high levels. It works under the notion that students learn best when they are taught at a level slightly above their functioning level, referred to as the zone of proximal development discussed in Chapter 3. Teachers in differentiated classrooms utilize a variety of pre-assessments to determine individual students' levels of readiness, interest, and learning style. They then adjust their content (by teaching to different levels of complexity), process, and product based on each student's pre-assessment data. These variances work together to provide every student with challenging and obtainable material, whether he or she needs remediation or enrichment (Tomlinson, 1999). When differentiation is incorporated with backward design, teachers develop a clear picture of where each student should be and how to get them there (Tomlinson & McTighe, 2006). The principles of differentiated instruction should be implemented in classrooms on an

Figure 4.1   Steps for Backward Design

1. Identify desired results.				
Consider:	Objectives/Standards/Goals	Themes	Enduring Understanding	Essential Questions
2. Design assessment evidence to match desired results.				
Consider:	Performance Tasks	Formative Assessments	Summative Assessments	
3. Develop the learning plan.				
Consider:	Strategies	Activities	Resources	Methods for Differentiation	Methods for Scaffolding

ongoing basis to address the different learning levels and needs within each classroom.

Although differentiated instruction is an established and accepted practice in most schools, we find quite a bit of misunderstanding about the concept. When teachers are asked to tell what they know about differentiation, they often respond that it means having students work in groups. We see this illustrated in the classroom where indeed, students are working in groups, but everyone is doing the same thing. As stated earlier, differentiation involves changing content, process, and product based on students' readiness, interests, and learning profiles (Tomlinson, 1999). Strategies for accomplishing this include the use of tiered instruction (Heacox, 2002), stations, complex instruction, orbital studies (Tomlinson, 1999), and numerous others. Teachers should receive ongoing staff development in the use of differentiated instruction in their classrooms. Their lesson plans should reflect the components of differentiation in content not by reducing or increasing the amount of work required but by showing that students are engaging in various levels of complexity of thought (Heacox, 2002). It becomes imperative for differentiated instruction to be a fundamental basis for every classroom as we move to implement Tier 2 strategies in the RTI process. Resource A of this book includes numerous resources on differentiated instruction.

Teachers must understand how to structure their classrooms for differentiation and should be given support to implement the process. In the elementary classroom, this often involves rethinking the schedule followed during the day. Both the language/reading block and the math block should be structured so that students work in a variety of groupings, allowing teachers to have opportunities to work with all students in small groups or individually. Resource B of this book provides a recommended reading block schedule developed from recommendations from No Child Left Behind and Reading First. Based on a ninety-minute reading block, it is one example of a method to provide for a variety of differentiated activities to students as well as allow time for progress monitoring.

In the upper grades, the provision of differentiated instruction also involves structuring the classroom for a variety of activities. Many high schools operate on schedules of ninety-minute blocks. During this type of class period, teachers should plan for two to four activities. Activities should vary by format, grouping, intensity, level of independence, and other variables. Flexible groupings should be formed based on ongoing progress monitoring. Even in classes that are forty-five to sixty minutes in length, teachers should provide a variety of instructional formats and activities for their students.

In summary, principals should take steps to ensure that quality instruction is in place in every classroom within the school. Teachers should demonstrate effective implementation of a research-based curriculum. Instruction should be grounded in the fundamentals of backward design and differentiated instruction to ensure that every student successfully masters content to deep levels of understanding. Pre-assessment should be utilized to form flexible instructional groups. Benchmark assessments and curriculum-based measurements should be implemented to monitor student progress and adjust instruction as needed. Teachers should structure their classrooms and schedules in a manner that promotes a variety of grouping and instructional strategies. It is not imperative that all of these elements be fully developed in every classroom in order to be considered to have quality Tier 1 instruction. However, research indicates that these are best practices for today's classrooms. We believe that schools should strive to incorporate them, always focusing on the goal of increased student achievement. When all these elements are implemented in the classroom, we can be assured that Tier 1 provides a quality core of instruction for all students. We may then take steps to identify students who are non-responders at this level and begin to develop specific strategies for those students.

Example of Quality Tier 1 Instruction

The following scenario depicts a classroom that incorporates all of the elements mentioned above. It may be applied to any grade level in all content areas.

Mrs. Smith teaches a ninety-minute Reading/Literature and Language Arts block. Her students come from a variety of backgrounds and cultures. Of the twenty-five students in the class, four are English language learners, three are served through special education for various disabling conditions, four are in the gifted program, and six are labeled slow learners. According to standardized assessment data from the previous spring, Mrs. Smith's students' reading abilities vary from three grade levels above to four grade levels below their present grade. Students also exhibit wide variance in their writing abilities.

On the first day of class, Mrs. Smith provides students with a brief learning style assessment that identifies students' preferred learning modality—visual, auditory, tactile, or kinesthetic. The students also complete a multiple intelligence inventory and an interest inventory, all of which were taken from online resources. These inventories are completed during the time that Mrs. Smith is performing record-keeping and clerical duties. The activities take approximately twenty minutes to complete.

Mrs. Smith also uses a quick exercise to assess readability of text to determine whether students can comprehend material from their textbook (Northey, 2005). Next, she asks students to write a one-page story when given the prompt "If I could grow up to be anything I wanted, it would be. . . . " Finally, Mrs. Smith has her students complete a pre-assessment she has developed for their first unit of instruction. She spends the remainder of her time on this first day teaching behavioral expectations to her students. She discusses various types of groupings that will be used in class and practices transitions from one setting to another.

Prior to the beginning of school, Mrs. Smith made a basic plan of her first instructional unit, designed to take four weeks to implement. She utilized the concept of backward design to determine exactly what she would want her students to know, do, and understand when the unit was completed. Next, she developed assessment tools that included daily Exit Cards, homework assignments, two formative quizzes, and a performance task. She developed a rubric that outlined the requirements of the performance task. With the content of these assessments in mind, she then developed a learning plan containing a variety of strategies and activities to teach the content.

Using the results from the assessments listed above, Mrs. Smith now takes that instructional unit plan and adjusts it to fit her specific students. She uses the content pre-assessment data to place students in flexible ability groups, which will be used for some activities. In doing so, she identifies three distinct functioning levels for this unit: exceeds mastery level, on or near mastery level, and far below mastery level. She forms additional flexible groupings using the learning style data, placing students in groups with peers who have similar styles. Finally, she develops mixed groups based on the results of the multiple intelligence inventories, matching one student's strength with another's weakness. These groups will be used for complex instruction groups that will work together to complete the performance task.

Next, Mrs. Smith reviews the activities and strategies in her learning plan. Again using her pre-assessment data, she adjusts activities to include multiple processes for teaching the content. She will use a number of graphic organizers, which will sometimes vary for different students based on their learning style. She plans to use learning stations on several occasions. Students will sometimes visit stations in ability groups. Even though all students will be working toward the same standard, they will perform different activities based on multiple levels of complexity of thought. At other times, students will visit stations in interest groups, where they will complete an activity based on similar interests within the group. Mrs. Smith will use tiered instruction during two small group activities. She will place students in ability groups. Each group will perform the same basic activity, but again the level of complexity will be adjusted. This will allow her to challenge her higher-performing students to work independently and move beyond the basic information, allow her to give support to her on-level students to begin moving into more complex thought, and then allow her to spend time with her lower-performing students to assist them in developing a firm grasp of the standard.

To help with organization, Mrs. Smith makes several sets of cards outlining membership in each type of group. She will place the cards in a pocket chart each day so that students can quickly find their group. She gathers all materials, resource books, and supplies that will be needed for the first few days of instruction and places them within easy reach. Finally, Mrs. Smith arranges the room so that transitions can be completed as quickly as possible.

During the next few days, Mrs. Smith implements her learning plan. She uses Exit Cards every three days to assess student mastery of the content. Based on those results, she adjusts her groupings and activities, providing more individual attention and time to some students while giving others more challenging tasks.

STEP 3: DEVELOP EFFECTIVE BEHAVIOR MANAGEMENT

Previously in this book, we discussed the use of RTI for addressing problem behaviors. Regardless of whether or not a school chooses to implement RTI for behavioral issues, development of appropriate behavior management techniques should be included in evaluation and strengthening of Tier 1. Our rationale for this goes back to our previous discussion on the weather of the classroom. One of the most common components identified by teachers as determining the weather of the classroom involves effective behavior management. Most teachers agree that it is very difficult to teach in the presence of disruptive classroom behaviors. The direct link between academic achievement and student behavior is well established and widely accepted (Sprick, 2006). Therefore, in order to ensure that Tier 1 instruction is effective, schools should evaluate and seek to strengthen the quality of school-wide and classroom behavior management.

When deficits in school-wide behavior management are identified, we recommend that schools implement a program based on the Positive Behavioral Interventions and Supports (PBIS) process. Outcome data for school-wide implementation reveals significant behavioral improvement

(Freeman et al., 2006). Establishing the process within a school or district requires preparation of a structural system to give support in critical areas. The National Technical Assistance Center on Positive Behavioral Interventions and Supports has identified four components essential to PBIS implementation:

1. A Leadership Team to actively coordinate implementation
2. An organizational structure to include adequate funding, broad visibility, and consistent support
3. A foundation for sustained and broad-scale implementation established through:
   a. a team of individuals who can provide coaching support for local implementation,
   b. a small group who can train teams on the practices and process of school-wide PBIS, and
   c. a system for ongoing evaluation
4. A small group of demonstration schools that documents the viability of the approach within the local fiscal, political, and social climate of the state/district (OSEP Technical Assistance Center on Positive Behavioral Interventions and Supports, 2007, p. 1)

After examining school-wide behavior management, we recommend that schools look at individual classroom management. Data on classroom management can usually be discerned from a cumulative report of office discipline referrals. After examining trends evident in data, principals can identify classrooms and teachers from whom most referrals come. It is important to follow up by determining whether referrals involve only one student or a multitude of students. Administrators should also visit the identified classrooms on several occasions to determine if the problem is poor management, one or more disruptive students, or a combination of factors. Support may then be provided to assist the teacher in developing an effective management plan.

One critical component of effective classroom management plans is the practice of directly teaching behavioral expectations to students for all types of instruction—for example, teacher-directed instruction, independent work, and small group work, as well as expectations for transitions. Rules and behavioral expectations should be clearly stated in a positive manner and posted in the classroom. Teachers should review expectations throughout the year, re-teaching as necessary (Sprick, Garrison, & Howard, 1998). Resource A of this book provides reference information for several resources to assist teachers in this process.

STEP 4: BEGIN STAFF DEVELOPMENT

As schools examine and strengthen their instruction and behavior management throughout general education classrooms, instructional leaders may begin implementation of training in the RTI process. All faculty members should be trained in the fundamentals and specifics of RTI implementation using the chosen model, whether Standard Protocol, Problem-Solving, or a combination. If the concepts of progress monitoring and curriculum-based measurement are new to teachers and paraprofessionals, they will need extensive staff development in these areas. Finally, they will almost certainly require ongoing training in specific research-based strategies for various areas of difficulty. We recommend that teachers have access to a variety of staff development formats that provide ongoing support and training. In Chapter 7, we will discuss professional development in greater detail.

Partnering With Parents (Chapter 4)

Effective instruction for students is a concern of parents. You must remember, however, that parents are not "trained teachers" and thus may not typically understand the educational practices. We have heard many times how education is conducted much different from other organizations. It is important to communicate the significance of best practices in education, such as differentiation and behavior management. Parents who do not understand the purpose of pre-assessments, backward design, behavior incentives, or school-wide discipline plans may not be effective team members. There are many teachers who still struggle with these same concepts. Why would you expect parents to fully understand unless you include and educate them in these processes?

Where there is very little parent involvement, educators should first look to increase parent participation at the school level. What would happen if we argued that 80 percent of parents should be actively involved before we moved to more intense parent participation practices? It truly goes back to how important each team member feels parents are to the educational process.

It is true that parents can be your greatest ally or your greatest barrier to interventions. This is most often true when the parents do not understand the process. We have worked with very educated, well-meaning parents who fight the system only because they do not fully realize the purpose behind the necessary strategies of reaching all children within a structured environment. Once parents recognize the importance of specific practices, such as planning, grouping, and assessing, they are more likely to support the team effort.

SUMMARY

In this chapter, we have discussed components of Tier 1 in the RTI process: effective instruction for all students. We recommend that school districts begin RTI implementation by devoting adequate time for developing foundational beliefs among all staff members. Administrators at the district and school levels share the responsibility for developing this vision of RTI as an effective school improvement process, with the major portion of the leadership falling to the building principal.

Next, schools should work to strengthen their core instruction and behavior management for all students. Failure to address this may result in over-identification of students for Tier 2 interventions, which in turn will eventually drain the school system's human and financial resources.

Finally, emphasis should be placed on providing training to faculty and staff in the identified areas of need. Staff development for the RTI process will need to be ongoing rather than a one-time session.

After these things are accomplished and schools have substantiated that Tier 1 instruction is indeed appropriate and that most learners are showing positive response, they may then turn to development of Tier 2 processes and strategies. We will discuss elements of Tier 2 implementation in the next chapter.

REFERENCES

Bender, W. N. (2005). *Differentiating math instruction: Strategies that work for K–8 classrooms*. Thousand Oaks, CA: Corwin Press.

Bender, W. N., & Shores, C. F. (2007). *Response to intervention: A practical guide for every teacher*. Thousand Oaks, CA: Corwin Press.

DuFour, R., DuFour, R., Eaker, R., & Karhanek, G. (2004). *Whatever it takes: How professional learning communities respond when kids don't learn*. Bloomington, IN: Solution Tree.

Freeman, R., Eber, L., Anderson, C., Irvin, L., Horner, R., Bounds, M., et al. (2006). Building inclusive school cultures using school-wide PBS: Designing effective individual support systems for students with significant disabilities. *Research & Practice for Persons with Severe Disabilities, 31*(1), 4–17.

Friend, M. (2005). *The power of 2: Making a difference through co-teaching* (2nd ed.). Bloomington, IN: Forum on Education.

Fuchs, D., & Deshler, D. (2007). What we need to know about responsiveness to intervention (and shouldn't be afraid to ask). *Learning Disabilities Research & Practice, 22*(2), 129–136.

Fuchs, L. S., & Fuchs, D. (2007). A model for implementing responsiveness to intervention. *TEACHING Exceptional Children, 39*(5), 14–20.

Harn, B. A., Kame'enui, E. J., & Simmons, D. C. (2007). The nature and role of the third tier in a prevention model for kindergarten students. In D. Haager, J. Klingner, & S. Vaughn (Eds.), *Evidence-based reading practices for response to intervention* (1st ed., pp. 161–184). Baltimore: Paul H. Brookes Publishing.

Heacox, D. (2002). *Differentiating instruction in the regular classroom: How to reach and teach all learners, grades 3–12.* Minneapolis, MN: Free Spirit Publishing.

Hilton, A. (2007). Response to intervention: Changing how we do business. *Leadership, 36*(4), 16–19.

Hollenbeck, A. F. (2007). From IDEA to implementation: A discussion of foundational and future responsiveness-to-intervention research. *Learning Disabilities Research and Practice, 22*(2), 137–146.

Huberman, A. M., & Miles, A. B. (1984). *Innovation up close: How school improvement works.* New York: Plenum.

Kamps, D. M., & Greenwood, C. R. (2005). Formulating secondary-level reading interventions. *Journal of Learning Disabilities, 38*(6), 500–509.

Marston, D., Muyskens, P., Lau, M., & Canter, A. (2003). Problem-solving model for decision making with high-incidence disabilities: The Minneapolis experience. *Learning Disabilities Research & Practice, 18*(3), 187–200.

Marzano, R. J. (2003). *What works in schools: Translating research into action.* Alexandria, VA: Association for Supervision and Curriculum Development.

McTighe, J., & Thomas, R. S. (2003, February). Backward design for forward teaching. *Educational Leadership, 60*(5), 52–55.

Northey, S. (2005). *Handbook on differentiated instruction for middle and high schools.* Larchmont, NY: Eye on Education.

OSEP Technical Assistance Center on Positive Behavioral Interventions and Supports (2007). *Overview of district-wide and state-wide Positive Behavior Support (PBS).* Retrieved September 2, 2007, from http://www.pbis.org/statewide.htm

Sindelar, P. T., Shearer, D. K., Yendol-Hoppey, D., & Liebert, T. W. (2006). The sustainability of inclusive school reform. *Exceptional Children, 72*(3), 317–331.

Sprick, R. S. (2006). *Discipline in the secondary classroom: A positive approach to behavior management* (2nd ed.). San Francisco: Jossey-Bass.

Sprick, R. S., Garrison, M., & Howard, L. M. (1998). *CHAMPS: A proactive and positive approach to classroom management.* Longmont, CO: Sopris West.

Tilley, W. D. (2003, December). *How many tiers are needed for successful prevention and early intervention? Heartland area education agency's evolution from four to three tiers.* Paper presented at the National Research Center on Learning Disabilities' Responsiveness-to-Intervention Symposium, Kansas City, MO.

Tomlinson, C. A. (1999). *The differentiated classroom: Responding to the needs of all learners*. Alexandria, VA: Association for Supervision and Curriculum Development.

Tomlinson, C. A. (2003). *Fulfilling the promise of the differentiated classroom: Strategies and tools for responsive teaching*. Alexandria, VA: Association for Supervision and Curriculum Development.

Tomlinson, C. A., & McTighe, J. (2006). *Integrating differentiated instruction and understanding by design*. Alexandria, VA: Association for Supervision and Curriculum Development.

U.S. Department of Education. (2001). *No Child Left Behind Executive Summary*. Retrieved August 21, 2007, from http://www.nationalreadingpanel.org/publications/nochildleftbehind.htm

Vaughn, S., & Fuchs, L. S. (2003). Redefining learning disabilities as inadequate response to instruction: The promise and potential pitfalls. *Learning Disabilities Research & Practice, 18*(3), 137–146.

Vaughn, S., & Roberts, G. (2007). Secondary interventions in reading: Providing additional instruction for students at risk. *TEACHING Exceptional Children, 39*(5), 40–46.

Wiggins, G., & McTighe, J. (2005). *Understanding by design* (2nd ed.). Alexandria, VA: Association for Supervision and Curriculum Development.

Establishing an Intervention Structure for At-Risk Students

Tier 2

Response to Intervention is regarded as having multiple benefits, most of which we have already discussed. These include the ability to rule out poor instruction as the cause of learning problems, directly apply outcome data to instruction, and rely on data for instructional decision making. Possibly the most beneficial characteristic of RTI, however, is its ability to provide early intervention in very specific areas of instruction.

As teachers instruct students in the general education classroom, it will become evident through formal and informal assessment, including benchmark assessment, that some students are not making adequate progress. It is here that decisions must be made regarding the best way to address student deficits. In this chapter, we will focus on a systematic process designed to provide early intervention services to students who are non-responsive at Tier 1. We will continue our discussion from Chapter 4 on system- and building-level factors for implementation. We will explore the implementation of both the Standard Protocol Model and the Problem-Solving Model and the implications for both in the school setting. We will also discuss the use of curriculum-based measurement to identify and monitor the progress of students in Tier 2. Finally, we will review the latest research findings on valid ways of determining responsiveness to Tier 2 interventions. As you read the chapter, we encourage you to apply the concepts and suggestions to your own students in your school and classroom.

DEVELOPMENT OF TIER 2 STRUCTURE

In Chapter 1, we outlined the Standard Protocol Model, the Problem-Solving Model, and the mixed model, which incorporates both into one process. After choosing the model that will best serve their students, schools must begin development of a systematic structure to ensure that the process will be implemented effectively and with fidelity. This involves identifying components necessary for the model to work and applying them to the school structure already in place. Implementation may involve restructuring of the schedule, reassignment of duties and responsibilities, and reallocation of resources. We recommend that the leadership team work from a well-developed action plan based on a thorough needs assessment.

We begin our discussion of program development by examining elements specific to each model. Later, we will explore components that are common to both and make suggestions for effective implementation.

Development of the Standard Protocol Model

The Standard Protocol Model involves development of standard interventions that are readily available for student access. This model is preferred by researchers for its ability to provide research-based interventions with fidelity. Practitioners, however, often disregard it as a feasible option because they lack the resources or knowledge of how to set up and staff the intervention groups. We believe this model can be used effectively within a school setting without additional staff requirements.

The first step for any school is to identify the most common deficit areas in student achievement. Examination of benchmark testing results, criterion-referenced test scores, and other school-wide assessment tools will reveal patterns of weaknesses. School leaders should closely examine these areas and, by looking at subtest results and individual competencies within those subtests, distinguish the areas in which students experienced the most significant problems. They may find, for example, students who met standards in a content area but displayed weaknesses in a particular skill area. Weakness areas may vary by grade level. There will be, however, students at multiple levels experiencing the same needs. School leaders should prioritize these findings from most to least significant, based on number of students affected. After identifying the most significant needs, they may then begin to develop a plan for addressing them.

The leadership team must begin to search for a variety of options for service delivery. Schools throughout the country are beginning to develop innovative delivery plans based on their own resources and needs. We will outline a few that we feel are most effective and practical to put into place.

At the primary and elementary level, we recommend that schools first take inventory of their personnel resources. The leadership team should examine the schedule of every general and special education teacher and teacher assistant on staff. They should also consider other personnel, such as instructional coaches, itinerant support personnel, and perhaps school psychologists. In looking at each component of the total scheduling picture, most teams find blocks of time in which teachers can be freed from their students to work with small intervention groups. For example, kindergarten students often have recess and/or relaxation time in the afternoon. If these students were supervised in slightly larger groups or by paraprofessionals working with a supervising teacher, the other kindergarten teachers would be available to provide Tier 2 instruction to groups of three to five students. According to recommendations from researchers, well-trained and supervised teacher assistants or paraprofessionals may also implement interventions (L. S. Fuchs & Fuchs, 2007; Vaughn & Roberts, 2007). However, schools must verify that this is permissible under state and district policies for meeting NCLB's qualifications for instruction from highly qualified teachers.

Another option for intervention time is to incorporate needs-based instruction (sometimes referred to as targeted assistance) into the weekly schedule. This is common among schools working within the Reading First framework. In designing the school schedule, time is allotted two or more days each week for all students in the school to go to targeted assistance groups (see Resource B of this book for a sample schedule). Students are assigned to these groups based on frequent administration of curriculum-based measurement. Numbers within the groups are kept small by utilizing every available staff member. Groups are available for Tier 2 intervention in reading, math, and language arts. Each of the interventions is research-based and designed to provide specific targeted assistance. Children who are working at grade level attend groups that provide extension and skill-building activities in reading, writing, and math. Finally, children who are working above grade level are provided enrichment activities in reading, writing, and math. Group size for students on or above grade level is increased in order to provide more faculty for targeted assistance groups. Targeted assistance occurs during the social studies/science block on the specified days. If students are receiving Tier 2 interventions more than the days allotted for targeted assistance, they are pulled from social studies/science for the recommended number of days. In our example in Resource B, you can see that the targeted assistance instructional block is forty-five minutes long. Actual instructional time, after allowing for transition, might be only thirty-five to forty minutes.

Yet another option for Tier 2 instructional time is the development of before-school and after-school tutoring programs. There are a number of schools using Early Intervention Funds, provided for in IDEA 2004, to fund these programs. Students identified as at risk are scheduled into groups before or after the school day. Teachers and paraprofessionals are paid an extended day to serve as tutors. This is a viable option only for students who can access the services outside the school day. If transportation or other issues impede this, or if parents do not agree to the extended day, the service must be provided during the school day.

At the middle school level, an option is to incorporate targeted assistance into the school day, similar to our example for elementary schools above (see Resource B for a description of a middle school RTI model). This is accomplished by including an extra period in the daily calendar. All students attend small group instruction in a specified area, as we described above. Progress monitoring is completed on a frequent basis and students' group assignments are re-evaluated every nine weeks.

Middle schools may also offer targeted assistance as a supplemental reading or math class during exploratory or connections time, taking the place of art, music, PE, or another exploratory area for Tier 2 students. However, we want to stress the importance of utilizing specific, research-based interventions in these classes. The classes should not be viewed as remedial classes where students receive more of the same instruction that has already been implemented in Tier 1 and found to be unsuccessful.

At the high school level, there is a growing trend to employ teachers certified in reading to provide targeted assistance throughout the school day. Schools are scheduling what is termed "zero period," which occurs during the instructional day. Targeted assistance may be delivered during this period while other students go to homeroom, advisement, or study hall. Many schools are also implementing "Freshman Academy" models in which ninth-graders are placed into teams, similar to middle school scheduling. Flexible scheduling within the Academy allows for targeted assistance time. Additionally, high schools are developing elective classes in which students receive content-specific tutoring and strategies or basic skills strategies, designed to fit the structures we outlined in Chapter 1.

Some schools are opting to provide extended learning time in order to address the needs of at-risk students. Extended learning time (ELT) is often viewed as being impractical at the high school level due to schedules for afterschool extracurricular and co-curricular activities. However, a study conducted by the Center for American Progress highlighted multiple schools that have used ELT as one component of a successful plan to raise student achievement. We spoke briefly about this study in our discussion of secondary RTI structures in Chapter 1. The full document can be obtained at www.americanprogress.org.

After the schedule for interventions is developed, the school must choose Standard Protocol interventions based on the priority of needs discussed earlier. In Chapter 3, we presented numerous research-based interventions. There is an ever-increasing collection of interventions available for reading and math. It is important to remember that interventions used in the RTI process may include either purchased supplemental materials or learning strategies appropriate across grade levels and content areas, or perhaps a combination of both. However, it is true that no strategy or curriculum will be effective for all students. Schools should carefully choose their interventions based on quality of research and application to the needs of students. D. Fuchs and Deshler (2007) state that "scientifically validated" means the intervention is a "good bet" for many children (p. 132); it is not a guarantee of success. Therefore, districts may want to choose two or more strategies for implementation in each deficit area, with one being the primary and first intervention. If children show minimal response, the second strategy may be implemented to rule out the possibility that the first was just not a good fit for the child.

As you can see, there are many creative options available, and we are certain more will be developed as schools seek to make the best use of the resources available to them. We want to encourage schools and districts to consider the feasibility of these options in relation to their students' needs. We believe that, with some creative planning, the Standard Protocol Model can be effectively implemented outside of the research domain.

Development of the Problem-Solving Model

As we explore the development of the Problem-Solving Model, it is helpful to begin by highlighting similarities and differences between it and the Standard Protocol Model (see Figure 5.1). We base our vision of the Problem-Solving Model on the general structure of the Heartland Area Educational Agency's problem-solving approach.

The most significant similarities between the models involve the use of research-based interventions and progress monitoring for determining student progress. These elements are essential if RTI is to function as an

Figure 5.1   Comparison of Standard Protocol Model and Problem-Solving Model

Standard Protocol Model	Problem-Solving Model
• Research-based interventions	• Research-based interventions
• Use of progress-monitoring data for decision making	• Use of progress-monitoring data for decision making
• Progression through tiers to increase intensity	• Progression through tiers to increase intensity
• Small group implementation	• Small group or individual implementation
• Instructional decisions made by person implementing strategy or other designee	• Instructional decisions made by assistance team
• Standard Protocol interventions established prior to need	• Interventions based on individual needs of learner
• Goals established for each student based on benchmark criteria	• Goals established for each student based on benchmark criteria or individual needs

effective tool. Traditionally, Problem-Solving Models have been much weaker in these areas and, in the absence of these elements, have become ineffective pre-referral processes (Fuchs, Mock, Morgan, & Young, 2003). By ensuring that these are key components in model implementation, school leaders may develop a Problem-Solving Model that can be effectively utilized for increased student achievement.

As you can see from our comparison chart, both models may involve instruction in small groups. It is a common misconception that the Problem-Solving Model involves interventions conducted for individual students. Although decisions are based on individual students' needs, there may be several students, perhaps within different grade levels in the school, who experience the same problems. Thus, it is feasible for schools to put together small groups of students to receive interventions. Schools can utilize some of the same recommendations that were presented for the Standard Protocol Model, although possibly on a much smaller scale.

One of the first steps in development of the Problem-Solving Model is to establish a team that will make instructional decisions for each student. The problem-solving team, often referred to as student support team, student assistance team, or building assistance team, will consider the needs of individual students and develop an intervention plan for them. There are options as to who serves on the assistance team. Teachers who work with the student or who teach similar students could compose the team. For example, several second-grade teachers could make up the team for a second-grade student. On the other hand, schools may choose to put in place a team of core membership that makes determinations for all students. Membership could include an administrator, curriculum specialist, school counselor, school psychologist, instructional coach, behavior specialist, or others with expertise in curriculum, behavior, and interventions. We recommend that a student's primary teacher be a member of the group, regardless of who the other members might be.

All team members should be trained in the problem-solving cycle and other key components of model implementation. They should have access to information on a variety of research-based interventions and their appropriateness for various student problems. This team will be charged with analyzing student weaknesses and identifying interventions to address those weaknesses. Therefore, they should be provided with time and extensive training for this process. In his description of the Problem-Solving Model utilized by Heartland Area Educational Agency, Tilley (2003) stressed the importance of extensive staff development to empower teachers in effective use of the cycle, research-based strategies, and progress monitoring.

One facet of Problem-Solving implementation that overwhelms both administrators and teachers is the large number of interventions that must be available to meet individual students' needs. Our recommendation is to divide this piece into manageable parts. Each school administrator may designate one or more faculty members to receive intensive training in a specific intervention. This person or group becomes the school's expert in that strategy. They train others in the use of the strategy as needed, being careful not to "water down" and thus negate the validity of the strategy. This person may also be the one who observes for fidelity of instruction. By assigning various interventions to individual or teams of staff members, teachers are more likely to feel empowered and "buy into" the process, thus enhancing the sustainability of implementation.

Development of the Mixed Model

If systems choose to employ a combination of the models, as described in Chapter 1, they must establish all of the components for both models. This is sometimes envisioned as a four-tiered model, with Tier 2 using Standard Protocol interventions and Tier 3 using individual interventions developed through the Problem-Solving Model (Bender & Shores, 2007). In other examples, the Standard Protocol Model is used for academic problems and the Problem-Solving Model is used for behavioral issues (L. S. Fuchs & Fuchs, 2007). Districts and schools should consider the efficacy of each and develop their vision for implementation while being true to the essential components for each.

Development of Elements Common to Both Models

As we pointed out using Figure 5.1, there are some elements common to both the Standard Protocol and Problem-Solving Models. In the Standard Protocol Model, these elements will be determined for each Standard Protocol intervention put in place in the school. In the Problem-Solving Model, they will be decided for each student. Resource D of this book contains an Intervention Plan form designed to guide this process, particularly in the Problem-Solving Model.

First, schools must identify a screening measure that will be utilized in identifying students at risk. This usually involves a benchmark assessment or universal screening given to all students in Tier 1. As we have previously discussed, a key component of a successful RTI process is to implement highly effective instruction in Tier 1, the general education classroom. If the majority of students are making adequate educational progress, it is easy to identify students in need of additional instruction and specific intervention.

Schools must establish a cut-point that is considered to be the demarcation line between satisfactory and unsatisfactory progress. This cut-point may be defined as a percentile score (e.g., <20th percentile) or a benchmark score (e.g., <25 wpm on Oral Reading Fluency; L. S. Fuchs & Fuchs, 2007). As this decision is made, leadership teams should keep in mind that percentile scores are making use of the bell curve, meaning that the students who fall into the at-risk category will vary depending on the overall performance of the class. With the benchmark score, however, students are not compared to each other but are instead compared to acceptable performance criteria. We recommend the use of benchmark scores whenever possible. If percentiles are used, we recommend making comparisons across a large group such as a grade level rather than across a single classroom. In many cases, this will provide a more heterogeneous comparison group.

Based on recent research findings, we also recommend the addition of progress monitoring for students identified as at risk before they are labeled as Tier 1 non-responders. Studies at the National Research Center on Learning Disabilities found that a large number of students who failed to meet acceptable criteria on one-time universal screenings showed acceptable progress when provided with Tier 1 instruction. They termed these students "false positives." The researchers then assessed the validity of implementing five weeks of weekly progress monitoring for these students. They found that this produced more reliable predictions of students in need of Tier 2 interventions (D. Fuchs & Deshler, 2007). In essence, when students are identified as at risk by benchmark testing, they remain in the general curriculum instruction and are administered weekly progress-monitoring probes. At the end of five weeks, only the students who have continued to perform below the cut-point are given Tier 2 interventions. Students who make sufficient progress are no longer considered at risk.

Whether interventions are provided individually or in groups, schools must make decisions about the intensity of instruction, including amount of time per session, number of sessions per week, and number of weeks for each intervention. While there are no absolutes in any of these variables, the intervention should be implemented with enough intensity for students to move toward grade-level performance (Vaughn & Roberts, 2007). Manipulation of each of the variables mentioned above can increase or decrease intensity. For example, intensity may be increased by providing instruction four times each week instead of two.

Recommendations for the number of weeks for implementation of academic interventions vary widely, ranging from ten to twenty weeks and more (L. S. Fuchs & Fuchs, 2007; Marston, 2005; Vaughn, Linan-Thompson, & Hickman, 2003). Vaughn and Roberts (2007) recommend that interventions be provided three to five times per week. In their studies, Vaughn and colleagues often use ten-week intervals of instruction, assessing students for readiness to exit instruction at the end of each interval. When this protocol is followed, students frequently receive instruction for thirty weeks (Vaughn et al., 2003). The time frame that produces the most valid results is yet to be determined and has been identified as an essential area of need in future research (D. Fuchs & Deshler, 2007). Until results are available, we recommend that schools utilize the ten-week intervals as outlined above as a general guideline. The ultimate decision for length of intervention will be determined by student response, which we will address shortly in our discussion of measuring progress.

In reality, there may be some students with severe deficits who make slow but sufficient progress for a number of years (Kovaleski, 2007). It is important to continually evaluate their progress to determine appropriateness of instruction. If progress is not considered sufficient, school personnel should explore other instructional options and perhaps seek additional evaluative information.

Schools must also establish procedures for ensuring fidelity of instruction, defined as implementation of the strategy as it was intended by the researchers. This is carried out through observation by someone who is knowledgeable about the intervention and can ascertain that it is being used correctly. The documentation generated during this observation serves as evidence that the student or students were provided effective instruction, ruling out the possibility that they have had lack of opportunity to learn (Bender & Shores, 2007). The observer may utilize a narrative summary that answers very basic questions about the quality and appropriateness of the instruction. If a strategy is used often by the school, educators may want to construct an Intervention Validity Checklist (IVC), which outlines the major components and requirements of the strategy (Vaughn et al., 2003). These often are in the form of a rubric, identifying key components and scoring through a range of compliance. This will simplify the observation while ensuring that all required elements from the strategy are in place. Resource C of this book provides a brief example of an IVC designed for a scripted reading program.

Next, schools must choose assessment tools for measuring student progress. This is most often accomplished in Tier 2 using a standardized curriculum-based measurement tool. There are a number of such tools on the market in the areas of reading and math for elementary and, to a lesser extent, middle grades. At the high school level, schools may have to develop their own until more standardized tools are available. In Chapter 2, we discussed procedures for developing these tools. Districts should carefully evaluate each available tool and choose the one most appropriate to the needs of their students. Assistance in this task has been provided by the National Center on Student Progress Monitoring. By visiting their Web site at www.studentprogress.org, school leaders may access a Tools Chart that rates numerous standardized assessment tools for reliability, validity, alternate forms, improving student learning, and other areas.

After choosing a tool, teams must decide how often these assessment tools will be administered to students receiving intervention. Recommendations for frequency of progress monitoring vary from biweekly (Vaughn et al., 2003) to weekly (D. Fuchs & Fuchs, 2005; Vaughn & Roberts, 2007) to daily (Bender & Shores, 2007). The key to answering this question lies to some extent in the degree to which the practice can be incorporated into the instructional routine. According to Deno (2003), many teachers fail to implement CBM on a regular basis, even though they understand the benefits of using it as a progress-monitoring tool. Summarizing two studies exploring barriers to implementation, Deno identified lack of time for implementation as the biggest barrier. In Resource B, we present a sample reading schedule that incorporates progress monitoring into the daily schedule. This same concept can be applied to Tier 2 progress monitoring, placing five minutes before or after each instructional session during which teachers can assess one or two students daily. Based on this scenario, we recommend biweekly to weekly progress monitoring in Tier 2.

Teams should also consider data management as they choose their assessment tool. Many tools are purchased as a package that includes computer-assisted data management. Teachers input their students' data, and a computer program compiles and analyzes the data, creating usable charts and graphs. If this is not a component of the chosen assessment tool, teachers may chart their data by hand or by using a tool such as Microsoft Excel. Regardless of how it is developed, this chart will provide a picture of student progress that will be utilized for instructional decision making.

This brings us to the next decision to be made: defining progress. We recommend the use of dual-discrepancy as the most valid means of defining progress (D. Fuchs & Deshler, 2007). This method has been found to be more valid than other methods in identifying poor readers at a younger age (Speece, Case, & Molloy, 2003). When utilizing dual-discrepancy, the teacher or team considers the student's level of performance in comparison to a benchmark, the class performance, or an established goal. Secondly, they consider the student's final level of performance in comparison to their original level of performance (referred to as slope).

In Figure 5.2 we see an illustration of dual-discrepancy being applied to data maintained on a kindergarten student. This student began instruction far below the benchmark. After five weeks of progress monitoring in Tier 1, she remained unresponsive and was placed into Tier 2 intensive instruction. With twelve weeks of intervention, the achievement gap between the student's performance and the benchmark remained significant. Judging this factor alone still places the student in a non-responder category because she did not achieve the benchmark. However, we find that the student showed marked improvement between her beginning and ending performance levels. Her slope of improvement was much greater with intervention than during Tier 1 instruction. Based on dual-discrepancy formula, we determine that the student is responding to the intervention but needs an instructional change in order to make the benchmark goal. The teacher or team must now decide the next instructional step for the student. Because the student showed positive response, but not enough to reach benchmark, the decision most likely would be to increase the intensity of the same intervention. If both the level and slope had revealed no improvement, the student would have been considered a non-responder to this intervention (L. S. Fuchs & Fuchs, 2007).

It is in this way that educators use data to make instructional decisions. The team must consider the overall slope and level of response to the intervention, comparing the slope of improvement to that made in

Figure 5.2   Dual-Discrepancy Model of a Kindergarten Student

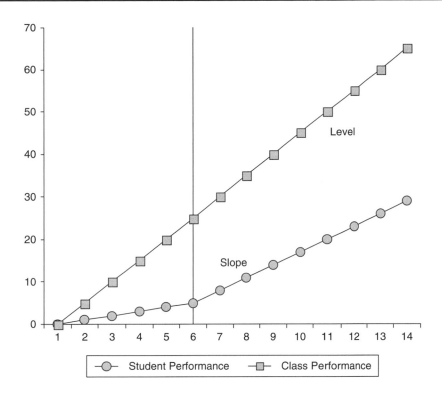

Tier 1 instruction. They must also consider whether the intervention was appropriate to the needs of the learner, considering any new information, such as learning style and skill strengths and weaknesses, gleaned from the child's performance. Using all available information, educators must determine what the next instructional step should be, whether moving to more intensive instruction in the next tier, changing or intensifying instruction in the current tier, or returning to a lower tier.

One related issue that has been identified by researchers is a tendency for some students to receive Tier 2 interventions, return to Tier 1, and then later be identified as needing Tier 2 intervention again (Hollenbeck, 2007; Vaughn et al., 2003). This indicates that there will be students who fail to thrive in the general education classroom but benefit from more intensive instruction in targeted assistance groups. Theoretically, if interventions are addressing broad skills such as reading fluency and the student receives appropriate instruction to meet the goal, this should happen only occasionally. However, we see this back and forth movement between Tiers 1 and 2 occurring frequently within schools. Students benefit from the instruction and begin performing at grade level. Later, they experience deficiencies in other areas as content becomes more complex.

There is nothing in the RTI structure that prohibits this movement. In fact, it is central to the foundations of the early intervention concept. However, more research will be necessary to determine whether these students experience long-term benefit from ongoing rounds of intervention. If this movement occurs frequently within a school, we recommend that leadership teams examine the needs of these students closely to determine whether Tier 1 instruction needs to be strengthened in order to increase achievement.

After choosing an appropriate assessment tool and deciding how to determine progress, school leaders must answer additional questions, including who will review student data to determine responsiveness. In the Standard Protocol Model, this may be the teacher implementing the strategy, school psychologists, instructional coaches, or others who have a thorough understanding of the system's definition of responsiveness. In the Problem-Solving Model, the decision would be made by the assistance team. School leaders must also decide how often student data will be reviewed. The answer to this question will depend on the number of weeks the intervention will be in place. Schools may decide to assess intermittently during that time frame, or only at the end.

As you have read through all of the elements presented here, you may have become overwhelmed with the magnitude of planning for and implementing RTI in Tiers 1 and 2. In fact, you may feel it is an impossible task. When implemented as a stand-alone project, each of these elements does require considerable planning and resources. However, when viewed as an overall school improvement plan, the elements work together to complement each other. Development of one step leads naturally into the next.

In our experience with school improvement, we have found that schools often launch into elaborate plans that later prove to be ineffective or the district decides to discontinue. Much time is wasted following plans that are later abandoned. RTI can be different if implemented well. Each of the steps outlined thus far has a strong research base supporting its effectiveness in raising student achievement. The RTI process encompasses instruction, assessment, scheduling, and allocation of resources. When implemented as part of a well-developed master plan, RTI can be the vehicle of change for overall school improvement.

Additional Recommendations for Behavioral Models

In general, the same basic procedures apply when implementing behavioral strategies as those for academic plans. However, there are a few points not already discussed that specifically address behavioral RTI models. First, the team may wish to review progress and analyze data more frequently. Problem-solving teams may meet every two to three weeks in order to carefully monitor the student's progress (Barnett et al., 2006). Although the team should always allow time for a strategy to make an impact, they may find it necessary to adjust or change interventions more often than the ten to twelve weeks commonly followed with academic models.

The intensity of behavioral interventions varies based on the type of strategy being implemented. When planning for interventions such as group counseling, the team may choose a frequency of one or more sessions per week. However, in determining frequency for behavior change strategies within the classroom setting, the interventions should be applied continuously throughout all applicable settings. Examples of this type of intervention include behavior charts, token economies, and other similar tools.

EXAMPLES OF TIER 2 PROCESSES

We will now provide examples of RTI processes in both the Standard Protocol and Problem-Solving Models in various grade levels. Each example incorporates the elements essential to RTI success.

Primary School Standard Protocol Model

Carrie is in first grade at Buchanan Primary School. In January, Carrie's teacher, Mrs. Price, used DIBELS as a benchmark assessment tool to evaluate reading progress of all her students. Carrie read 12 words per minute on the Oral Reading Fluency subtest. The class average was 20 words per minute. The ORF goal for end of first grade is 40 words per minute. Mrs. Price distinguished Carrie and several other students as possibly being at risk for reading failure. She continued to administer the ORF subtest weekly for five weeks. At the end of that time, two of the students had made adequate progress and were no longer considered at risk. Carrie showed no significant gains. Mrs. Price consulted with her school's literacy coach and arranged to place Carrie into targeted assistance for reading fluency. A goal of 30 words per minute was set, defining weekly progress as approximately 2 words per week.

Carrie attended this instructional period, taught by Ms. Jones, a kindergarten teacher, for thirty minutes four days per week. The targeted assistance group received intensive instruction through a research-based supplemental reading program proven effective for increasing reading fluency. Ms. Jones was observed twice during this time by the literacy coach, who documented appropriate instructional fidelity. Carrie's progress was monitored once each week using the DIBELS ORF. After ten weeks of intervention, Ms. Jones and Mrs. Price reviewed Carrie's progress. As seen in Figure 5.3, Carrie's ORF score was now 26 words per minute. Although she did not achieve her goal, Carrie's data showed improvements in level and slope. This indicates that Carrie was responsive to the intervention, but not significantly enough to exit the group. It was decided that Carrie would continue in the targeted assistance group for an additional ten weeks with weekly progress monitoring. The assistance would continue to be provided for thirty minutes four times each week. A new goal of 40 words per minute was established, based on increased expectations for this point in the year.

Figure 5.3 Carrie's ORF Data

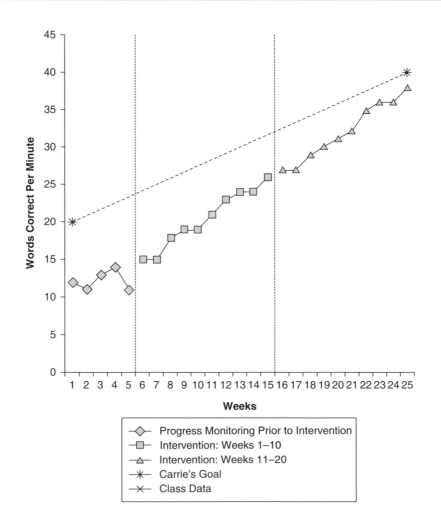

Review at the end of the second ten weeks revealed that Carrie's ORF score was now 38 words per minute. Carrie had come within 2 wpm of meeting her goal. She was now considered to be ready to return to Tier 1 instruction.

Elementary School Standard Protocol Model

Terrence is in fourth grade at Madison Elementary. It was early December, and Terrence's class was learning to simplify, add, and subtract fractions and mixed numbers. Terrence was having a very difficult time with the concept. His teacher, Ms. Hammers, evaluated his performance on recent curriculum-based measurement probes. She found that he scored significantly below the benchmark on the past three assessments. She also reviewed formative assessment and saw that Terrence was having significant difficulty with math problems involving abstract concepts. These same difficulties had been documented by previous teachers.

Ms. Hammers scheduled Terrence to attend supplemental math instruction four days per week, thirty minutes per session, for fourteen weeks. He would receive supplemental and strategy instruction from a trained teaching assistant during these sessions. Progress would be monitored weekly using CBM probes.

During the intervention sessions, Terrence was given intensive instruction using the Concrete-Representational-Abstract strategy. The strategy was embedded in supplemental math materials based on state standards and similar to the ones used in general education instruction. The teaching assistant was observed weekly by the math coach to ensure fidelity of instruction. As we see in Figure 5.4, Terrence showed little gain in his CBM scores. Ms. Hammers met with the school's math coach to discuss instructional options. They decided that Terrence may require more intensive instruction than can be provided through general education. They decided to move Terrence to Tier 3. In this tier, the school psychologist would complete an evaluation to identify learning deficits and possible eligibility for special education services.

Middle School Problem-Solving Model

Jamie is an eighth-grade student at Lakemont Middle School. He has a history of school failure dating from first grade. Recently, his teachers reported that he seemed unmotivated to attempt any assignments. During the first week of school, the language arts teacher, Mr. Hastings, asked Jamie to read a short maze passage (see Chapter 2). While reading the passage, Jamie was asked to choose the correct word from a choice of three in

Figure 5.4 Terrence's Math Data

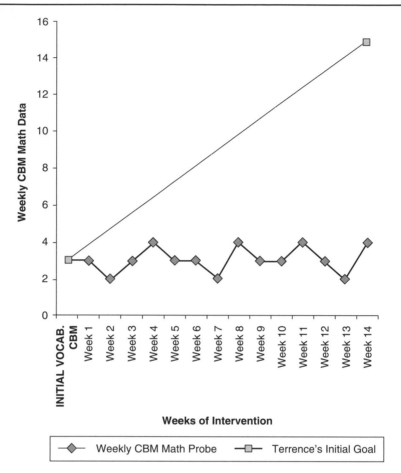

order to complete sentences. In a reading passage with 38 possible correct answers, Jamie obtained a score of 5—Mr. Hastings stopped administration of the assessment after five incorrect answers in a row.

The following week, Mr. Hastings met with the student assistance team and discussed the data related to Jamie's performance. The student assistance team spent time reviewing Jamie's school and personal history. It was found that Jamie lives with his mother and four younger brothers and sisters. There has been little communication between Jamie's mother and his teachers throughout his school history. After discussing numerous issues that might possibly relate to Jamie's school failure, the team decided to address his reading problems first and placed him in a reading tutorial program operated during the school's exploratory classes. Jamie would be moved from art into the tutoring program, where he would receive instruction using Making Connections Interventions from Educators Publishing Services, a research-based middle school reading comprehension program designed for struggling readers. A goal was set for Jamie to correctly answer 25 of 40 items on the maze passage assessment. Jamie would attend the program every day for thirty minutes. During the remaining fifteen minutes of the block, Mr. Hastings would utilize additional research-based learning strategies to teach Jamie skills that could be used in all his classes. The tutoring program would be reevaluated after twelve weeks.

Jamie's progress-monitoring data is displayed in Figure 5.5. At the end of twelve weeks, Jamie reached his goal of 25 correct items. Mr. Hastings also reported to the team that Jamie had turned in all assignments in language arts during the last eight weeks. The team determined that, based on dual-discrepancy criteria of improvement in level and slope, Jamie had responded positively to the intervention. They developed another goal of 40 correct items and recommended that Jamie continue to attend the tutoring sessions. The team also recommended that Jamie's social studies and science teachers integrate many of the comprehension strategies into their content area instruction.

Figure 5.5 Jamie's Maze Data Chart

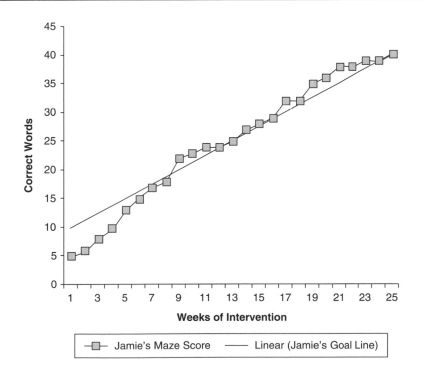

High School Basic Skills Structure

Jiwon is a first-semester freshman at Taylor High School. She is a Korean exchange student who has been educated in American schools for four years. Jiwon was having significant difficulty in her American Literature class. Her teacher, Mrs. Hardy, initiated a student assistance team meeting to discuss Jiwon's needs in high school. Jiwon attended the meeting, along with her geography teacher, the school counselor, and the English language learner specialist.

The team first discussed Jiwon's English language skills. Jiwon was considered to be conversationally proficient in English. However, she still struggled with academic English, specifically in the area of vocabulary. She was not considered eligible for ELL services but did need support in classes requiring extensive reading. Mrs. Hardy noted that in her class she always provides a vocabulary list containing definitions and sample sentences with each word. She also incorporates numerous literacy strategies, such as self-questioning, visual imagery, and think-alouds, which are used with all students. Jiwon stated that, although the list is helpful, she has a very difficult time understanding what she is reading. In benchmark testing administered to all students in the class, Jiwon scored in the lowest 10 percent of the class on a vocabulary CBM, with 5 out of 20 possible points. After some discussion, the team hypothesized that although Jiwon had become a sufficiently fluent reader in English, she had not mastered essential comprehension strategies necessary for success in reading-intensive classes.

The team developed an educational plan for Jiwon in which she would receive supplemental instruction in reading comprehension strategies. The interventions would be taught daily during the school's zero period, a thirty-minute block set aside for advisement/homeroom and Tier 2 strategies. Jiwon would attend the zero period instead of her homeroom for a period of twelve weeks. She would be taught comprehension strategies from the Strategic Instruction Model developed at the University of Kansas. A goal was set for 18 of 20 correct answers on the vocabulary assessment tool. Instruction would be provided by a locally funded intervention specialist. The strategies would also be integrated into instruction in the Literature class and any other class that required extensive reading. Progress would be monitored weekly using a vocabulary assessment.

Figure 5.6 illustrates Jiwon's progress while receiving Tier 2 interventions. Her vocabulary assessment scores showed marked increase during the instructional period, with her final outcome being at her goal. The team determined that Jiwon would no longer receive Tier 2 interventions during the zero period. However, the strategy instruction would continue in her content area classes.

Figure 5.6   Jiwon's Vocabulary Data

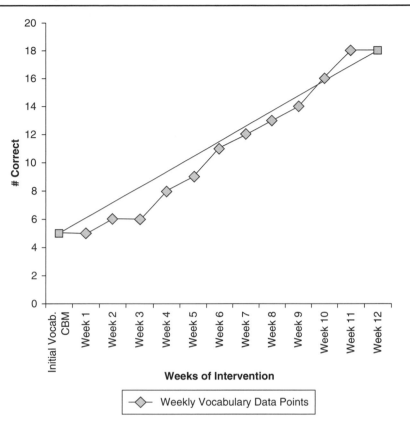

Elementary School Behavior Problem-Solving Model

Kristin is a third-grade student identified by her teacher, Ms. McCollum, as having frequent verbal outbursts. Specifically, Kristin yells out answers to questions before being called on and argues when given assignments that she does not like. These behaviors have worsened over the past few weeks, prompting Kristin's teacher, Ms. McCollum, to bring the matter to her school's problem-solving team. The following is a summary of the team's application of RTI elements and the problem-solving cycle.

Quality of Tier 1 instruction: Ms. McCollum has developed a generally effective behavior management plan in her classroom. Students were taught behavioral expectations each day during the first few weeks of school. Direct teaching of expectations was not phased out until the class followed the rules on a consistent basis. Rules and consequences for breaking them are posted in the classroom. There are five rules, all stated in a positive manner.

Ms. McCollum also has a small bulletin board in the classroom dedicated to social skills development and behavioral expectations. Each week, she teaches one or more twenty-minute lessons on appropriate social skills. A reward system is in effect in which students earn a token each day for compliance with the rules. In addition, all students and their parents signed a behavior contract at the beginning of the school year. Ms. McCollum has referred no students to the office this school year.

Tier 2 Intervention Plan

Define the problem:

- Verbal outbursts—defined as any verbal communication that interrupts the teacher or other person without the student being called on (Fairbanks, Sugai, Guardino, & Lathrop, 2007).
- Compliance—defined as accepting assignments from the teacher without verbal or physical opposition.
- External contributing factors—Kristin has a history of excessive talking documented by previous teachers. Her parents report behaviors at home that are similar to those seen in the classroom. She is the second of four children. She often aggressively competes for her parents' attention.
- Data analysis—Before the initial meeting, the school counselor observed Kristin for thirty minutes during a ninety-minute reading block. During the observation, Kristin exhibited twelve verbal outbursts and two acts of noncompliance.

Plan the intervention:

- Intervention: Daily Behavior Report Card (Fairbanks et al., 2007)—The instructional day will be divided into fifteen-minute segments with a daily total of sixteen segments (excluding recess, lunch, and other non-instructional segments). Kristin has the potential of earning two possible points during each segment: one point for no incidences of verbal outbursts, and one point for compliance. In addition, Ms. McCollum will provide Kristin with a visual cue reminding her to raise her hand when she would like to speak. There will be a picture taped to Kristin's desk showing Kristin with her hand raised. If Kristin has a verbal outburst, Ms. McCollum will silently point to the picture as she walks past Kristin's desk.
- Person responsible for implementation and progress monitoring: classroom teacher with consultation by school counselor
- Time frame: daily for all segments

- Goal: Initially, Kristin will receive a reward for earning 75 percent of all possible points. The goal will be increased in five-point increments as she meets the previous goal. Additionally, Kristin will receive verbal praise each time she earns a point.
- Progress monitoring tool: number of points earned
- Frequency of progress monitoring: daily
- Review of progress: every three weeks

Implement the intervention:

- Ms. McCollum implemented the intervention as specified. The school counselor observed for fidelity of instruction during the first week. He found that the plan was being implemented consistently and appropriately.

Evaluate the student's progress:

- Results of the intervention are illustrated in Figure 5.7. During the second week of implementation, Kristen earned 75 percent of her points on two days. During the third week, she earned 75 percent on four days.
- The goal will be raised to 80 percent for an additional three weeks. Progress will again be reviewed at that time.

Figure 5.7   Kristin's Behavior Chart

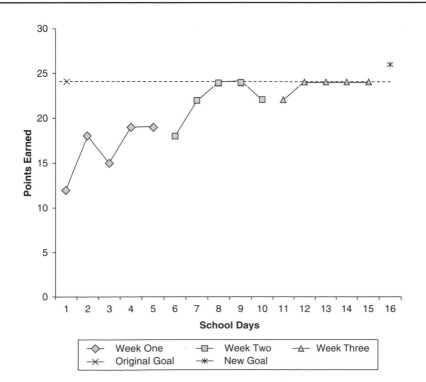

Partnering With Parents (Chapter 5)

Most parents are concerned when their child struggles academically. However, they often do not understand why we now have a system for providing more intense interventions for these children. Some parents do not want any part of having their child identified as different, while others want to totally skip this tier and move immediately to evaluation for special education services. Either perspective can inhibit the school's attempt to intervene and meet specific student needs.

Again, as seen throughout the process, communication is key. Parents need to understand that rejecting the intervention will not make the student's difficulty go away. Rather, denying that a weakness exists is the worst thing a teacher or parent can do. Similarly, insisting that a child is disabled based on identified weaknesses can also be harmful for the student. Parents and teachers alike should be aware that weaknesses in educational performance do not necessarily constitute a disability.

The pyramid of interventions is designed to provide a system of supports to meet individual students' needs at all levels. It is not designed to label a child for life or pretend the problem does not exist. Helping parents understand this process can be difficult, as this approach is a shift in how we have traditionally worked with struggling students. The best way to communicate this to parents is to include them in every step of the process.

SUMMARY

In this chapter, we have outlined specific steps in the implementation of Tier 2 interventions in both the Standard Protocol and the Problem-Solving Models. At the district or school level, leaders should first choose between these models, or perhaps design a mixed model that combines elements of both. The choice of models should be based on available resources and the overall needs of the students.

When implementing a Standard Protocol Model, schools must first take inventory of the most significant deficit areas identified by their student achievement data. This will point toward the Standard Protocol interventions that should be developed within the school. Schools should then explore a variety of scheduling options for providing the targeted assistance. This may occur before, during, and after the instructional day.

Should the school choose to implement the Problem-Solving Model, an assistance team must be formed that will apply the problem-solving process to individual students' needs. Schools may need to develop a structure for training teachers in the problem-solving approach and in numerous research-based strategies. Finally, but most importantly, the school must choose and implement effective progress monitoring for instructional decision making.

Regardless of the model chosen, schools must choose assessment tools, establish cut-points for determining progress, and take steps to ensure fidelity of instruction. In order for the RTI process to be effective, schools should begin with a well-developed action plan and incorporate the process into the overall school improvement plan.

REFERENCES

Barnett, D. W., Elliott, N., Wolsing, L., Bunger, C. E., Haski, H., McKissick, C., et al. (2006). Response to intervention for young children with extremely challenging behaviors: What it might look like. *School Psychology Review, 35*(4), 568–582.

Bender, W. N., & Shores, C. (2007). *Response to intervention: A practical guide for every teacher*. Thousand Oaks, CA: Corwin Press.

Deno, S. L. (2003). Developments in curriculum-based measurement. *The Journal of Special Education, 37*(3), 184–192.

Fairbanks, S., Sugai, G., Guardino, D., & Lathrop, M. (2007). Response to intervention: Examining classroom behavior support in second grade. *Exceptional Children, 73*(3), 288–310.

Fuchs, D., & Deshler, D. (2007). What we need to know about responsiveness to intervention (and shouldn't be afraid to ask). *Learning Disabilities Research & Practice, 22*(2), 129–136.

Fuchs, D., & Fuchs, L. S. (2005). Responsiveness-to-intervention: A blueprint for practitioners, policymakers, and parents. *TEACHING Exceptional Children, 38*(1), 57–61.

Fuchs, D., Mock, D., Morgan, P. L., & Young, C. L. (2003). Responsiveness-to-intervention: Definitions, evidence, and implications for the learning disabilities construct. *Learning Disabilities Research & Practice, 18*(3), 157–171.

Fuchs, L. S., & Fuchs, D. (2007). A model for implementing responsiveness to intervention. *TEACHING Exceptional Children, 39*(5), 14–20.

Hollenbeck, A. F. (2007). From IDEA to implementation: A discussion of foundational and future responsiveness-to-intervention research. *Learning Disabilities Research & Practice, 22*(2), 137–146.

Kovaleski, J. F. (2007). Response to Intervention: Considerations for research and system change. *School Psychology Review, 36*(4), 638–646.

Marston, D. (2005). Tiers of intervention in responsiveness to intervention: Prevention outcomes and learning disabilities identification patterns. *Journal of Learning Disabilities, 38*(6), 539–544.

Speece, D. L., Case, L. P., & Molloy, D. E. (2003). Responsiveness to general education instruction as the first gate to learning disabilities identification. *Learning Disabilities Research & Practice, 18*(3), 147–156.

Tilley, W. D. (2003, December). *How many tiers are needed for successful prevention and early intervention? Heartland Area Education Agency's evolution from four to three tiers.* Paper presented at the National Research Center on Learning Disabilities' Responsiveness-to-Intervention Symposium, Kansas City, MO.

Vaughn, S., Linan-Thompson, S., & Hickman, P. (2003). Response to instruction as a means of identifying students with reading/learning disabilities. *Exceptional Children, 69*(4), 391–408.

Vaughn, S., & Roberts, G. (2007). Secondary interventions in reading: Providing additional instruction for students at risk. *TEACHING Exceptional Children, 39*(5), 40–46.

Delivering Intensive Intervention to Non-Responders

Tier 3

As described in the majority of the current research, Response to Intervention has two primary purposes: early intervention and identification of learning disabilities. Thus far in this book, we have focused on its application to early intervention. The purpose for this focus was to present RTI as a process for improving schools and raising student achievement. Our discussion has centered around Tiers 1 and 2 and how instruction and intervention at these levels should look. We now turn our attention to Tier 3 and the use of RTI for learning disabilities (LD) identification.

After a student is provided with interventions at Tier 2 and is found to have made insufficient progress, he or she may be considered for Tier 3 interventions. Tier 3 of the RTI pyramid involves the most intensive level of intervention and progress monitoring. In most models, this tier is considered to be individualized instruction provided through special education services (Bender & Shores, 2007; L. S. Fuchs & Fuchs, 2007; Vaughn & Fuchs, 2003). Throughout this chapter, we will present issues related to assessment, identification, and instruction of students who were considered "non-responders" to instruction in the earlier tiers and who have been placed in Tier 3.

DETERMINATION OF TIER 2 NON-RESPONSE

In Chapter 5, we outlined the use of dual-discrepancy formula to determine whether a student has made adequate response. Using this procedure, a small number of students in a school will be identified as non-responders. IDEA regulations identify non-responders as follows:

> The child does not make sufficient progress to meet age or State approved grade-level standards in one or more of the areas identified in paragraph (a)(1) of this section when using a process based on the child's response to scientific, research-based intervention. . . . (U.S. Department of Education, 2006, Sec. 300.309(a)(2)(i))

This determination should be made based on careful interpretation of the data and consideration of the appropriateness of the interventions provided. Some students may receive multiple interventions or multiple rounds of a single intervention prior to reaching this point. Essentially, the data must indicate that the student has made inadequate progress and is unable to meet grade-level mastery without more intensive evaluation and/or intervention. At that point, the teacher or team may consider the need for further information to determine the presence of a disability. The way in which this additional information is obtained may vary considerably from state to state.

INITIAL ASSESSMENT FOR LEARNING DISABILITIES ELIGIBILITY

In its provision to allow RTI for evaluative purposes, IDEA 2004 calls for a multidisciplinary evaluation to be conducted in order to determine specific learning disability (SLD) eligibility. There has been much discussion among researchers and practitioners as to what exactly should be included in this evaluation and what role RTI data should play in eligibility determinations. Basically, the discussion revolves around three critical issues:

1. Should the multidisciplinary evaluation be a comprehensive battery of tests or should it simply seek to answer questions raised in the RTI process?

2. Should significant discrepancy be eliminated from the eligibility criteria?

3. Should the multidisciplinary evaluation distinguish between specific eligibility categories, such as LD or behavior disorder, or should the evaluation use non-categorical placement for students

needing special education services? (L. S. Fuchs & Fuchs, 2007; Hollenbeck, 2007)

On the first issue, IDEA regulations provided some additional guidance in the requirement that multidisciplinary evaluations should include aptitude and achievements tests (U.S. Department of Education, 2006). In a discussion of this requirement, Zirkel cited commentary accompanying the regulations which reads as follows: "An RTI process does not replace the need for a comprehensive evaluation, and a child's eligibility for special education services cannot be changed solely on the basis of data from an RTI process" (U.S. Department of Education, p. 46648, as cited in Zirkel, 2007). In essence, further evaluation in some form is required. This is consistent with previous IDEA requirements that eligibility decisions cannot be based on a single determining factor. The question then becomes, what will be included in that evaluation? Specifically, what additional assessment must be conducted in order to effectively determine eligibility?

Leading researchers and practitioners, particularly in the field of school psychology, have expressed very different opinions on these issues. There is much disagreement about the validity and usefulness of information obtained from comprehensive psychoeducational assessments, most of which usually include IQ tests, measures of cognitive abilities, and individually administered achievement tests (Wodrich, Spencer, & Daley, 2006). The inclusion of IQ scores is often the most controversial aspect of the evaluation process. Some argue that Full Scale IQ is valid in predicting general achievement only and cannot distinguish specific learning problems (Flanagan, Ortiz, Alfonso, & Dynda, 2006). There is also considerable argument that IQ assessment adds little to the type of instruction a child will receive following the evaluation (Vaughn & Fuchs, 2003). Along these lines, many researchers have recommended that evaluations be conducted only for the purpose of answering questions raised during the RTI instructional process. They reason that full assessments provide no guidance or utility in planning for instruction and therefore are unnecessary (L. S. Fuchs & Fuchs, 2007). In this scenario, the evaluation does not involve a standard battery of tests given to every child being considered for special education eligibility. Instead, the evaluation is designed for each child in order to answer the specific instructional questions that surface during Tier 1 and Tier 2 instruction and may or may not include IQ testing.

However, the case is also made that cognitive ability testing and subscores in IQ testing contribute a great deal of knowledge as to the child's strengths, weaknesses, and instructional needs (Flanagan et al., 2006;

Mastropieri & Scruggs, 2005; Willis & DuMont, 2006). This has impact not only in distinguishing between eligibility categories (e.g., SLD vs. MiMR), but in instructional planning as well. For instance, a student with mild mental retardation may need functional skills instruction and specific vocational training as part of classroom and transition instruction. Most students with specific learning disabilities do not need this type of instruction. As Wodrich and colleagues point out, this information may be more important to the family in long-range planning than to the school (Wodrich et al., 2006).

This ongoing debate often raises more questions than it answers. Despite some extreme opinions completely for or completely against traditional assessment, the consensus seems to be settling in on a combined approach in which RTI is combined with some level of additional testing (Flanagan et al., 2006; Willis & DuMont, 2006; Wodrich et al., 2006). Indeed, the combination approach reduces the complete reliance on specific test results while ruling out lack of instruction as the cause of the student's learning problems. This certainly seems to be the most logical approach.

The debate then focuses on our second question. Should significant discrepancy be eliminated from the eligibility criteria? At first look, this seems to be answered by a resounding "yes" from the research community, based on ongoing research substantiating the poor ability of discrepancy to predict reading ability (Speece, Case, & Molloy, 2003). However, there are those who disagree. For example, Scruggs and Mastropieri (2002) recommended utilizing RTI in conjunction with, rather than instead of, the discrepancy model. Basically, if a student was a non-responder to Tier 1 and Tier 2 instruction and exhibited an achievement–IQ discrepancy, he would be considered eligible for LD. If he was a non-responder but did not exhibit a discrepancy, he would receive interventions outside of special education. The reasoning behind this argument is that heavy reliance on RTI data would conceivably change the definition of learning disability (Kavale, Holdnack, & Mostert, 2005). Without additional assessment of processing deficits and discrepancy to distinguish between students with LD and those with generally low achievement, often referred to as "slow learners," it is conceivable that the characteristics of children served through the learning disabilities category of LD would change considerably.

The exact definition of multidisciplinary evaluation and LD eligibility will ultimately be determined by individual states and will, more than likely, vary greatly between states. This variability is quite evident in an October 2007 survey of state laws regarding SLD eligibility. This survey, completed by state directors of special education, revealed that approximately half of the states had finalized their requirements for RTI use in eligibility decisions, while the other half were still in the proposal stages. Within both groups, considerable differences were noted in the criteria used for eligibility determination, namely in the decision to require, permit, or prohibit significant discrepancy in the decision process (Zirkel & Krohn, 2008).

We agree that the evaluation should be useful in guiding future instruction and that the RTI process is essential in providing early intervention and appropriate instruction. However, we are cautious about abandoning previous methods in favor of moving to new methods in which there are so many unknowns. For example, in a comparison of evaluation methods involving low achievement alone versus low achievement coupled with IQ criteria, Speece et al. (2003) found that the makeup of the identified groups was very different. However, they could not discern from the data which was the "right" group of children to identify as LD. In the years since this study, researchers have still not identified absolutes in determining the presence of a learning disability using RTI data.

In the previously discussed survey of state implementation, it was found that the majority of states are taking a transitional approach to the use of RTI for LD eligibility. Although RTI has a strong research base and history for school improvement, the research base is not so extensive for identifying students with learning disabilities (Bender & Shores, 2007). Until we know more about the most appropriate cut-points, the most effective amounts of time for intervention, and appropriateness of various interventions, it is our recommendation that states and districts follow this transitional approach from previous methods rather than abandon them. We feel this is necessary particularly during the training phase of the RTI process, when there is uncertainty of the quality of RTI processes and fidelity of implementation within individual settings. The decision to place an LD label on a child is life-changing and should be made using the best information available.

This brings us to our third issue, that of categorical or non-categorical placement. Here, too, there is disagreement. Some argue that placements should be made based on the need for services without defining a specific eligibility category. Approximately one-fifth of the states have implemented some non-categorical or cross-categorical placement for students with high-incidence disabilities (Reschly, Hosp, & Schmied, 2003). This was the case in Minneapolis Public Schools (Marston, Muyskens, Lau, & Canter, 2003). The most significant impact of this type of decision is most often a change in state funding formulas. Because many states provide varying amounts of funding based on eligibility category, a change of this sort would be warranted only after considerable work to alter this formula. However, it also may have a profound impact on services and instruction provided to students, as referenced in our earlier example. Again, this is an issue that will almost certainly vary by state and should be carefully considered in its entirety.

One additional question to be addressed about the evaluation is whether it will take place at the end of Tier 2, between Tiers 2 and 3, or as part of Tier 3. Again, we find significant variance between researchers' recommendations and state-by-state practices. On one hand, it is a matter of semantics based on the structure adopted by the state. On the other hand, it is important in that due process is initiated at the point when the school system or parents suspect that the child needs special education (Zirkel, 2007). Regardless of the point on the pyramid where evaluation takes place, it is important to ensure that the child continues to receive intervention and progress monitoring during the evaluation. In our experiences with pre-referral intervention models, children received limited (albeit often ineffective) interventions prior to referral for evaluation. During the evaluation process, interventions often ended while the school waited for evaluation results. This should not occur. In the RTI process, after the child has proven unresponsive to an intervention at Tier 2, the school must determine the next level of intervention and the need for additional evaluation procedures.

RTI AS AN EVALUATIVE TOOL FOR OTHER AREAS OF ELIGIBILITY

In our discussion of evaluation procedures, we have focused on eligibility issues for students with specific learning disabilities. This is the only eligibility area in IDEA 2004 that employs RTI in evaluation procedures. However, as we have discussed in previous chapters, RTI is an appropriate framework for addressing behavioral problems as well. There may, then, be some states that incorporate RTI into evaluation procedures for determining the existence of possible behavioral disorders. In that instance, RTI may be one important piece of information in the overall evaluation process. It would be accompanied by information from teachers and parents obtained through behavior checklists, projective measures, observations, functional behavioral assessments, and/or cognitive assessments.

We are aware of at least one state that has incorporated RTI procedures into many areas of eligibility in order to rule out inadequate instruction and provide high-quality intervention prior to evaluation. This may be easily incorporated when RTI is used as a school improvement framework. Essentially, all students who are at risk of not meeting standards (academic or behavioral) would have access to Tier 2 interventions. Documentation of responsiveness to these interventions would serve as pre-referral interventions, regardless of the eventual eligibility determination. However, it is important to note that RTI has not been researched for use in determining eligibility for any categories other than specific learning disabilities.

TIER 3 INSTRUCTION

As a result of the assessment process, some children will be determined eligible for special education services, delivered through Tier 3 in our model. In previous chapters, we have presented numerous interventions and teaching practices appropriate for Tiers 1 and 2 of an effective RTI pyramid. As we turn our focus to Tier 3, we will explore ways in which this tier is similar to and different from the first two. Tier 3 instruction should involve the most intensive level of intervention and progress monitoring. Teachers providing Tier 3 instruction should utilize the information regarding the student's lack of responsiveness to previous instruction and additional information gained during evaluation procedures to develop a highly specific plan for addressing deficit areas. The urgency of this was illustrated in the following observation: "The odds of reaching the next literacy goal for students given an instructional recommendation of intensive [as measured by DIBELS] are poor (i.e., less than 40%) unless significant additional instructional support is provided immediately, relentlessly, explicitly, and continuously" (Harn, Kame'enui, & Simmons, 2007, p. 165).

In their presentation of a model RTI process, L. S. Fuchs and Fuchs (2007) call for a restructuring of special education in order to provide a viable and effective third tier. In their model, special education teachers would have lower student–teacher ratios, increased instructional time coupled with intensive progress monitoring, reduced caseloads, and reduced paperwork. They envision special education as being a more intensive and individualized version of Tier 2 where students move into the tier, receive intensive individualized instruction specific to their needs, and then move back into Tier 1 or 2 (L. S. Fuchs & Fuchs, 2007).

This restructuring of special education is receiving more attention as school systems nationwide implement the RTI process. It is a logical assumption that general education should not be the only component of the school that is transformed by RTI. In most districts, full implementation of this type of Tier 3 model will require a major shift in policy and procedures. In the current special education structure, students generally enter special education and remain there indefinitely. In some instances, more emphasis is placed on meeting procedural requirements than providing high-quality instruction to students with disabilities (L. S. Fuchs & Fuchs, 2007).

In a multi-year study of the effectiveness of a three-tier intervention model, Harn, Kame'enui, and Simmons identified three features that were critical in effective Tier 3 instruction: (1) protected time and grouping for intensive intervention, (2) ongoing performance monitoring for instructional decision making, and (3) the provision of prioritized content selection coupled with purposeful design and delivery (Harn et al., 2007). We will discuss each of these elements as they relate to the provision of special education services in Tier 3.

If special education is to serve a valuable place in the RTI pyramid, it must mirror and exceed the requirements in Tiers 1 and 2. If students do indeed receive high-quality general education instruction in Tier 1 and research-based interventions specific to their needs coupled with frequent progress monitoring in Tier 2, should they receive less in Tier 3? No—quite the opposite.

Special education teachers and administrators are faced with a perplexing problem. They must seek to provide high-quality instruction to students who have not responded to research-based interventions that were effective with most learners. They must also provide access to the general education curriculum in the least restrictive environment. This presents a significant challenge and poses the question: How special is special education?

As we explore this question, we make recommendations with full knowledge that this component of the RTI pyramid may require more of a shift in beliefs and processes than any we have discussed thus far. It will require a shift from the perception of special education services provided in many schools. It will certainly require a shift in policies at the state and district levels. For this reason, we believe it is critical that leadership teams work toward establishing the vision for Tier 3 with the same intensity and forethought that was required for Tiers 1 and 2. We encourage districts to develop a multi-year plan for systematic implementation. With that in mind, there are many components of the process that can be implemented immediately (e.g., increased use of progress monitoring for instructional decision making). Others will require extensive preparation and policy development. As we explore the quality of Tier 3 instruction, we encourage you to evaluate each suggestion and think about ways to apply processes immediately and long term to your district and/or school.

Protected Time and Grouping for Intensive Intervention

Service Delivery

Over the past decade, there has been increased emphasis on providing access to the general curriculum through the inclusion model. We wholeheartedly agree with this emphasis. The achievement gap between students with and without disabilities is showing a steady decrease because of this emphasis (U.S. Department of Education, 2003). However, one result of increased inclusion may be decreased intensive, skill-specific instruction. When students with disabilities receive all instruction in the general education classroom, they may have limited access to research-based interventions designed to address their specific learning needs.

Skill-specific interventions should be in addition to, not instead of, general curriculum access. Students must continue to receive access to the general curriculum in general education settings. However, in order to receive more intensive high-quality, skill-specific interventions than are provided in Tier 2, students will need additional intensive instruction. Otherwise, we may be faced with a situation in which students receive more intensive intervention at Tier 2 than at Tier 3.

This brings up the question of how and when to provide this intensive intervention. When schools use the tiered framework to provide targeted assistance to all at-risk learners, they have flexibility in scheduling and resources, which should make Tier 3 service delivery much easier. Previously discussed formats for needs-based instruction and extended learning time can be provided for students with disabilities in the same manner as for Tier 2 students. The instructional period may provide more intensity by meeting more often and/or for longer segments (Stecker, 2006). Groupings should be kept small. The makeup of the group should include only children working on the same skill, avoiding the pitfalls seen in many traditional interrelated resource rooms (e.g., large numbers of students working at different levels on different subjects).

Early Intervention

Key to the RTI concept is the idea that students benefit most from early intervention at the first signs of learning problems. NCLB stresses the importance of early intervention in its appropriation of Reading First funding (U.S. Department of Education, 2001). Ongoing research identifies early reading intervention as being necessary for optimal success in teaching reading (Good, Simmons, & Kame'enui, 2001). RTI research has demonstrated that reading intervention provided in kindergarten could reduce or eliminate the need for reading intervention in later grades (Vellutino, Scanlon, Small, & Fanuele, 2006). In other research, children who received early intervention through RTI and were later found to be non-responsive to Tier 2 interventions performed better at Tier 3 than students who did not receive Tier 2 interventions (Denton, Fletcher, Simos, Papanicolaou, & Anthony, 2007; Speece et al., 2003).

Using information obtained through the evaluation and eligibility process, special education teachers can deliver Tier 3 instruction that focuses on very specific deficit areas. For example, students' abilities in phonological awareness and rapid automatic naming ability have been found to be valid early indicators of risk for reading disability (Wagner et al., 1997). They are also central to reading problems in older students (Fletcher et al., 1994). If students with reading disabilities receive interventions intensively focused on phonemic awareness and decoding skills during the earliest stages of reading development, they show improved reading ability (Torgesen et al., 1999; Vellutino et al., 2006). Based on these studies and many others like them, evidence strongly suggests that early intervention offered through RTI has the potential to make a significant impact on eventual outcomes for students at risk for reading failure and may possibly eliminate reading disability in some children (Coyne, Kame'enui, & Simmons, 2004).

In an effective RTI process, children who progress through Tier 2 should have received early intervention since first being identified as at risk for failure. Non-response to Tier 2 should signal the implementation of more intensive interventions to be implemented just as quickly. Evaluation processes should not postpone or delay access to intensive instruction.

In order to get the most benefit from early intervention, research indicates that students should have access to the most intensive interventions in kindergarten and first grade (Vellutino et al., 2006). One possibility for accomplishing this involves a sort of "front-loading" of special education services for young students. This is evident in our targeted assistance schedule example included in Resource B of this book. In this schedule, instruction is offered in reading and math only. Concepts from social studies and science are incorporated into reading and math instruction but may not be taught as separate subjects. This allows time for needs-based instruction to be offered daily for at-risk students.

In theory, the early intervention aspect of RTI is impossible with older children. In reality, many students will continue to need services past the primary grades and perhaps throughout their school career, even though there may be times when even students identified early require no services. Elementary, middle, and high schools must explore options for providing intensive interventions while giving students access to the general curriculum. For example, there are secondary schools that are providing freshmen with intensive intervention through reading and math electives and then developing five-year, rather than the traditional four-year, programs for these students to meet graduation requirements. Additionally, if schools have developed programs of intensive intervention for students prior to placement in special education, then perhaps these could be integrated with programs designed for children after placement (Coyne et al., 2004).

Movement Between Tiers

If Tier 3 is to be a viable part of the RTI process, there must be flexible movement into and out of the tier. Intensive special education services should be provided to students as needed and discontinued when adequate progress is made (L. S. Fuchs & Fuchs, 2007). We are not suggesting that disabilities come and go as time passes; however, the impact of the disability on educational performance may change on a regular basis. For many students, intensive intervention should reduce the negative impact of the disability. In other words, the child does indeed have a learning disability, but the intensive instruction received remediates the learning deficits. At that point, he or she may be able to benefit from Tier 1 or Tier 2 instruction without intensive Tier 3 instruction, but perhaps with support in inclusive classrooms. However, as learning becomes more complex, the disability may again severely affect the student's progress (Vaughn & Fuchs, 2003). When this occurs, Tier 3 instruction would be appropriate once again. Depending on state requirements, it may not be necessary to redetermine eligibility each time a change of this type is made. Instead, the individualized education program (IEP) committee would need to be reconvened in order to make adjustments to the instructional plan. When being instructed in Tier 1 or Tier 2, the child still has a disability but can benefit from general education instruction with possible special education and related services provided in a less restrictive setting. With the flexibility for this type of adjustment, special education services can be available to all children with disabilities through general education and intensive intervention as appropriate for individual students' needs.

Ongoing Performance Monitoring for Instructional Decision Making

We have demonstrated the positive effects of frequent progress monitoring using curriculum-based measurement in the general education classroom. Those same positive effects can be found when implementing CBM and progress monitoring with students with disabilities (Deno, Fuchs, Marston, & Shin, 2001; Harn et al., 2007). First, CBM data can be utilized to write present levels of performance that accurately describe student ability in measurable, observable terms (Stecker, 2006). IEPs written with progress-monitoring goals will more accurately reflect classroom instruction than if they are written using a summative assessment tool (Safer, Donaldson, & Oxaal, 2005). When teachers chart students' progress-monitoring data, they can use the information to continually adjust instruction in order to work toward maximum student gain.

As IEP teams develop student IEPs, they can use progress-monitoring data in a variety of ways. At the outset, they can use this data to specifically describe a student's present level of performance. This is most often accomplished by averaging the first three to six CBM scores in an area. Teams can then use this data to develop goals for anticipated student performance at the end of the instructional year. These goals may broken down into incremental targets to create short-term objectives, which are then measured through progress monitoring. Figure 6.1 provides examples of a present level of performance, an annual goal, and a short-term objective based on student data.

Figure 6.1   IEP Components Based on Progress-Monitoring Data

Present Level of Performance (Oral Reading Fluency segment only): Megan is beginning her second-grade year. Benchmarks for oral reading fluency are a minimum of 40 words per minute at the end of first grade and 90 words per minute at the end of second grade. Megan currently reads 18 words per minute as measured by the DIBELS.

Oral Reading Fluency Goal: Megan will read 90 words per minute by the end-of-year benchmark assessment. (Based on average gain of 2.0 words per week × 36 weeks of instruction = 72 words per minute added to the present level of 18 words per minute)

Short-Term Benchmark Objective: Megan will read 38 words per minute after 10 weeks of instruction.

Teachers should monitor student progress by charting each data point because it clearly illustrates progress to teachers, parents, and the students themselves. Dual-discrepancy formula, as described in Chapter 5, should be applied to determine appropriate progress. Decision rules should be applied at least monthly to determine when instructional adjustments should be made (Harn et al., 2007). Many factors should be considered in making these decisions. A general guideline involves counting the number of data points above or below the aimline. If three consecutive weekly data points fall below the aimline, an instructional change may be necessary (Stecker, 2006). If a student is showing growth in performance but an insufficient growth rate, then the intensity of the current instruction may need to be increased. Data points above the aimline are significant data as well. At times, our expectations for students need to be raised. If six consecutive data points are above the goal line, consider raising the goal to increase expectations.

Teachers' responsiveness to data is a key factor in determining success. According to research, goal ambitiousness positively affected student achievement. When teachers and students set high goals and increased them based on response, student progress was more rapid than with students who had lower performance goals that remained fixed (L. Fuchs, Fuchs, & Deno, 1985). It is essential that educators use data for instructional decision making to improve student learning. This process makes the IEP a usable, effective planning document for instructing students with disabilities.

The Provision of Prioritized Content Selection Coupled With Purposeful Design and Delivery

Research-Based Interventions

After the IEP is developed, the next critical component of RTI Tier 3 instruction involves, as with the earlier tiers, the use of research-based interventions. During instructional segments, students should receive intensive, specific interventions designed to address their identified deficit areas. Many special education teachers are asking the question "If the students didn't respond to Tier 2 instruction using research-based interventions, what am I going to do that will be different?" There is a growing body of research that indicates that students with reading disabilities benefit from reading instruction based on the recommendations of the National Reading Panel, just as do other students with reading deficits. However, students with reading disabilities need instruction that is much more intense, much more systematic, and sustained for longer periods of time (Kovaleski, 2007; Torgesen et al., 2001). This indicates that, in some instances, special education intervention will not necessarily involve strategies that are completely different from those available to students in Tier 2. It may, instead, provide more access to quality interventions on a more individualized and intense level than could be provided through general education (Stecker, 2006).

Interventions should be chosen based on information gained about the student during the RTI process and evaluation. Teachers must have knowledge of how to interpret all available data to make precise instructional decisions about their students. They must thoroughly review student data from Tier 2 instruction in order to distinguish the types of strategies to which students have or have not responded. Teachers should use this information to identify interventions that may prove to be more effective. If the student showed poor response to one method of improving reading fluency, a different method should be chosen. As we discussed in Chapter 3, these interventions may include purchased programs designed for students with disabilities as well as learning strategies. In order to fully address the needs of non-responders, special education teachers must have access to a variety of interventions.

It is important to note that not all special education teachers have been thoroughly trained in research-based interventions. Due to teacher shortages, there are many teachers currently working in the special education field who are not fully certified in methods of teaching students with disabilities. Even teachers with specialized and advanced training in teaching students with disabilities often report that training in specific research-based interventions was not part of their program. The perceived knowledge base required for providing highly specific instruction to a variety of students is overwhelming to many teachers.

Special education teachers will have to be trained in a number of research-based interventions appropriate for their students' needs. We feel it is imperative for colleges and universities to examine their teacher preparation programs and address areas of weakness, such as a possible lack of instruction in research-based interventions and progress monitoring. School districts must also develop inventive and timely processes for inservice training of all educators. Again, we recommend improved collaboration between general education and special education for sharing of resources and expertise. States and districts must invest time and resources into evaluating, choosing, and training their teachers in highly effective interventions.

Fidelity of Instruction

Just as in Tiers 1 and 2, it is imperative for a system to be in place to observe for fidelity of instruction in Tier 3. It should begin with appropriate and ongoing training for service providers. Structures should be developed within the school to support teachers in learning and implementing new programs and strategies. Administrators should set clear expectations for instruction (Kovaleski, 2007). Documentation for fidelity of specific strategy implementation may be accomplished in the same way as with previous tiers, with a fidelity checklist or narrative summary. Overall effectiveness of instruction can be monitored through lesson plan review, administrator walk-throughs, and peer observations. The person observing implementation should document that the intervention is being used as designed and researched. This documentation can be used as evidence that the IEP was properly implemented and can provide additional information regarding student response.

Tier 3 Intervention Studies

In the rapidly growing body of RTI research, most attention has been given to Tiers 1 and 2. Even studies that address the issue of LD identification rarely move to the next step to explore the actual instruction that takes place in Tier 3. In order to provide a clearer picture of Tier 3, we will briefly review two studies which addressed this next step.

Denton and colleagues provided interventions to Tier 2 non-responders during a sixteen-week period (Denton et al., 2006, as cited in Denton et al., 2007). During the first half of Tier 3 instruction, students received two hours daily of intensive instruction in phonemic awareness and decoding using a program called Phono-Graphix. After eight weeks, the intervention was reduced to one hour of reading fluency instruction using Read Naturally. The instruction was provided by teachers who had received one week of training on Phono-Graphix and two days of training on Read Naturally. Fidelity of instruction was considered good.

The results demonstrated significant growth in decoding, fluency, and reading comprehension during the first half of the study. In the second phase of instruction, students demonstrated significant gains in their ability to "fluently and accurately read words in lists and connected text" (Denton et al., 2007, p. 113). However, there was a great deal of variability among individual students' gains. Students who had received Tier 2 intervention prior to this study performed better than children who had not. First- and second-graders also made more gains than third-graders. Some students showed minimal gains, indicating the need for different and/or more intensive intervention (Denton et al., 2007).

The second study involved students who were identified by DIBELS as being at high risk for reading failure. Instructional programs were designed for each student based on specific needs. Students were provided with ninety minutes or more of reading instruction per day, most of which was delivered in small groups. Students in three control groups received different types of instruction: (1) Code Emphasis program developed specifically for the students by the researchers; (2) Code and Comprehension Emphasis, again developed by the researchers; and (3) Commercial Program with a strong research base. Progress was monitored using CBM every two weeks. Additionally, problem-solving teams met every other week to make instructional adjustments based on results of progress monitoring (Harn et al., 2007).

Students receiving the Code Emphasis intervention made more significant gains than the Commercial Program group and the Code and Comprehension Emphasis group in several areas. Overall, the Code Emphasis and Code and Comprehension Emphasis groups outperformed the Commercial Program group (Harn et al., 2007). However, the researchers pointed out that they were not recommending that schools design their own reading programs. The knowledge required to develop these programs goes beyond the training of most teachers. They did, however, stress the importance of carefully evaluating any programs considered for implementation.

It is evident from these studies that Tier 3 instruction must be intensive in its focus and amount of intervention in order to be effective. In the second example, when students were far below grade-level expectations, this intervention took place instead of the Tier 1 reading instruction (Harn et al., 2007). However, many of the students only required the sixteen weeks of intervention. As outlined in our earlier discussion, these students would be able to return to Tier 1 or Tier 1 and Tier 2 instruction. The remainder of the students would need additional Tier 3 intervention. As Tier 3 intervention models are further developed, it will be important to find appropriate methods of providing this intensive intervention while also providing access to and support in the general education curriculum.

Example of Quality Tier 3 Instruction

James is a second-grade student who has shown poor response to interventions at Tiers 1 and 2 in his school's RTI pyramid. In November, the school psychologist began assessment procedures to determine whether James might have a learning disability. In early January, the team met to discuss the results. Test data, coupled with RTI data, verified that James exhibited sufficient evidence of a specific learning disability in reading fluency.

It is now January 12 and the IEP committee is meeting to develop an individualized education plan and determine appropriate services to enable James to benefit from instruction. Their first step is to describe his current educational performance. When presented with second-grade reading passages, James is able to orally read 18 words in one minute as measured by DIBELS. With this knowledge, the committee sets out to establish a reading fluency goal for him. Based on an average growth rate for second-graders of 1.5 words per week (Stecker, 2006), the team sets a goal for James to orally read 45 words per minute at the end of eighteen weeks, which will coincide with the end of the school year. This was established by multiplying eighteen weeks by 1.5 words per week, then adding the product (27) to his current 18 words.

Instruction for James will consist of forty-five-minute sessions four days per week. He will work in a group with two other children who are functioning at the same level. The special education teacher, Mr. Harding, will utilize a reading program designed to provide intensive instruction in decoding skills. Progress will be monitored twice weekly using DIBELS. Figure 6.2 shows James' progress-monitoring data.

Figure 6.2   James' Oral Reading Fluency (ORF) Data

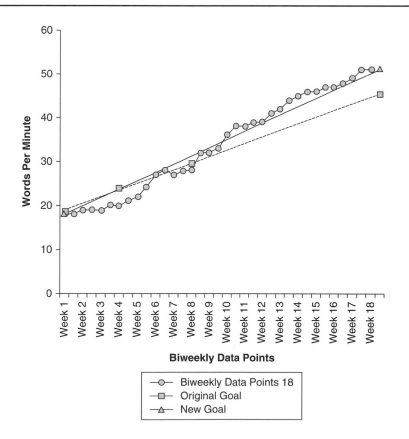

After four weeks of intervention, Mr. Harding applies the three-point decision rule to determine whether instructional adjustments are necessary for James to meet his goal. James currently reads 20 words per minute (wpm). His goal for four weeks into intervention is 24 wpm. Mr. Harding determines that James is responding to the intervention, but progress is not sufficient. He adjusts instruction by adding sight words, blending, CVC pattern words, and repeated oral readings of first-grade passages. Instruction will continue four days each week. Progress monitoring will be performed twice each week.

At the end of eight weeks, James orally reads 28 words per minute. His goal for this point was 30 words. Despite the fact that he is just under his goal, James did surpass the aimline on two occasions within the past two weeks. Mr. Harding decides to continue the current instructional plan.

At the twelve-week point, James is reading 39 wpm. He has surpassed the aimline on the last four data points. There are six weeks left in the school year. Mr. Harding decides to raise James' goal by basing it on an ambitious growth rate of 2 words per week (Stecker, 2006). The new goal is set at 51 wpm. At week 16, James is at the aimline with a fluency rate of 47 wpm. Instruction continues until the end of the year. James meets his adjusted long-term goal of 51 wpm.

Partnering With Parents (Chapter 6)

Certainly, parents should be involved at the final tier in which special education services either are being considered or are being provided. In the past, this has been the typical point of entry for parent participation. For parents who have been involved from the beginning, this tier will be easier to process and support. Remember, however, that some parents may still be in a denial phase and should be given every opportunity to provide input and ask questions. No parent dreams of having a child with a disability, but given time, support, and an opportunity to truly participate on the team, they can accept and move forward with the challenges that await.

It is important to remember that while educators most certainly care about the welfare of their students, it is the parent who is ultimately responsible for the decisions made. From the beginning to the end, parents should be welcome members of the team. Keep open communication as a priority. Think about how you would feel if this were *your* child. Listen to concerns and ideas. Lastly, make every decision with the child's best interest at heart. We understand how easy it is for team members to focus on irrelevant or uncontrollable factors. Remember, we can only control what is in our power to control. When we come together as a team, we accomplish so much more. In the end, the child benefits immensely, which most certainly affects every person in society.

SUMMARY

This chapter has focused on Tier 3 instruction: assessing students for learning disabilities and providing intensive instruction for those who qualify. Tier 3 should be seen as an extension of Tier 2 with increased intensity. The dilemma for special education teachers lies in providing instruction that is more specialized than was delivered in the earlier tiers. We recommend that educators look to the interventions attempted in Tier 2 to gain insight in planning for Tier 3 instruction. They should take into account all diagnostic information generated by previous instruction and assessment to develop an IEP and instructional program that specifically and intensively addresses the learning needs of each student. Progress monitoring through curriculum-based measurement should yield an ongoing picture of student performance. All instruction should be provided with fidelity to the original design. We also recommend that schools and districts work to provide increased collaboration between special education and general education professionals. When all of these elements are combined, Tier 3 intervention can be considered instructionally sound and appropriate for students with disabilities.

REFERENCES

Bender, W. N., & Shores, C. (2007). *Response to intervention: A practical guide for every teacher*. Thousand Oaks, CA: Corwin Press.

Coyne, M. D., Kame'enui, E. J., & Simmons, D. C. (2004). Improving beginning reading instruction and intervention for students with LD: Reconciling "all" with "each." *Journal of Learning Disabilities, 37*(3), 231–239.

Deno, S. L., Fuchs, L. S., Marston, D. B., & Shin, J. (2001). Using curriculum-based measurement to develop growth standards for students with learning disabilities. *School Psychology Review, 30*, 507–524.

Denton, C. A., Fletcher, J. M., Simos, P. G., Papanicolaou, A. C., & Anthony, J. L. (2007). An implementation of a tiered intervention model: Reading outcomes and neural correlates. In D. Haager, J. Klingner, & S. Vaughn (Eds.), *Evidence-based reading practices for response to intervention* (1st ed., pp. 107–137). Baltimore: Paul H. Brookes Publishing.

Flanagan, D. P., Ortiz, S. O., Alfonso, V. C., & Dynda, A. M. (2006). Integration of response to intervention and norm-referenced tests in learning disability identification: Learning from the Tower of Babel. *Psychology in the Schools, 43*(7), 807–825.

Fletcher, J. M., Shaywitz, S. E., Shankweiler, D. P., Katz, L., Lieberman, I. Y., Stuebing, K. K., et al. (1994). Cognitive profiles of reading disability: Comparisons of discrepancy and low achievement definitions. *Journal of Educational Psychology, 90*, 37–55.

Fuchs, L., Fuchs, D., & Deno, S. (1985). The importance of goal ambitiousness and goal mastery to student achievement. *Exceptional Children, 52*(3), 63–71.

Fuchs, L. S., & Fuchs, D. (2007). A model for implementing responsiveness to intervention. *TEACHING Exceptional Children, 39*(5), 14–20.

Good, R. H., III, Simmons, D. C., & Kame'enui, E. J. (2001). The importance and decision-making utility of a continuum of fluency-based indicators of foundational reading skills for third grade high-stakes outcomes. *Scientific Study of Reading, 5*, 257–288.

Harn, B. A., Kame'enui, E. J., & Simmons, D. C. (2007). The nature and role of the third tier in a prevention model for kindergarten students. In D. Haager, J. Klingner, & S. Vaughn (Eds.), *Evidence-based reading practices for response to intervention* (1st ed., pp. 161–184). Baltimore: Paul H. Brookes Publishing.

Hollenbeck, A. F. (2007). From IDEA to implementation: A discussion of foundational and future responsiveness-to-intervention research. *Learning Disabilities Research & Practice, 22*(2), 137–146.

Individuals with Disabilities Education Act of 2004. (2004). *Federal Register, 71*, pp. 46539–46845. Retrieved August 30, 2006, from http://www.ed.gov/policy/speced/guid/idea/idea2004.html

Kavale, K. A., Holdnack, J. A., & Mostert, M. P. (2005). Responsiveness-to-intervention and the identification of specific learning disability: A critique and alternative proposal. *Learning Disability Quarterly, 27*, 77–88.

Kovaleski, J. F. (2007). Response to Intervention: Considerations for research and system change. *School Psychology Review, 36*(4), 638–646.

Marston, D., Muyskens, P., Lau, M., & Canter, A. (2003). Problem solving model for decision making with high-incidence disabilities: The Minneapolis experience. *Learning Disabilities Research & Practice, 18*(3), 187–200.

Mastropieri, M. A., & Scruggs, T. E. (2005). Feasibility and consequences of response to intervention: Examination of the issues and scientific evidence as a model for the identification of individuals with learning disabilities. *Journal of Learning Disabilities, 38*(6), 525–531.

Reschly, D. J., Hosp, J. L., & Schmied, C. M. (2003, August). *And miles to go . . . : State SLD requirements and authoritative recommendations.* Retrieved July 20, 2006, from http://www.nrcld.org

Safer, N., Donaldson, W., & Oxaal, I. (2005, March). *Using progress monitoring to develop strong IEPs.* Retrieved September 15, 2007, from http://www.studentprogress.org

Scruggs, T. W., & Mastropieri, M. A. (2002). On babies and bathwater: Addressing the problems of identification of learning disabilities. *Learning Disability Quarterly, 25*(2), 155–168.

Speece, D. L., Case, L. P., & Molloy, D. E. (2003). Responsiveness to general education instruction as the first gate to learning disabilities identification. *Learning Disabilities Research & Practice, 18*(3), 147–156.

Stecker, P. M. (2006). Monitoring student progress in individualized educational programs using curriculum-based measurement. Retrieved September 15, 2007, from http://www.studentprogress.org

Torgesen, J. K., Alexander, A. W., Wagner, R. K., Rashotte, C. A., Voeller, K. K., & Conway, T. (2001). Intensive remedial instruction for children with severe reading disabilities: Immediate and long-term outcomes from two instructional approaches. *Journal of Learning Disabilities, 34*, 33–38.

Torgesen, J. K., Wagner, R. K., Rashotte, C. A., Lindamood, P., Rose, E., Conway, T., et al. (1999). Preventing reading failure in young children with phonological processing disabilities: Group and individual responses to instruction. *Journal of Educational Psychology, 91*(4), 579–593.

U.S. Department of Education. (2001). *Improving literacy by putting reading first: No Child Left Behind executive summary.* Retrieved August 21, 2007, from http://www.nationalreadingpanel.org/publications/nochildleftbehind.htm

U.S. Department of Education. (2003). *Twenty-fifth Annual Report to Congress on the Implementation of the Individuals with Disabilities Education Act.* Retrieved December 7, 2007, from http://www.ed.gov/about/offices/list/osers/osep/research.html

U.S. Department of Education. (2006). *IDEA Regulations. 71 Federal Register* 46540 et seq.

Vaughn, S., & Fuchs, L. S. (2003). Redefining learning disabilities as inadequate response to instruction: The promise and potential pitfalls. *Learning Disabilities Research & Practice, 18*(3), 137–146.

Vellutino, F. R., Scanlon, D. M., Small, S., & Fanuele, D. P. (2006). Response to intervention as a vehicle for distinguishing between children with and without reading disabilities: Evidence for the role of kindergarten and first-grade interventions. *Journal of Learning Disabilities, 39*(2), 157–169.

Wagner, R. K., Torgesen, J. K., Rashotte, C. A., Hecht, S. A., Barker, T. A., Burgess, S. R., et al. (1997). Changing causal relations between phonological processing abilities and word-level reading as children develop from beginning to fluent readers: A five-year longitudinal study. *Developmental Psychology, 33*, 468–479.

Willis, J. O., & DuMont, R. (2006). And never the twain shall meet: Can response to intervention and cognitive assessment be reconciled? *Psychology in the Schools, 43*(8), 901–908.

Wodrich, D. L., Spencer, M. L., & Daley, K. B. (2006). Combining RTI and psychoeducational assessment: What we must assume to do otherwise. *Psychology in the Schools, 43*(7), 797–806.

Zirkel, P. A. (2007). What does the law say? *TEACHING Exceptional Children, 39*(5), 65–66.

Zirkel, P. A., & Krohn, N. (2008). RTI after IDEA: A survey of state laws. *TEACHING Exceptional Children, 40*(3), 71–73.

Bringing It All Together

A Model for System Implementation

Throughout this book, we have sequentially presented the RTI process as a vehicle for school improvement. We have presented all the components essential for successful implementation of the process. However, actual implementation at the district or building level requires much more than a thorough understanding of RTI. It requires a well-organized, systematic plan for long-term change.

As we work with school districts across the country, we are disheartened to see instances in which the first step of RTI implementation is development of Tier 2 interventions. This minimizes the importance of the knowledge base required to build the foundation of the pyramid. In fact, the pyramid in these schools is best illustrated by very large Tiers 2 and 3 resting on a much-too-small Tier 1. In these schools, we fear that the RTI process will never be anything more than an ineffective pre-referral process for special education. It is this example that we strive to transform.

Thus, the focus of this chapter will be to bring together all of these essential components into a realistic implementation plan. We will highlight features of system change and sustainability that must be taken into account in any effective school improvement effort. These include changes in roles and responsibilities and requirements for staff development. We will explore the national outlook for RTI implementation, including areas for future research. We will also discuss barriers to full implementation and options for overcoming those barriers. Finally, we will provide a model for system-level implementation based on best practices and our experiences with school districts.

SYSTEM CHANGE AND SUSTAINABILITY

In earlier chapters, we discussed the importance of the role of educational leaders in developing the RTI process. This cannot be stressed enough. It is imperative for leaders from general education and special education departments to unite to develop a system plan. Developing an effective Response to Intervention framework requires expertise in curriculum, instruction, assessment, staff development, personnel, budget, student support, and special education. One person or department in a school district or building cannot bring about this type of change on his or her own.

In most school districts, RTI implementation will require a significant change of mind-set for everyone involved in the process. It is unlikely that RTI will fulfill any of its potential benefits without a change in practices, policies, and goals of the school and district (Danielson, Doolittle, & Bradley, 2007). When districts seek to implement RTI processes too quickly with little or no foundational preparation, the result is often confusion at best and rejection at worse. Teachers may view the process as another useless paperwork procedure that will fail to meet the lofty claims of its presenters.

Research on system change has identified several important features of sustainable reform efforts. They include the following:

1. Creating readiness by using key stakeholders to develop an organizational climate that is receptive to change. This includes sharing the vision for the change and establishing buy-in. It also includes development of action plans.
2. Performing initial implementation through sequential training, practice, support, and evaluation. This includes ongoing, effective staff development. It also includes initial phases of implementation and continual evaluation of progress.
3. Institutionalizing new approaches through system policies to maintain the reforms.
4. Providing ongoing evolution and renewal to allow stakeholders to adapt and engage in problem solving to refine changes as needed (Adelman & Taylor, 1997).

Creating Readiness Through Vision and Buy-In

Our first step in creating change involves creating readiness through sharing of vision and achieving buy-in from those who will be implementing the process (Adelman & Taylor, 1997; Huberman & Miles, 1984; Sindelar, Shearer, Yendol-Hoppey, & Liebert, 2006). This must first be established for district and building leaders. As we have stated several times, RTI cannot be viewed as a special education initiative. District administrators in general education and special education should work together in system-wide implementation. Building administrators must be clear about and committed to the process. All persons in leadership positions must develop their own understanding, acceptance, and belief systems. Special care should be taken to examine the benefits and barriers that will be experienced by all levels of personnel. Time must be spent putting together a well-developed plan of goals and expected outcomes for the process.

Therefore, every implementation plan should begin with the establishment of a foundation of acceptance and buy-in from key stakeholders. This can be accomplished by first establishing a district RTI leadership team. Membership on this team should be representative of all groups involved in the process. It should be facilitated by someone who clearly understands and is committed to RTI—this may or may not be an employee of the district. As consultants, we often facilitate these first steps in order to assist leadership teams in developing a thorough action plan.

The team should explore the RTI process, develop a thorough understanding of all of the components through training opportunities, and synthesize the information to determine how best to proceed with implementation. All team members should understand which model, whether Problem-Solving, Standard Protocol, or mixed, will be used. If this has not been decided by state requirements, the team will have to determine which model is most suited to its needs. The team should have a clear understanding of state RTI requirements. Team members should be made aware of state timelines for implementation and determine how they will meet those timelines. Their work may be facilitated with completion of a needs assessment to determine system needs and priorities. We have included one such assessment tool in Resource E of this book.

Part of the agenda for this group should include addressing the concerns and fears of team members. Ignoring concerns will undermine the buy-in that should eventually prevail. In reality, implementing RTI is not an easy process. There will be obstacles that will be overcome only through strong commitment and perseverance. Team members should be given the opportunity to voice their concerns and have them legitimately addressed. In the end, each member of this team should feel comfortable enough with the process to be able to share the vision with others.

Ultimately, the district team should develop an action plan that prioritizes long-term and short-term goals. Based on information obtained from the needs assessment, student performance data, and other methods of information gathering, the plan should cover a workable and realistic time frame. It should identify barriers for implementation and include plans to overcome these barriers. It should also allow for refinement and customization at each school while maintaining consistent expectations and policies throughout the district.

If the state implementation plan allows for gradual phase-in of the RTI process, we recommend that districts take advantage of this by developing multi-year plans to include pilot schools before full district implementation. This allows program refinement on a small scale and reduces the number of problems down the road.

Once this core group has learned about and embraced RTI as a tool for school improvement, the process may be repeated at individual schools. This should begin in earnest in pilot schools. However, all schools in the district should be made aware of the program and the district implementation plan.

Building implementation may begin with a leadership team before proceeding with the entire staff. The principal should serve an active role in this phase of the process, although he or she may not actually deliver the content information. The principal should, however, make it very clear that he or she supports and believes in the process and its ability to raise student achievement.

Our experience, validated by research, reveals that it is the building principal who has the most impact on school-level success of a new program (Gorton, Alston, & Snowden, 2007; Klingner, Arguelles, Hughes, & Vaughn, 2001; Praisner, 2003; Sindelar et al., 2006). The building principal will be the person ultimately responsible for ensuring fidelity of implementation. If he or she embraces the program and shares his or her vision and expectations with the staff in a positive manner, it will usually be received in a positive light. While studying innovation in schools, Demeter (as cited in Gorton et al., 2007, p. 179) made the following observation: "Building principals are key figures in the innovation process. Where they are both aware of and sympathetic to an innovation, it tends to prosper. Where they are ignorant of its existence, or apathetic, if not hostile, it tends to remain outside the bloodstream of the school."

Strong teacher leaders who are respected by other faculty members should also be part of the leadership team. This may include individuals who are somewhat resistant to change. Involving them in initial decision making may help them to more thoroughly understand the process and see the potential benefit. They may also be very influential in working with other teachers who are resistant. Each grade and/or department should be represented.

Figure 7.1 presents a sequential plan for process development, beginning with development of district- and building-level leadership teams. Throughout the chapter, we will continue to add to the plan as each area is discussed. The complete plan can be seen in Resource F.

Essentially, this building leadership team should follow the same general path as that taken with the district team. They must develop a good understanding of the components involved. They should evaluate the district plan and apply it to their own faculty and students. School, classroom, and individual student data will be essential in determining areas of strength and weakness. The needs assessment may again be used to develop long-term and short-term goals that are closely aligned with the district goals. Once again, members should have an opportunity to work through their own concerns.

Eventually, the vision for RTI implementation will be shared with the entire faculty of each school. This is effective when approached from the district and building level. As the principal shares his or her vision for RTI, he or she must help teachers understand how it will impact them and their students. In order to see the value of an initiative, teachers must recognize that it will raise student achievement and that it can be feasibly implemented within the context of their classrooms (Gersten, Chard, & Baker, 2000). It is not enough to be told something will work. They must see the value for themselves and believe that it will work.

For many teachers, implementation of the RTI process will be a natural next step. These teachers may already use formative assessment, including benchmark assessment and progress monitoring, to drive instruction for their students. They may already use differentiated instructional practices and flexible grouping to teach all students. They may recognize the importance of using research-based interventions in their classrooms. Many will have already been trained in several of these strategies—in fact, we find that school faculties who have been trained in the Reading First model are well on their way to successful RTI implementation.

However, there are many teachers who have not had the benefit of this type of training or experience. The components of RTI, especially in

Figure 7.1 System Change Phase 1—Creating Readiness Through Vision and Buy-In

1. Form a district level leadership team composed of key stakeholders.
   a. Superintendent
   b. District-level administrators in curriculum, instruction, assessment, special education, student support services, ELL, Title I, human resources, fiscal services, etc.
   c. Building principals
   d. Building-level curriculum experts including instructional coaches
   e. Student support services personnel, such as school psychologists
   f. Key teacher leaders
   g. Community representatives
   h. Parent representatives
2. Develop readiness for change with district leadership team.
   a. Identify the need for change. Evaluate student performance to determine how many students could receive benefit from the process.
   b. Develop vision for the expected outcomes.
   c. Analyze data to determine strengths, weaknesses, and potential impact.
   d. Identify state requirements and timelines.
3. Develop district action plan for RTI implementation.
   a. Provide thorough training in the RTI process and its essential components to members of the leadership team.
   b. Complete needs assessment to determine current levels of implementation.
   c. Identify RTI model to be used.
   d. Identify and address concerns and barriers for implementation.
   e. Identify which schools will be involved in initial and secondary phases of implementation.
   f. Identify necessary commitments in terms of staff development, materials, assessment tools, and additional resources.
   g. Identify barriers to implementation and develop plans for resolution.
   h. Develop timeline for implementation.
4. Develop building leadership team composed of key stakeholders.
   a. Core membership from school that served on district team.
   b. Additional members to represent all groups involved.
5. Develop building action plan for implementation.
   a. Follow procedures similar to district team.
   b. Adjust and refine plan for individual school needs.

SOURCE: Adelman & Taylor, 1997; Gorton, Alston, & Snowden, 2007; National Staff Development Council, 2001

the area of assessment, are foreign and seem impossible to implement. This is particularly true for many secondary teachers. Middle and high schools have not, as a whole, been part of the formative assessment initiatives that have been so prevalent in the elementary grades over the past few years. Standardized assessment tools are not readily available at these levels. Most high school teachers are under such pressure to deliver large amounts of content that they feel they do not have time to incorporate data-based decision making into their already hectic routines. Requiring these teachers to implement RTI without significant preparation, support, and policy change is unfair and unproductive. They must be given an understanding of the value of the process and be ensured of support when putting it in place in their classrooms.

Performing Initial Implementation

Schools should begin training teachers through effective, ongoing inservice opportunities. Effective staff development provides essential information at the outset and throughout the duration of implementation. It also provides modeling, opportunities for practice and feedback, and on-site coaching (Deshler, 2007; National Staff Development Council, 2001). One staff development session providing an overview, however in-depth, will not be sufficient to meet training needs. Certainly, initial training should be provided that gives leadership teams and administrators a thorough understanding of each critical RTI component. However, we find that with new concepts such as RTI, it takes repeated exposure to the information in order to make sense of it. Leadership team members should be knowledgeable about each component and be able to redeliver the information often so that teachers have multiple learning opportunities. Teachers should then be provided with opportunities to participate in group discussions, application, modeling, and coaching. This can be facilitated at the district and building level and should be repeated throughout all stages of implementation.

The National Staff Development Council has developed standards and guidelines for inservice training based on research-supported practices. We encourage leadership teams to review these standards and guidelines (found at www.nsdc.org) when putting together comprehensive plans for staff development. We have also compiled a list of the core concepts that must be addressed through teacher training:

The Problem-Solving process

- Benchmark assessment
- Curriculum-based measurement

- Progress monitoring
- Research-based interventions
- Differentiated instruction
- Data-driven instruction
- Positive behavior supports
- Cultural diversity

An important part of this initial implementation phase will be to provide parents with a general overview of the RTI structure. We feel it is very important to include parents at the beginning, helping them to understand RTI's impact on all students, rather than waiting until their child is identified for Tier 2 interventions. This will help parents to see that the school is not willing to let children struggle and fall behind. Instead, they will know that interventions will be provided at any point that their child is at risk of not meeting standards. We feel strongly that this will go a long way in improving relations between parents and the school. This can be accomplished through informational meetings, such as PTA, and including information in the student handbook and newsletters.

The next area to be addressed in initial implementation is the quality of Tier 1 instruction. This was discussed in detail in Chapter 4. In this part of our discussion, we will briefly refer back to the most important points and discuss how they fit into the system plan. Essentially, the leadership teams must evaluate whether or not the majority of students are meeting achievement and/or behavioral standards through Tier 1 instruction. We recommend a goal of 80 percent of general education students meeting or exceeding standards through Tier 1 instruction. This is based on researcher recommendations, best practices, and common sense. If fewer than 80 percent of students are successful here, the school will be faced with the task of providing Tier 2 interventions to large numbers of students. As a result, the quality and intensity of those interventions may be greatly reduced.

At this point, districts should identify and begin using benchmark assessment and progress monitoring tools if they have not done so already. This will enable teachers to identify students who will need Tier 2 interventions. Again, schools that already have formative assessment in place, even if it is only informal assessment, will be more prepared for this step. If no formative assessment has been used to drive instruction, we recommend that teachers first be taught to use simple tools such as Exit Cards (also called "Ticket out the Door") to determine which students did not understand the day's lesson and then adjust instruction to address those deficit areas. It is a small step that lays an important foundation for data-driven instruction.

As Tier 1 instruction is strengthened, schools may begin looking toward Tier 2. The thought processes and specific areas to be addressed were discussed in detail in Chapter 5. The leadership team will need to develop a schedule structured for providing targeted interventions. This may be done by the district or building leadership team. For example, if all elementary schools will adopt a similar schedule, it is best to establish this at the district level. We recommend that the schedule be developed at this point so that the team may determine who will deliver Tier 2 interventions and, therefore, will need training in those interventions.

Teams will need to spend time exploring and examining research-based interventions that will meet the needs of at-risk students. In doing so, it is very helpful to examine the Tier 1 curriculum to determine where weakness areas exist and to find interventions that complement the curriculum. These interventions may involve learning strategies, supplemental materials, or both. Again, this may take place at the district and/or building level.

All persons who will carry out Tier 2 instruction will need to be thoroughly trained in the interventions. If the school is using a Standard Protocol Model, this usually involves a core group of teachers, paraprofessionals, or tutors. The Problem-Solving Model, however, may require that every teacher and service provider in the school be trained. We want to reiterate that it is not necessary, nor is it productive, to attempt the implementation of a large number of interventions in a short period of time. We recommend that schools choose interventions that meet the most significant learner needs first. Additional interventions can be added over time. We see training in this area, particularly, as being an ongoing process broken into manageable parts each year.

This process is made easier if the district or school has available an intervention specialist such as an instructional coach. This person should be knowledgeable about numerous interventions and resources and should provide that information to teachers. He or she should also have frequent opportunities to go into classrooms and intervention groups to assist teachers in refining interventions and to ensure fidelity of instruction.

After the intervention training phase has progressed to a point where teachers are proficient in an acceptable number of strategies or materials, Tier 2 instruction may begin. Curriculum-based measurement should be used biweekly or weekly to assess student progress and make ongoing instructional decisions. Steps should be taken to ensure fidelity of instruction through observation and other means already discussed. This seems to be a minor issue at first glance. However, it is important to remember that this rules out lack of instruction as the cause for students' learning problems.

Teachers and interventionists should communicate with parents in all phases of Tier 2 implementation. When a child is identified as at risk, teachers should meet with parents to review data and to develop or explain the Tier 2 intervention plan. Results of progress monitoring should be shared with parents on a regular basis. The very nature of data management through charting of CBM results will make communicating with parents much easier. Our Partnering With Parents section of this chapter provides additional ways to involve parents in the process.

The district and/or building leadership teams may begin examination and restructuring of Tier 3 concurrently with or after the completion of Tier 2 implementation. Some schools find that addressing both tiers concurrently allows for better integration of services. Others feel that it is overwhelming to address both tiers at the same time. Members of the leadership team should carefully consider options so that they make the best decision for their teachers and students. There are, however, some elements of these tiers that could easily and most effectively be accomplished concurrently. For example, both general education and special education staff can be trained in CBM and research-based interventions at the same time. The element that we see may best be accomplished separately involves changes in structure such as service delivery.

Figure 7.2 summarizes all of these points in the next portion of our district implementation plan. The timeline for this initial implementation phase may be spread over two or more years and is best if taken in small, sequential steps. For example, after service providers have been trained in several interventions and have implemented them for some time, the school may begin the process again by choosing more interventions. Student data should be reviewed on an ongoing basis to refine instruction in each tier. Staff development should be ongoing in all areas. The district and building leadership teams should not be assembled only for initial implementation. We view them as essential in providing guidance for refinement each year.

In Resource F of this book, we have provided a sample multi-year timeline for RTI implementation, including specific staff development topics. The purpose of this sample is to provide you with a starting point to develop your own system's plan. The actual timelines and staff development needs will vary based on where your system currently stands in each of the areas. We have also included a blank action plan form that you may use in your planning process.

Figure 7.2   System Change Phase 2—Performing Initial Implementation

6. Begin initial training for participating faculty and staff.

   a. Provide inservice training in small segments, providing time to synthesize and apply information to curricular requirements.

   b. Provide opportunities for practice, modeling, and coaching of new skills.

7. Communicate information to parents regarding the overall structure of the RTI model.

   a. Include information in student handbook.

   b. Share information at parent meetings, such as PTA.

   c. Highlight interventions that could be utilized by parents in regular communication tools, such as newsletters.

8. Evaluate and strengthen Tier 1 instruction, ensuring fidelity of curriculum implementation.

   a. Ensure that instruction is differentiated and appropriate for at least 80 percent of general education students.

   b. Identify staff development needs to strengthen Tier 1.

   c. Provide identified staff development.

   d. Choose benchmark assessment and progress-monitoring tools.

   e. Implement benchmark assessment to identify students at risk.

9. Develop structure for Tier 2 targeted interventions.

   a. Identify research-based interventions appropriate for students' needs.

   b. Develop schedule that provides time and resources for Tier 2 interventions.

   c. Provide intervention training to individuals who will carry out Tier 2 instruction.

10. Implement Tier 2 interventions with at-risk students.

    a. Evaluate progress using curriculum-based measurement.

    b. Ensure fidelity of interventions.

    c. Communicate plan and results with parents on a regular basis.

11. Develop structure for Tier 3 practices.

    a. Identify research-based interventions appropriate for student needs.

    b. Develop schedule that provides time and resources for Tier 3 interventions.

    c. Use student data to develop data-driven IEPs.

    d. Implement Tier 3 interventions with students with disabilities.

    e. Evaluate progress using curriculum-based measurement.

    f. Ensure fidelity of interventions.

    g. Communicate plan and results with parents on a regular basis.

SOURCE: Adelman & Taylor, 1997; Gorton, Alston, & Snowden, 2007; National Staff Development Council, 2001

Institutionalizing New Approaches

As RTI becomes embedded in the school improvement framework, it should be seen as "the way we do school." As one administrator put it, "Everything we do in the school, from hiring new teachers, to developing our schedules, to looking at curriculum, to developing behavioral expectations, refers back to the pyramid." When RTI is viewed from this perspective, it can transform schools to the highly effective arenas of learning that we discussed in Chapter 1. In fact, we believe it is the way that RTI truly makes sense. Otherwise, it exists outside of the norm, as something to do in addition to teaching and learning, and it cannot reach its potential to raise student achievement.

During the transformation process, districts need to evaluate policies and procedures to see how they fit into the RTI structure. For example, retention policies may be adjusted to include RTI language and procedures. Teacher evaluation programs should include the critical elements for RTI implementation. Student grading procedures may need to be examined in light of Tier 2 implementation. Certainly, pre-referral procedures should reflect the RTI process.

Another significant change that often occurs with RTI implementation is a change in roles and responsibilities for various staff members. The separation between special education and general education personnel that exists in many schools under the traditional structure should be significantly decreased. We see the potential for better integration of services as being beneficial to teachers and students alike.

The group to be affected most by changes in roles and responsibilities may be school psychologists. The basis of this assertion stems from our earlier discussion of the amount of testing required for eligibility determination. If school psychologists move away from full psychoeducational assessments and provide more focused evaluations, they should require fewer hours of testing. The school psychologist community, including the National Association of School Psychologists (NASP), is engaged in a great deal of debate about whether or not RTI will indeed create new roles for them and what types of activities should be included in that new role. These activities include:

1. System design, including the task of designing Tier 2 interventions
2. Team collaboration, including consulting with teachers about those interventions, providing training in interventions and progress monitoring

3. Serving individual students, including consulting with teachers about individual student plans and data (National Association of School Psychologists, 2006)

Some districts are utilizing their school psychologists to implement Tier 2 interventions and/or administer progress-monitoring tools. However, this may require significant retraining efforts for some practicing school psychologists. In a 2005 survey of a representative sample of NASP members, 43.7 percent of respondents rated their knowledge of early indicators of reading problems in the low to moderately low range. Similar ratings were reported when participants were asked to rate their expertise in remediation of reading problems (58.8 percent low to moderately low), research-based interventions for reading (55.9 percent low to moderately low), and ability to work within an early intervention reading program (62.8 percent low to moderately low). One of the most surprising results was that 45.6 percent of respondents rated their ability to identify, interpret, and explain phonological processing deficits as low to moderately low (Nelson & Machek, 2007). It is clear from these results that preservice and inservice training is as essential for school psychologists as it is for other personnel. Because their role has not traditionally included most of these elements, they must also be given the tools to adapt and participate in the RTI process.

Ongoing Evolution and Renewal

The final step in our change model involves a continual process of evaluation and refinement. You may think of it as progress monitoring for the RTI process. As districts and schools progress through various stages

Figure 7.3   System Change Phase 3—Institutionalizing New Approaches

12. Provide support for continual evaluation and improvement of process.
   a. Provide ongoing staff development.
   b. Engage in continuous evaluation of quality of instruction in Tiers 1, 2, and 3.
   c. Evaluate effectiveness of interventions.
   d. Evaluate student data to refine action plan.
   e. Allocate additional resources as needed.
   f. Adjust district policies as needed.

SOURCE: Adelman & Taylor, 1997; Gorton, Alston, & Snowden, 2007; National Staff Development Council, 2001

of implementation, educators will need to continually assess their strengths and weaknesses and allow student achievement data to drive the next steps of the process. As administrators, teachers, and other service providers grow in their knowledge base of critical RTI elements, they will move to higher levels of understanding and application. At the same time, preservice programs at both undergraduate and graduate levels will include enhanced training of research-based interventions and progress-monitoring techniques, resulting in better preparation for new teachers.

Leadership teams should stay current on the latest research findings. Components of RTI may well be the most heavily researched topics in educational history. There are many educational journals that contain research articles related to RTI in almost every one of their new issues. As we have discussed throughout this book, there are many unanswered questions related to the specifics of RTI implementation. These questions involve the issues raised above and others critical to LD identification, including standard definitions for operationalizing responsiveness, valid measures for progress monitoring, and research on utilizing the process with older students (Fuchs & Fuchs, 2006; Hollenbeck, 2007; Mellard, Byrd, Johnson, Tollefson, & Boesche, 2004). For example, there is no agreed-upon cut-point that indicates lack of responsiveness to secondary interventions and signals the presence of LD (Vaughn & Fuchs, 2003). Therefore, as districts develop their own cut-points, there will be great variance in placement criteria for LD. If we are to implement the RTI process as a whole with fidelity, we must answer these questions based on valid research findings (National Joint Committee on LD [NJCLD], 2005).

Following is a list of some topics for future research (Danileson et al., 2007; Glover & DiPerna, 2007; Kovaleski, 2007; Wodrich, Spencer, & Daley, 2006). This is not meant to be an exhaustive list. As the process evolves, there are sure to be more. It will be imperative to continue the translation of research into practice in order to make the best use of the knowledge and tools available.

- Development of assessment tools appropriate for all content areas at all grade levels
- Identification of appropriate levels (cut-points) and rates of progress on various assessment tools
- Development of larger pool of research-based interventions appropriate across content areas and grade levels
- Identification of effects of varying intervention components and intensity at each tier
- Improvement of accuracy and validity of assessment systems

- Comparisons of validity of Standard Protocol and Problem-Solving Models for academics and behavior in typical school settings
- Application of interventions to culturally diverse populations
- Validity of using RTI to identify students with various disabling conditions
- Evaluation of effectiveness of various supplemental materials
- Evaluation of effectiveness of the RTI model to meet the goals of No Child Left Behind

NATIONAL RTI PERSPECTIVE

We now turn our focus to the future of Response to Intervention. Despite the fact that tiered instructional models have been researched for more than thirty years, RTI as a process is in its infancy. There is much to be done in working toward maturity. In some ways, RTI is developing rapidly, as evidenced by the volume of research and discussion in the educational community. However, there are numerous barriers and unresolved issues that must be addressed before RTI can be fully and effectively implemented across the country.

The RTI process receives support from most national organizations whose focus is special education, including the Council for Exceptional Children (CEC), which is the largest international professional organization that advocates for students with disabilities. In 2007, the CEC published a position statement that outlines its support for RTI, stressing the importance of using it as a school improvement process. In addition, it stresses the importance of each of the critical components of RTI outlined in this book and recommends that RTI data be used as one part of a comprehensive evaluation. The CEC provides support for the process by hosting numerous training opportunities, including national and international conferences, regional workshops, and Web seminars. This type of advocacy and support from the CEC and other professional organizations is critical to future policy development and regulations.

However, there is not the same level of involvement and understanding from organizations that focus on general education professionals and issues. In March 2008, we explored the official Web sites of six national organizations generally associated with content instruction or professional organizations for administrators: the National Council of Teachers of Mathematics, the National Council of Teachers of English, the International Reading Association, the National Association of Elementary School Principals, the National Association of Secondary School Principals, and the Association for Supervision and Curriculum Development. We typed "Response to Intervention" into the search tool of each organization's Web site. The International Reading Association site returned a significant number of matches (over 900 articles and informational links), as did the National Association of Elementary School Principals site and the Association for Supervision and Curriculum Development site. On the National Association of Secondary School Principals site, there were a small number of informational articles. It is understandable that the International Reading Association would have so much information, considering RTI's roots and heavy research in the area of reading. It is also logical that organizations serving administrators would have information available to their members, though that on the Secondary School Principals site was minimal.

Alarmingly, however, there was little specific information available on RTI on the National Council of Teachers of English site or the National Council of Teachers of Mathematics site. The information that was provided pertained to progress monitoring and, to some extent, research-based interventions. Very few search results pertained to the RTI process specifically. We found no RTI position papers on any of the six Web sites.

We find this trend interesting. This is indicative of significant differences in technical language between general educators and special educators. This language barrier, so to speak, is a source of frustration for many. It was especially pronounced in a statement from an article posted on the National Council of Teachers of English site. The article focused on the fact that, until IDEA 2004, educational improvement referred to differentiation and supplemental programs to address the requirements of NCLB. IDEA brought an entirely new vocabulary to the educational community. The authors expressed their frustration in the following statement: "Thanks to IDEA and our colleagues in special education, the focus is now on what is called an improved version of Response-to-Intervention (RtI or Responsiveness-to-Intervention)" (Berkas & Pattison, 2007, p. 1).

This statement also reflects what we see in schools: Response to Intervention is seen as a special education initiative. This may seem a minor point, but the lack of a common language and support for RTI is a significant barrier to implementation. As we have discussed throughout this book, RTI must be supported through general education or it cannot be effective. Leaders at the national level agree.

In October 2006, the National Association of State Directors of Special Education held an informational forum, called Project Forum, for the purpose of identifying critical needs and developing recommendations for RTI research and national policy. The group identified a list of specific barriers to full implementation. Included on the list were issues such as lack of knowledge and skills for service providers at all levels, including families; lack of consistency and clarity in defining high-quality instruction; misaligned policies, including lack of alignment between NCLB and IDEA; conflicting beliefs and values between general education and special education professionals; and insufficient funding (Project Forum's Recommendations full report may be obtained from www.projectforum.org.). Based on the identified barriers, the forum developed the following policy recommendations:

- Embed RTI language into NCLB reauthorization.
- Provide comprehensive training.
- Focus on implementation of high-quality instruction at the classroom level.
- Encourage research syntheses and the development of implementation tools.
- Develop a national coordinating body to support implementation of RTI.
- Develop a common understanding to encourage interdisciplinary collaboration.
- Develop state and local implementation infrastructures.
- Develop and implement a marketing strategy (Burdette, 2007).

Implementation of these policies at the national, state, and local levels would provide an excellent foundation for the RTI process. They are all critical to success in using RTI to improve schools and raise student achievement. It is unfortunate that they were not addressed prior to implementation at the national level. Had they been developed into a national action plan prior to IDEA 2004, we believe local districts would not have many of the difficulties they are having now. However, we believe it is not too late to address these issues.

In looking at these recommendations, we believe the one with the most potential for immediate impact will be embedding RTI into the reauthorization of NCLB. The most significant barrier that we as consultants face in working with school districts to build vision and buy-in is the conflict between the components of RTI and Adequate Yearly Progress (AYP) requirements. High-stakes testing dominates much of the decision-making process when choosing instructional components. Administrators and teachers see AYP requirements as being in direct conflict with progress monitoring and tiered interventions. That is an unfortunate perception, because the two can easily work together. Formative assessment, when used to drive instruction, is strongly related to higher student achievement (Black & William, 1998; Wiggins, 1998). Specifically, CBM reading assessments have been highly correlated with performance on high-stakes assessment (Marston, Reschly, Lau, Muyskens, & Canter, 2007). Response to Intervention addresses the underlying issues that cause student failure. It is not a quick fix. Instead, it is a long-term solution.

Partnering With Parents (Chapter 7)

As school districts and individual schools are developing and implementing their RTI process, it is tempting to avoid collaborating with parents initially—after all, school employees are often still trying to organize the framework. However, including parents even at the early stages can in fact help to clarify common misconceptions as well as broaden perspectives to aid in developing an effective program. For example, one particular elementary school was discussing the need for more personnel to deliver interventions. A parent on the team quickly suggested that the parents who line up to pick up their children thirty to forty-five minutes early each day could park their cars in the line and come in to the school to provide assistance in the classroom while teachers are providing intervention to small groups of students. Not only did this assist in a school need, the parents felt they were helping the school to make a real difference in overall student achievement.

It is equally important to include parents at all levels of the RTI pyramid. Initially, parents need to be familiar with the overall structure and purpose of RTI. A parent should not hear about the process for the first time when his or her child is identified as at risk. In summary, effective collaboration relies upon open communication and parental involvement at every stage of the learning process. The team approach is most assuredly the only way to successfully address the varied needs of students.

As we have worked with parents within an RTI framework, there have been common areas of misconception and concern. The following tables identify common parent factors that should be addressed in school handbooks, parent meetings (PTO/PTA), and parent–teacher conferences.

Issues to Communicate With Parents:

Provide written materials to explain the school's overall RTI process including:

✓ Specific ways parents can be involved at each stage

✓ A description of school screening procedures

✓ Examples of school interventions and resources for home use of similar interventions

✓ A timeline of events, such as estimated length of time interventions are administered and frequency of progress monitoring

✓ The importance of monitoring progress and using the data to make decisions

✓ IDEA Due Process Parental Rights, specifically highlighting their right to request an evaluation to determine special education eligibility and when parental consent is required

Issues to Address Within the Intervention Plan:

Provide the following information to parents of children who are found to be at risk:

✓ The data that led to awareness of student need

✓ Instructional intervention(s)

✓ Number of weeks anticipated with intervention(s)

✓ Schedule for delivering interventions: minutes per day, days per week, name of person delivering instruction, and location of instruction

✓ Type(s) of assessments used and criteria for determining success

✓ Methods for supporting school efforts at home

Terms and Concepts Parents Should Understand:

1. Response to Intervention (RTI)	RTI is a collaboration between various school personnel and parents to provide high-quality instruction with specific interventions matched to a student's needs. Many schools provide a written action plan to address the areas(s) of concern, review data to determine effectiveness, and make educational decisions based on the data.
2. Universal Screening or School-Wide Screening	Screenings are methods of identifying struggling students who are "at risk" for failure. The screenings can be large-scale tests, such as Criterion Reference Competency Test (CRCT) or academic grade-level probes, such as DIBELS. Students who perform below grade-level expectations receive more frequent progress monitoring to determine whether the need truly exists. If the screening and progress-monitoring tools confirm a child's need, the student receives more intensive interventions. Benchmark assessments are given three to four times per year to gauge student progress and identify at-risk students throughout the school year.
3. Curriculum-Based Measurements (CBM)	CBM determine basic skill proficiency in the areas of reading fluency, reading comprehension, math, spelling, writing, and vocabulary.
4. Student Progress Monitoring	Progress monitoring is a research-based practice for determining the academic progress of students and the effectiveness of instruction. The information obtained through formal and informal methods of progress monitoring is used to make educational decisions for improving learning.

5. Scientific, Research-Based Instruction	Scientific, research-based instruction includes curricula and interventions that have a base of research and have been proven to be effective. Interventions may be standard for a group of students with similar needs or may be individualized for a particular student.
6. No Child Left Behind (NCLB)	NCLB is the education law that governs all education in the United States. NCLB requires schools to incorporate research-based strategies for school improvement.
7. The Individuals with Disabilities Education Act (IDEA)	IDEA is the education law that governs special education issues. IDEA encourages schools to use an RTI process that determines whether struggling students respond to research-based interventions as a part of the formal evaluation to determine eligibility as a student with a learning disability in need of special education services. Throughout the RTI process, IDEA allows parents to request a formal evaluation to determine eligibility for special education services; therefore the RTI process cannot deny or delay formal evaluation procedures. While RTI practices may continue, the evaluation timeline of sixty days from parental consent to evaluate must be kept. The data received during the sixty days can be considered by the eligibility team as part of the comprehensive evaluation.

Parent Resources:

National Center for Learning Disabilities (NCLD)	www.ncld.org www.ncld.org/images/stories/downloads/parent_center/ rti_final.pdf
National Joint Committee on Learning Disabilities (NJCLD)	www.ldonline.org/about/partners/njcld
National Research Center on Learning Disabilities (NRCLD)	www.nrcld.org
National Center on Student Progress Monitoring	www.studentprogress.org

The Center on Accelerating Student Learning (CASL)	http://kc.vanderbilt.edu/casl
Schwab Learning	http://schwablearning.org/articles.aspx?r=1057
Dynamic Indicators of Basic Early Literacy Skills (DIBELS)	http://dibels.uoregon.edu
Institute for the Development of Educational Achievement	http://reading.uoregon.edu
Reading Rockets	http://www.readingrockets.org
National Association of School Psychologists (NASP)	http://www.nasponline.org/families

SUMMARY

Throughout this book, we have presented a framework for school improvement using RTI as the driving force. The essential elements of Response to Intervention do not represent a buffet from which schools can pick and choose what they prefer to implement. Instead, the overall process must be systematically developed and carried out through thoughtful long-range planning.

In her address to Project Forum, Alexa Posny, director of the Office of Special Education and Rehabilitative Services, made the following statement: "RTI and EIS [early intervening services] are absolutely the future of education—not the future of special education, but of education" (Burdette, 2007, p. 3). Some may say this is a dream. Perhaps it is. It will only become a reality when schools commit to long-term change in their structure, infrastructure, and goals.

For so long, we as an educational community have drifted from one fad to the next, rarely basing our new programs on research evidence. We see this trend changing significantly as schools work to translate research into practice. It can continue to change with a concentrated focus on working together to raise achievement of all students. The concepts presented in this book are the backbone for making this change. With the combined efforts of all teachers, administrators, families, researchers, and higher education faculty, Response to Intervention can fulfill the promise of creating highly effective arenas of learning in which all children achieve to their potential.

REFERENCES

Adelman, H. S., & Taylor, L. (1997). Toward a scale-up model for replicating new approaches to schooling. *Journal of Educational and Psychological Consultation, 8,* 197–230.

Berkas, N., & Pattison, C. (2007, July/August). *What is intervention and why is everyone talking about it?.* Retrieved March 14, 2008, from http://www.nctm.org

Black, P., & Wiliam, D. (1998). Inside the black box: Raising standards through classroom assessment. *Phi Delta Kappan, 80*(2), 139–148.

Burdette, P. (2007, April). *Response to Intervention as it relates to Early Intervening Services: Recommendations.* Retrieved March 5, 2008, from http://www.projectforum.org

Danielson, L., Doolittle, J., & Bradley, R. (2007). Professional development, capacity building, and research needs: Critical issues for response to intervention implementation. *School Psychology Review, 36*(4), 632–637.

Deshler, D. (2007, April). *The scaling of innovations: Factors to consider beyond professional development.* Presentation at the National Council for Exceptional Children's Conference, Louisville, KY.

Fuchs, D., & Fuchs, L. S. (2006). Introduction to response to intervention: What, why and how valid is it? *Reading Research Quarterly, 41,* 93–99.

Gersten, R., Chard, D., & Baker, S. (2000). Factors enhancing sustained use of research-based instructional practices. *Journal of Learning Disabilities, 33,* 445–457.

Glover, T. A., & DiPerna, J. C. (2007). Service delivery for response to intervention: Core components and directions for future research. *School Psychology Review, 36*(4), 526–540.

Gorton, R., Alston, J. A., & Snowden, P. (2007). *School leadership & administration: Important concepts, case studies, & simulations* (7th ed.). New York: McGraw Hill.

Huberman, A. M., & Miles, A. B. (1984). *Innovation up close: How school improvement works.* New York: Plenum.

Hollenbeck, A. F. (2007). From IDEA to implementation: A discussion of foundational and future responsiveness-to-intervention research. *Learning Disabilities Research & Practice, 22*(2), 137–146.

Klingner, J. K., Arguelles, M. E., Hughes, M. T., & Vaughn, S. (2001). Examining the school wide "spread" of research-based practices. *Learning Disability Quarterly, 24,* 221–234.

Kovaleski, J. F. (2007). Response to Intervention: Considerations for research and system change. *School Psychology Review, 36*(4), 638–646.

Marston, D., Reschly, A. L., Lau, M. Y., Muyskens, P., & Canter, A. (2007). Historical perspectives and current trends in problem solving. In D. Haager, J. Klingner, & S. Vaughn (Eds.), *Evidence-based reading practices in Response to Intervention* (1st ed., pp. 265–285). Baltimore: Paul H. Brookes Publishing.

Mellard, D. F., Byrd, S. E., Johnson, E., Tollefson, J. M., & Boesche, L. (2004). Foundations and research on identifying model responsiveness-to-intervention sites. *Learning Disabilities Quarterly, 27,* 243–256.

National Association of School Psychologists. (2006). *The role of the school psychologist in the RTI process.* Retrieved March 7, 2008, from http://www.nasponline.org

National Joint Committee on LD. (2005). Responsiveness to intervention and learning disabilities. *Learning Disabilities Quarterly, 28,* 249–260.

National Staff Development Council. (2001). *NSDC's Standards for Staff Development.* Retrieved March 5, 2008, from http://www.nsdc.org

Nelson, J. M., & Machek, G. R. (2007). A survey of training, practice, and competence in reading assessment and intervention. *School Psychology Review, 36*(2), 311–327.

Praisner, C. L. (2003). Attitudes of elementary school principals toward the inclusion of students with disabilities. *Exceptional Children, 69*(2), 135–145.

Sindelar, P. T., Shearer, D. K., Yendol-Hoppey, D., & Liebert, T. W. (2006). The sustainability of inclusive school reform. *Exceptional Children, 72*(3), 317–331.

Vaughn, S., & Fuchs, L. S. (2003). Redefining learning disabilities as inadequate response to instruction: The promise and potential pitfalls. *Learning Disabilities Research & Practice, 18*(3), 137–146.

Wiggins, G. (1998). Educative assessment: *Designing assessments to inform and improve student performance.* San Francisco: Jossey-Bass.

Wodrich, D. L., Spencer, M. L., & Daley, K. B. (2006). Combining RTI and psychoeducational assessment: What we must assume to do otherwise. *Psychology in the Schools, 43*(7), 797–806.

Resource A

DIFFERENTIATED INSTRUCTION

Benjamin, A. (2002). *Differentiated instruction: A guide for middle and high school teachers.* Larchmont, NY: Eye on Education.

Gregory, G. H., & Kuzmich, L. (2004). *Data driven differentiation in the standards-based classroom.* Thousand Oaks, CA: Corwin Press.

Heacox, D. (2002). Differentiating instruction in the regular classroom: *How to reach and teach all learners, grades 3–12.* Minneapolis, MN: Free Spirit Publishing.

Northey, S. (2005). *Handbook on differentiated instruction for middle and high schools.* Larchmont, NY: Eye on Education.

Thousand, J. S., Villa, R. A., & Nevin, A. I. (2007). *Differentiating instruction: Collaborative planning and teaching for universally designed learning.* Thousand Oaks, CA: Corwin Press.

Tomlinson, C. A. (1999). *The differentiated classroom: Responding to the needs of all learners.* Alexandria, VA: Association for Supervision and Curriculum Development.

Tomlinson, C. A. (2003). *Fulfilling the promise of the differentiated classroom: Strategies and tools for responsive teaching.* Alexandria, VA: Association for Supervision and Curriculum Development.

Tomlinson, C. A., & McTighe, J. (2006). *Integrating differentiated instruction and understanding by design.* Alexandria, VA: Association for Supervision and Curriculum Development.

Wiggins, G., & McTighe, J. (2005). *Understanding by design* (2nd ed.). Alexandria, VA: Association for Supervision and Curriculum Development.

BEHAVIOR

Crimmins, D., Farrell, A. F., Smith, P. W., & Bailey, A. (2007). *Positive strategies for students with behavior problems.* Baltimore: Paul H. Brookes Publishing.

Jenson, W., Rhode, G., & Reavis, H. K. (1994). *Tough Kid Tool Box*. Longmont, CO: Sopris West.

Marzano, R. J. (2003). *Classroom management that works: Research-based strategies for every teacher*. Alexandria, VA: ASCD.

Sprick, R. S. (2006). *Discipline in the secondary classroom: A positive approach to behavior management* (2nd ed.). San Francisco: Jossey-Bass.

Sprick, R. S., Garrison, M., & Howard, L. M. (1998). *CHAMPs: A proactive and positive approach to classroom management*. Longmont, CO: Sopris West.

- Dr. Terry Alderman
  http://www.resourcesforprofessionals.com

- Center for Evidence-Based Practice: Young Children with Challenging Behavior
  http://challengingbehavior.fmhi.usf.edu

- Florida's Positive Behavior Support Project
  http://flpbs.fmhi.usf.edu

- Intervention Central
  http:/www.interventioncentral.org

- Positive Behavioral and Interventions and Supports
  http://www.pbis.org

- A Research Synthesis on PBS
  http://rrtcpbs.fmhi.usf.edu/rrtcpbsweb/Products/research_synthesis_brief.pdf

- Turning Point Effects for Students with and without Disabilities Who Are Involved in School Disciplinary Actions
  http://www.education.ucsb.edu/turningpoints

- Vanderbilt University Center on the Social and Emotional Foundations for Early Learning
  http://www.vanderbilt.edu/csefel

VARIED INSTRUCTIONAL PROGRAMS AND STRATEGIES

Marzano, R., Pickering, D., & Pollock, J. (2001). *Classroom instruction that works: Research-based strategies for increasing student achievement*. Alexandria, VA: McREL.

Montague, M., & Jitendra, A. K. (2006). *Teaching mathematics to middle school students with learning difficulties*. New York: The Guilford Press.

Muschla, J. A., & Muschla, G. R. (2006). *Hands-on math projects with real-life applications*. San Francisco: Jossey-Bass.

Oczkus, L. D. (2003). *Reciprocal teaching at work: Strategies for improving reading comprehension*. Orinda, CA: International Reading Association.

Posamentier, A. S., & Jaye, D. (2006). *What successful math teachers do, grades 6–12: 79 research-based strategies for the standards-based classroom.* Thousand Oaks, CA: Corwin Press.

Rathvon, N. (1999). *Effective school interventions: Strategies for enhancing academic and social competence.* New York: Guilford Press.

Rogers, S., & Graham, S. (2006). *The high performance toolbox: Succeeding with performance tasks, projects, and assessments.* Evergreen, CO: Peak Learning Systems, Inc.

- The Access Center
  http://www.k8accesscenter.org

- Best Evidence Encyclopedia
  http://www.bestevidence.org

- Florida Center for Reading Research
  www.fcrr.org/FCRRReports

- Focus on Effectiveness
  http://www.netc.org/focus/strategies

- Intervention Central
  http://www.interventioncentral.org

- Making Connections Interventions Reading Program for middle school students – Educators Publishing Service
  http://www.epsbooks.com

- Promising Practices Network
  http://www.promisingpractices.net

- Promising Practices Network: Programs that Work
  http://www.promisingpractices.net/programs.asp

- System 44 Reading Program for grades 3–12 – Scholastic
  http://www.scholastic.com

- Vanderbilt University
  http://kc.vanderbilt.edu/pals

- What Works Clearinghouse through the Institute for Education Sciences
  http://ies.ed.gov/ncee/wwc

ASSESSMENT

Hosp, M. K., Hosp, J. L., Howell, K. W. (2007). *The ABCs of CBM: A practical guide to curriculum-based measurement.* New York: Guilford Press.

LEGAL ISSUES

Council for Exceptional Children. (2005). *What's new in the new IDEA 2004: Frequently Asked Questions and Answers.* Arlington, VA: Council for Exceptional Children.

- National Center on Education, Disability, and Juvenile Justice
  http://www.edjj.org

LEADERSHIP

- Council of Administrators of Special Education
  http://www.casecec.org/rti.htm

- National Association of Secondary School Principals
  http://www.nassp.org

- National Center on Response to Intervention
  http://www.rti4success.org

COMPUTER-ASSISTED INSTRUCTION

- AplusMath
  http://www.aplusmath.com

- BrainPOP
  http://www.brainpop.com

- Coolmath4kids
  http://www.coolmath4kids.com

- Dositey
  http://www.dositey.com

- EDinformatics Kids and Teens Math Site
  http://www.edinformatics.com/kids_teens/kt_math.htm

- ExploreLearning
  http://www.explorelearning.com/index.cfm?method=cResource
  .dspResourceCatalog

- FunBrain.com
  http://www.funbrain.com

- iKnowthat.com
  http://www.iknowthat.com

- Illuminations—Illuminating NCTM's Vision for School Mathematics
  http://illuminations.nctm.org

- Math Playground
  http://www.mathplayground.com

- National Library of Virtual Manipulatives
  http://nlvm.usu.edu/en/nav/vlibrary.html

- Online Graphing Calculator
  http://www.coolmath.com/graphit

- StarFall—Learn to Read
  http://www.starfall.com

- Woodlands Junior School Educational Games and Activities Zone
  http://www.woodlands-junior.kent.sch.uk/Games/educational

TEACHER AND PARENT TOOLS

- 4Teachers
  http://www.4teachers.org

- Balanced Assessment in Mathematics
  http://balancedassessment.concord.org

- Bookmarking Web site (organizing bookmarks for teacher and student use)
  http://del.icio.us

- edHelper.com
  http://www.edhelper.com

- Figure This! Math Challenges for Families
  http://www.figurethis.org

- Giant Calculator
  http://www.mrjennings.co.uk/teacher/maths/giantcalc1024x768.htm

- Google for Educators
  http://www.google.com/educators

- Graphic Organizers
  www.region15.org/curriculum/graphicorg.html

- Library of Congress: America's Story from America's Library
  http://www.americaslibrary.gov

- Math Trails
  http://www.saskschools.ca/~otl_el/grassroots/mathtrail

- Math Trails—Shape Walk
  http://www.saskschools.ca/~otl_el/grassroots/mathtrail/trail10/index.html

- Microsoft Photo Story for Windows (free software)
  http://www.microsoft.com/windowsxp/using/digitalphotography/photostory/default.mspx

- National Education Telecommunications Network: Elementary Education links
  http://www.netn.net/14113.htm

- The National Math Trail
  http://www.nationalmathtrail.org

- Online Graphing Calculators
  http://webgraphing.com

- Heifer International Read to Feed
  http://www.readtofeed.org

- Rubistar—Create Rubrics for Your Project-Based Learning Activities
  http://rubistar.4teachers.org

- SMART Technologies
  http://education.smarttech.com

- Exemplars: Standards-Based Performance Assessment & Instruction
  http://www.exemplars.com

- Sylvan Book Adventure
  http://www.bookadventure.org

- Tools for Teachers
  http://www.suelebeau.com/freetools.htm

- United Streaming (Discovery Education)
  http://streaming.discoveryeducation.com/teacherCenter/index.cfm
  http://streaming.discoveryeducation.com/professionalDevelopment/
  teachingTips/index.cfm

- Virtual Stopwatch and Virtual Timer
  http://www.timeme.com

- Windows Movie Maker (free software)
  http://www.microsoft.com/windowsxp/using/moviemaker

Resource B

Part 1

PRIMARY SCHOOL SCHEDULE INCORPORATING NEEDS-BASED INSTRUCTION

This schedule illustrates integration of one segment of needs-based instruction or extended learning time. It may be implemented two to five days per week. The same concept may be used at all grade levels to provide extended learning time for targeted assistance.

NBI = Needs-Based Instruction

Explo = PE/Art/Music and Character Education

Grade/Time	8:00–8:10	8:10–8:55	8:55–9:40	9:40–10:25	10:25–11:10	11:10–11:55	12:15–1:00	1:00–1:45	1:45–2:30
	Homeroom	1	2	3	4	5	6	7	8
2a	Morning	Explo P A M	Read	Read	Read	Math	Lunch	Math	NBI
2b	Morning	Read	Explo P A M	Read	Read	Math	Lunch	Math	NBI
1a	Morning	Math	Math	Explo P A M	Read	Lunch	Read	Read	NBI
1b	Morning	Read	Read	Math	Explo P A M	Read	Lunch	Math	NBI
1c	Morning	Read	Read	Math	Math	Explo P A M	Lunch	Read	NBI
Ka	Morning	Read	Read	Math	Math	Lunch	Explo C A M P	Read	NBI
Kb	Morning	Read	Read	Math	Math	Lunch	Read	Explo C A M P	NBI

SOURCE: Bender, W. N. & Shores, C. (2008). *Response to intervention: A Multimedia Kit for Professional Development.* Thousand Oaks, CA: Corwin Press.

Topic Areas for Needs-Based Instruction Group

- Reading Needs: Students grouped according to weakness
  - Phonemic Awareness
  - Phonics
  - Fluency
  - Vocabulary
  - Comprehension

- Math Needs: Students grouped according to weakness
  - Numeration
  - Measurement
  - Patterning/Geometry
  - Data Collection
  - Problem Solving

- Language Arts Needs: Students grouped according to weakness
  - Sentence Recognition
  - Punctuation
  - Parts of Speech
  - Writing Process

- Above Level: Enrichment of all skills areas
  - Fluency
  - Vocabulary
  - Writing
  - Mathematics

- On Level: Extending and Building skills
  - Fluency
  - Vocabulary
  - Writing
  - Mathematics

Resource B

Part 2

RECOMMENDED ABILITY-GROUPED READING SCHEDULE

Based on guidelines from the federal law, No Child Left Behind

Text Courtesy of the Iris Center, Peabody College of Education, Vanderbilt University

Time	Group 1 (Typically Lower-Performing Students)	Group 2 (Typically Average-Performing Students)	Group 3 (Typically Higher-Performing Students)
9:00–9:10	Whole Group Instruction Engaging and motivating . . . connected to one of five components of reading		
9:10–9:30	Small Group Instruction Core Reading Instruction—differentiated	Learning Centers Individual or small groups practicing skills . . . listening center, computer, writing center, vocabulary . . . reinforcement of previously introduced skills	Independent Practice Reinforce, Enhance, Enrich
9:30–9:50	Independent Practice Reinforce, Enhance, Enrich	Small Group Instruction Core Reading Instruction—differentiated	Learning Centers Individual or small groups practicing skills . . . listening center, computer, writing center, vocabulary . . . reinforcement of previously introduced skills
9:50–10:10	Learning Centers Individual or small groups practicing skills . . . listening center, computer, writing center, vocabulary . . . reinforcement of previously introduced skills	Independent Practice Reinforce, Enhance, Enrich	Small Group Instruction Core Reading Instruction—differentiated
10:10–10:20	Paired Instruction (Mixed Ability) Practice, Modeling, and Corrective Feedback—PALS—Peer Assisted Learning Strategy (Dr. Lynn Fuchs) (Complete progress monitoring with 5 students per day.)		
10:20–10:30	Whole Group Instruction Read story aloud . . . connect to first 10 minutes		

Resource B

Part 3

DESCRIPTION OF A MIDDLE SCHOOL RTI PROCESS

Lakeview Middle School (LMS), Fort Oglethorpe, Georgia, developed a schedule to address Tier 2 deficiencies through Standard Protocol Interventions. The process they used is described below.

Determining Areas of Weakness

The first step used at Lakeview Middle School was to look at cumulative standardized assessment data to determine areas of weakness. In looking at the data, it was noted that math scores were an issue, and the achievement gap between regular and special education students was quite large. Only 46 percent of special education students were passing the assessment. The domains were then disaggregated. We use a program from Pearson Learning (Inform) that allows us to look at the data by domain. We looked at the weight of each domain and determined that Numbers & Operations and Algebra were domains with more items. We then decided to begin with the Numbers & Operations domain. Our Extended Learning Time (ELT) program runs four days per week, with ten minutes borrowed from each period of our block schedule. We have forty minutes between first and second periods that we use for this intervention.

We disaggregated the data by the Numbers & Operations domain. We looked at all the students who failed that domain (even if their overall score in math was passing). We also looked at the students we consider "bubble" students. These students scored between 800 and 815. These are students who need additional instruction to ensure they continue to meet standards. We had more than half our students at LMS who needed math ELT.

Our next step was to determine the group sizes and placement. We decided that students who scored at the lowest end of the scale (0 percent to about 38 percent) would be put in groups of ten. As student scores got higher, more students were placed in those groups. We also paired up teachers. We used language arts teachers and made sure they were paired with another teacher for support. Our math teachers were working with those students closest to the bubble, because we felt they would make progress more quickly.

We are providing professional development to teachers on a weekly basis. Each week, teachers come to ELT training during their planning period on Wednesday. Because we are asking teachers to teach conceptually, which is new to many, and because we are asking language arts teachers to teach math, we come together to work the tasks that we will be asking students to do in ELT classes. This is proving very helpful to ensuring teachers feel comfortable with the content and tasks. We also began with a focus on math only, since data showed it as the greatest area of need.

For the second nine weeks, we will begin to incorporate reading comprehension into ELT. To do this, we have again disaggregated the CRCT data by domain and identified students according to three groups: those who need only math, those who need only reading, and those who need both. We are able to get the groups to fifteen students or smaller. Our groups will be a bit different for the second nine weeks. Those who are teaching only math or teaching only reading will keep those same students all the time. We are creating two-person teams to rotate the students who need both reading and math. Each teacher will keep half the group (about ten students) for four days and teach their subject (e.g., math). Then the math teacher will get the other half and teach the same lessons again. The reading teacher will do the same—repeating lessons every four days with half the group. We feel that the structure will benefit the students, and they will develop a better relationship with a two-person team.

For language arts, we will focus on reading comprehension using research-based strategies. We will develop lessons that highlight the comprehension strategies that research has shown to be most effective: Making Connections, Summarizing (Synthesizing), Visualizing, Making Inferences, Asking and Generating Questions, and Making Predictions. We will then begin using Reciprocal Teaching, a strategy that enables students to apply the strategy in text they are reading.

We will also use QAR (Question Answer Response) to help students understand the four types of questions. They will apply this to test-taking, as they decide which types of questions would be efficient to search the text to answer, and which they must use prior knowledge to answer. They will then begin to generate questions (of each type) as they read text. This will reinforce the comprehension strategies mentioned above.

We plan to focus a good bit of attention on non-fiction text structures. Many students are not as comfortable with non-fiction, and helping them analyze the structure will enable them to realize the need to read this text differently than narrative text. In addition, we will implement writing into ELT, helping students write in response to what they are reading as well as writing in the genres of the GPS (narrative, expository, persuasive, and response to literature). We will use the rubrics from the eighth-grade writing assessment to evaluate work, helping students to score their work according to the rubric.

Resource C

FIDELITY CHECKLIST

Teacher Behavior	Most of the Time 3	Some of the Time 2	Rarely 1	Not at all 0
Intervention				
Teacher follows lesson outline or script as presented in teacher's edition.				
Teacher implements each component of the prescribed plan.				
Instruction				
Teacher maintains appropriate pacing to keep students actively engaged.				
Teacher provides corrective feedback immediately as needed.				
Teacher models new information for students.				

Resource D

Part 1

RTI INTERVENTION PLAN

Student Name:	Date:

Define the presenting problem:

Are there external contributing factors?	☐ Yes	☐ No

If yes, please describe.

Analyze available data:

List research-based intervention:

Is this standard protocol intervention established in the school currently? ☐ Yes ☐ No

Person responsible for implementation:

Person responsible for progress monitoring:

Specify time frame for implementation:
minutes per session _____ sessions per week _____ weeks of intervention _____

Student achievement goal:

Progress-Monitoring Tool:

Frequency of Progress Monitoring ☐ daily ☐ bi-weekly ☐ weekly ☐ bi-monthly ☐ monthly

Fidelity of instruction plan:

Observer:

Timeline for observation:

Observation tool:

Progress-Monitoring Data
Attach progress-monitoring graph with plotted baseline, goal, and aimline.

Summarize the graphed data:

BEHAVIOR ABC DOCUMENTATION

Behavior Documentation

Dates of observation: _____ Completed by: _____

The chart on the following page should be completed for a period of five to ten consecutive school days. If the student is absent, the date of absence should be noted and the data collection should continue on the day the student returns to school. The information should be compiled by each of the student's teachers.

Analysis of data

After completing the behavior documentation for a period of time, use the following questions to identify patterns revealed in any area during the data-collection period.

Day: Do the problem behaviors occur more often on specific days of the

week? _____ If yes, which ones? _____

Setting: Do the problem behaviors occur more often in specific settings or types of

settings (e.g., structured vs. unstructured)? Describe. _____

_____

_____

_____

Activity: Do the problem behaviors occur more often during similar types of

activities (e.g., when student is asked to read or write)? Describe. _____

_____

_____

_____

Are there any settings where the behavior does not occur? _____

Who is present when the behavior occurs? _____

Day	Date	Setting	Activity	Description of Behavior	Frequency of Behavior	Time/ Duration	Strategy or Consequence Imposed by Teacher	Response to Strategy or Consequence

Types of behavior: Can the behaviors be categorized into specific categories?

_____ impulsivity _____ distractibility _____ withdrawal

_____ aggression toward others _____ aggression toward self

_____ other _____

Frequency of behavior: How many times does the behavior occur during a time period? _____ times in a _____ -minute period

Time/duration: Is there a pattern in the time of day the behavior occurs? How long does the episode last? _____

Strategy or consequence: What types of strategies are most often being implemented with this student?

_____ proactive, designed to prevent the behavior from occurring

_____ reactive, designed to punish and correct the behavior after it occurs

_____ positive reinforcement, designed to reward the student for appropriate behavior

_____ punishment, designed to remove

Student response to strategy or consequence: What types of strategies are providing positive outcomes?

_____ proactive, designed to prevent the behavior from occurring

_____ reactive, designed to punish and correct the behavior after it occurs

_____ positive reinforcement, designed to reward the student for appropriate behavior

_____ punishment, designed to remove

Based on the information outlined above, please answer the following questions.

Is the problem behavior linked to a behavioral skill deficit?

Does the student understand the behavioral expectations for the situation?

Does the student realize that he or she is engaging in unacceptable behavior, or has that behavior simply become a "habit"?

Is it within the student's power to control the behavior, or does he or she need support?

Suggested strategies:
- Explicitly teach behavioral expectations to the student (Sprick, 1998: CHAMPs).
- Conference with the student, making him aware of the number of times the behavior has occurred. Use a phasing technique to reduce the behavior in small increments.
- Use specific strategies to increase the probability of positive behaviors while extinguishing negative ones.

Does the student have the skill but, for some reason, not the desire to modify his or her behavior?

Is it possible that the student is uncertain about the appropriateness of the behavior?

Does the student find any value in engaging in appropriate behavior?

Is the behavior problem associated with certain social or environmental conditions?

Suggested strategies:
- Conference with the student and make him aware that the behavior is inappropriate for the setting.
- Remove the positive reinforcement that the student receives for the inappropriate behavior (e.g., peer approval, escape from work).
- Give the student attention and positive reinforcement for appropriate behavior.
- Use a reward system such as MYSTERY MOTIVATORS (Jenson, 1993).

Is there a more acceptable behavior that might replace this behavior? List: _____

How will you teach that behavior? _____

What seems to be the purpose of the behavior?

_____ gain attention   _____ avoid instruction

_____ seek excitement   _____ avoid a low-interest subject

_____ other _____

How will you change this cycle? _____

Resource E

RTI NEEDS ASSESSMENT

*Current level of implementation:

1 = None
2 = Some or beginning stages
3 = Most or advanced stages
4 = All or completed

**Priority Level

1 = No
2 = Medium
3 = High

General Education Curriculum	Current Level of Implementation?*	Priority Level**	Comments: What does that mean for your school? What resources are required to achieve this?
All teachers are effectively trained in the curriculum standards for the grade level and content area in which they teach.			
Curriculum standards are implemented as designed in each content area.			
Teachers have a thorough understanding and knowledge of the principles and strategies of differentiated instruction.			
Instruction is differentiated by content, process, product, and learning environment on a consistent and ongoing basis.			
Curriculum mapping is utilized to align the curriculum across grade levels and content areas.			
Progress Monitoring			
Curriculum-Based Assessment/ Measurement is used frequently to assess student progress.			
Teachers are trained in the use of Curriculum-Based Assessment/ Measurement to evaluate student learning.			

Progress Monitoring	Current Level of Implementation?*	Priority Level**	Comments: What does that mean for your school? What resources are required to achieve this?
Teachers have Curriculum-Based Assessment/Measurement tools available to them in their content area and appropriate grade level.			
Teachers understand how to analyze, chart, and interpret data.			
Teachers utilize data from ongoing CBM to drive instructional decisions on a daily and/or weekly basis.			
Research-Based Strategies			
Teachers have knowledge base of multiple research-based strategies to address a wide variety of learning and behavior problems.			
Teachers have resources available to train them in specific research-based strategies.			
Teachers are trained in multiple research-based strategies.			
Teachers implement research-based strategies in their classroom with integrity and fidelity.			
A process is in place to ensure research-based strategies are implemented with integrity and fidelity.			
Standard Protocol Interventions			
The school has in place standard protocol interventions designed to address common and/or frequent learning or behavior problems.			
Flexible scheduling for students and staff is utilized to enable student access to standard protocols.			
Job responsibilities have been restructured to enable student access to standard protocols.			
Standard protocols are designed to assertively and intensively address student needs.			

Standard Protocol Interventions	Current Level of Implementation?*	Priority Level**	Comments: What does that mean for your school? What resources are required to achieve this?
Teachers are knowledgeable about or have resources available to inform them about appropriate interventions.			
Administrative Factors			
The entire administration portrays to the staff, students, and parents the importance of the RTI process for increased student achievement.			
The school schedule is designed to provide for flexibility and restructuring of resources to meet student needs.			
Various strategies including walk-throughs, extended observations, teacher conferences, lesson plan evaluations, and others are used to monitor implementation of research-based strategies.			
A variety of resources are identified and provided to address deficit areas in curriculum, behavior management, and instructional strategies.			
Teachers are provided with time and incentives for collaboration, professional growth, and staff development.			
Inventive programs for teacher training (e.g., action research, strategy sharing, publishing) are utilized.			
Partnerships are formed with local organizations (e.g., colleges, retired teacher associations, senior groups) for programs that directly impact teacher training and student performance.			
School and class data are utilized to determine areas of need.			
Adequate and appropriate resources to address identified needs are provided to staff.			

Knowledge of English Language Learners	Current Level of Implementation?*	Priority Level**	Comments: What does that mean for your school? What resources are required to achieve this?
Staff members have a good understanding of language acquisition theory and the effects of L1 on L2.			
An expert in the area of English Language Learners is included in Tier 2 intervention decisions for all ELLs.			
An expert in ELLs is included in RTI meetings for all ELLs.			
Cultural Responsiveness			
Staff members utilize parent interviews, questionnaires, student records, previous teachers, and all other available resources to learn about students and factors which may contribute to their learning and/or behavior problems.			
Staff members are trained in understanding African American culture.			
Staff members are trained in understanding poverty and its effect on school performance.			
Staff members utilize their understanding of cultural differences to form relationships with students and to guide instruction.			

SOURCE: Bender, W. N. & Shores, C. F. (2007). *Response to intervention: A practical guide for every teacher*. Thousand Oaks, CA: Corwin Press.

Resource F

Part 1

RTI ACTION PLAN

Response to Intervention

Action Plan

Goal or Area of Need:	Activities to Accomplish Goal:	Persons Responsible:	Timeline:	Resources Needed:

Resource F

Part 2

SAMPLE MULTI-YEAR PLAN FOR DISTRICT IMPLEMENTATION

X: full implementation

P: implementation in pilot schools only

RTI Component	Year 1	Year 2	Year 3	Year 4
Form district leadership team.	X			
Develop readiness for change with district team.	X			
Develop and refine district action plan.	X	X	X	X
Develop building leadership teams.	P	X		
Develop building action plan.	P	X		
Begin initial training for faculty and staff.	P	X		
Communicate information to parents.	X	X	X	X
Evaluate and strengthen Tier 1 instruction.	X	X	X	X
Identify and acquire/develop benchmark assessment tools.	X			
Implement benchmark assessment.	P	X		
Identify and acquire/develop progress-monitoring tools.	P	X		
Develop structure for Tier 2 targeted interventions.		P	X	
Identify research-based interventions.	X	X	X	X
Train service providers in research-based interventions.	P	X	X	X
Implement Tier 2 interventions.		P	X	
Implement progress monitoring.		P	X	
Develop structure for Tier 3.		P	X	
Implement Tier 3 structure.			P	X

SAMPLE MULTI-YEAR PLAN FOR STAFF DEVELOPMENT

DL: District Leadership
BL: Building Leadership
P: Pilot Schools
A: All Schools

Staff Development Topic	Year 1	Year 2	Year 3	Year 4
RTI Process Overview	A			
RTI Intensive Training	DL, BL, P	A		
Differentiated Instruction and Tier 1 Instructional Components (will vary based on needs of district)	A	A	A	A
Problem Solving and Collaboration	A	A	A	A
Benchmark Assessment	DL, BL, P	A		
Curriculum-Based Measurement and other Progress-Monitoring Tools	DL, BL, P	A	A	A
Research-Based Interventions	DL, BL, P	A	A	A
Data-Driven Instructional Practices	DL, BL, P	A	A	A
Positive Behavior Supports School-Wide Behavioral Plan		DL, BL, P	A	A
Targeted Behavioral Interventions		DL, BL, P	A	A

Index

CORWIN PRESS

The Corwin Press logo—a raven striding across an open book—represents the union of courage and learning. Corwin Press is committed to improving education for all learners by publishing books and other professional development resources for those serving the field of PreK–12 education. By providing practical, hands-on materials, Corwin Press continues to carry out the promise of its motto: **"Helping Educators Do Their Work Better."**

The worldwide mission of The Council for Exceptional Children is to improve educational outcomes for individuals with exceptionalities.

CEC, a non-profit association, accomplishes its mission, which is carried out in support of special education professionals and others working on behalf of individuals with exceptionalities, by advocating for appropriate governmental policies, by setting professional standards, by providing continuing professional development, by advocating for newly and historically underserved individuals with exceptionalities, and by helping professionals achieve the conditions and resources necessary for effective professional practice.